D1621377

XB00 000002 1013

THE GREAT BRITISH
STORECUPBOARD
COOKBOOK

WOLVERHAMPTON
PUBLIC LIBRARIES

XB000000021013	
Bertrams	08/10/2009
641.5941	£25.00
B	625983

THE GREAT BRITISH
STORECUPBOARD
COOKBOOK

PAUL HARTLEY

First published in Great Britain
in 2009 by
Absolute Press
Scarborough House
29 James Street West
Bath BA1 2BT
Phone 44 (0) 1225 316013
Fax 44 (0) 1225 445836
E-mail info@absolutepress.co.uk
Website www.absolutepress.co.uk

Publisher Jon Croft
Commissioning Editor Meg Avent
Designer Matt Inwood
Photography Matt Inwood
Food Styling Andrea O'Connor

© Paul Hartley, 2009
Photography © Absolute Press,
2009

All rights reserved. No part of this
publication may be reproduced,
stored in a retrieval system or
transmitted in any form or by any
means, electronic or otherwise,
without the prior permission of
Absolute Press.

A catalogue record of this book
is available from the British Library

ISBN 13: 9781906650117

Printed and bound by
Oriental Press, Dubai.

Marmite, Colman's Mustard,
Lea & Perrin's Worcestershire
Sauce, Lyle's Golden Syrup,
HP Sauce and Bovril are all
registered trademarks.
All copyright material and
registered trademarks are
reproduced with the permission
of the respective companies.

Any information contained within
this book has been based upon
the research and the opinions
of the author and publisher.

The recipes in this collection were
previously published separately as:
The Marmite Cookbook
The Colman's Mustard Cookbook
**The Lea & Perrins Worcestershire
Sauce Cookbook**
**The Lyle's Golden Syrup
Cookbook**
The HP Sauce Cookbook
The Bovril Cookbook

CONTENTS

THE ADVENTURES OF THE MUSTARD CLUB

Being a selection of the famous advertisements of the MUSTARD CLUB, together with many interesting cartoons and hitherto unpublished documents.

PRICE
6D.

MARMITE
FOR GOOD PEOPLE
OF GOOD TASTE

"MARMITE" IS GOOD FOR SOUPS SANDWICHES ETC.

"BE A SANDWICH-MAN"
USE
MARMITE

H.P.

AN OPEN SECRET—

GOOD GOOD

MARMITE

MARMITE

LYLE'S
GOLDEN SYRUP

SAUCE

Good with bacon

LEA & PERRINS' SAUCE

The Original and Genuine Worcestershire

LEA & PERRINS' SAUCE

WAS INTRODUCED OVER SIXTY YEARS AGO AND NEVER VARIES IN EXCELLENCE OF QUALITY.

BOVRIL puts BEEF into you.

PRESS CAP

TEASPOONFUL TO A T LING WATER & STIR

BOVRIL

TWO HOUSEHOLD FAVORITES — ALWAYS IN HOT WATER

LYLE'S GOLDEN SYRUP

IN 1 lb. 2 lb. 4 lb. & 14 lb. TINS

Abram Lyle & Sons Ltd. London

HP SAUCE

By Royal Warrant to His Majesty the King

THE LABEL

THE ONLY SECURITY against deception is to see that

LEA & PERRINS

is printed in WHITE across the label — THE ORIGINAL WORCESTERSHIRE.

BY SPECIAL APPOINTMENT TO THE KING

Colman's

Mustard

THE MARMITE RECIPE COLLECTION

Seared Beef and Beansprout Wrap

SERVES 2

150g rump steak, thinly sliced
$\frac{1}{2}$ red pepper, cut into strips
1 tablespoon sesame oil
1 teaspoon Marmite
1 pack beansprouts
2 Chinese pancake wraps

Firstly put two plates in the oven to warm. Put the beef and the red pepper into a bowl. Add the sesame oil and Marmite and mix all together roughly so that the meat and the pepper become well coated.

Heat a wok or frying pan to a high heat and add the mixture, cooking quite quickly to sear the ingredients and to just cook the beef. At this point add 2 handfuls of beansprouts and toss it all together for 2 minutes.

Place a Chinese pancake on each warmed plate and then pile on the steak, beansprouts and peppers. Wrap up the pancake and devour immediately.

LOVE

MARIE E. VILMOT
Hamburg, Germany

'The yummiest thing ever to come out of the UK.'

Pasta Primavera

SERVES 2

50g broad beans, fresh or frozen
50g unsalted butter
50g green beans
75g mangetout
200g pasta ribbons
    (fettuccine or tagliatelle)
1 heaped teaspoon Marmite
1 tablespoon chopped
    fresh chives
1 tablespoon chopped
    flatleaf parsley
black pepper

Cook the broad beans in a little boiling water for about 2–3 minutes (slightly longer if frozen), drain them and pop them out of their shells with your thumb and finger. Put them into a medium-sized saucepan with the butter and keep to one side. Cook the green beans in boiling water for 3–4 minutes, adding the mangetout to cook for the last minute. Then drain and add them to the broad beans. Don't compromise the sweet taste of the vegetables by adding salt when you cook them.

Cook the pasta in boiling water for about 10 minutes until just tender. Drain, leaving a little moisture on the pasta, return it to the hot pan and add the Marmite and stir until the pasta is well coated. Now add the warm vegetables and chopped herbs to the pasta and give the whole mixture a gentle stir over a very low heat, seasoning with plenty of freshly ground black pepper. Serve on hot plates and enjoy the wonderful fresh flavours.

HATE
MARTIE MATHER
Romsey, Hampshire

'It tastes like old socks.'

Roasted Onions with Marmite Sausages

SERVES 4

8 medium onions
50g dried prunes, stoned and finely chopped
350g good quality sausagemeat
2 teaspoons Marmite
1 level teaspoon chopped rosemary
fresh black pepper
1 tablespoon olive oil
25g unsalted butter

Bring a large pan of water to the boil and cook the whole and unpeeled onions, for 15–20 minutes. Drain the onions and allow them to cool until easy to handle.

Put the prunes, sausagemeat, Marmite, rosemary and black pepper into a bowl and mash thoroughly – using the back of a spoon is an easy way to do this.

Pre-heat the oven to 200C/400F/ Gas 6. Cut off the lid of each onion and scoop out the middle third of each onion with a teaspoon – you can always use this for a soup – and fill the hole with the sausage mixture. Drizzle with the olive oil and roast in the oven for 30–35 minutes. Great served with a leafy salad and some good crusty bread.

MARMITE SHRINE

Contrary to popular belief, Marmite does have its fans in the US. Possibly its chief flag bearer is Missouri-based Doug Schneider, who established his very own shrine to the yellow-lidded stuff in the form of the Missouri Marmite Museum. Doug's collection started humbly enough, way back in 1973, when he was living in the UK. He held onto the 'adorable' metal-capped jar, keen to retain this memento that struck him as so very British. Doug's travels took him to many countries, and he began to pick up more Marmite jars – from Canada, Sri Lanka and Hong Kong to name a few. That's when the collecting bug really started to drive him: he dug up an antique jar from a Welsh trash heap; he located tins that used to house Marmite stock cubes, and, of course, he discovered the internet and a worldwide homage – hundreds of Marmite items, from the bespoke to the mass-produced to the outright weird (Marmite candle, anyone?). The museum is located in Valley Park and, via prior arrangement with Doug, is open to the public.

Savoury Waffles with Pumpkin and Pancetta

MAKES 8 WAFFLES

200g pumpkin or butternut
 squash, peeled, deseeded and
 diced
100g cubed pancetta
a drizzle of olive oil
180g plain flour
120g fine cornmeal
2 teaspoons baking powder
2 eggs, separated
225ml milk
200ml natural yoghurt
1 teaspoon Marmite
maple syrup
freshly ground pepper

**You will need an electric waffle
iron or waffle maker
for this recipe.**

Mix together the pumpkin or butternut squash and pancetta, drizzle with a little olive oil and roast in a medium-hot oven (190C/375F/Gas 6) for 20 minutes.

To make the waffles; sift the flour, cornmeal and baking powder into a large bowl. Put the egg yolks into another bowl, add the milk, yoghurt, Marmite and 2 tablespoons of olive oil and whisk well. Add the flour mixture and beat well. Put the egg whites into a clean bowl and whisk until you have stiff peaks. Then using a large metal spoon gently fold the egg whites into the waffle batter.

Depending on the size of your waffle maker, spoon about 125ml of the batter into a heated and lightly oiled waffle iron, or follow the instructions of your waffle maker. Cook until crisp – about 4–5 minutes, keep warm and repeat until all the batter is used. Place a waffle on each plate and using a slotted spoon pile the roasted pumpkin or butternut squash and pancetta on top, drizzled with lashings of maple syrup. Serve immediately.

~1866~

**A German chemist by the
name of Justin Liebig
discovered that the waste of
brewers' yeast in the beer
brewing process could be
made into a concentrate that
resulted in a protein-rich
paste with a meaty flavour.**

Croustades of Seared Salmon and Tarragon Mayonnaise

FOR A FEW FRIENDS

2 tablespoons mayonnaise
sprig of tarragon, finely chopped
1 teaspoon Marmite
1 small French stick
250g fresh salmon fillet
olive oil for brushing
handful rocket leaves
4 cherry tomatoes
black pepper

Mix together the mayonnaise, tarragon and Marmite in a small bowl and set aside. Slice the French bread into rounds about 1cm thick and lightly toast on both sides. Take the salmon and cut into thin slices a little smaller than the toast rounds they are going to nestle on. Brush each side of the salmon with a little olive oil and sear on a griddle for a couple of minutes.

Take the toasted breads and spread each with a teaspoon of the Marmite mayo then lay a piece of salmon on each. Top the salmon with a couple of rocket leaves, slices of cherry tomatoes and a good flourish of fresh black pepper. Lovely eaten warm but also delicious cold.

~1902~

The Marmite Food Extract Company Limited started life as a public company on June 13th. With the acquisition of the patents for their yeast extract negotiated, the directors set up a small factory in Burton-on-Trent, centre of the British brewing industry where the all-important yeast was readily available.

Crispy Roasted Fennel and New Potato Salad

SERVES 4

16 baby new potatoes
salt and black pepper
1 pack Walkers Marmite crisps
2 large fennel bulbs
A drizzle of olive oil
dressed mixed salad leaves

Boil the new potatoes in salted water for 15–20 minutes until cooked through. Drain and keep warm.

Take the pack of Marmite crisps, make a small hole at one end of the packet to let the air escape, and crush the contents with a rolling pin. Empty the contents onto a plate. Cut each fennel bulb into about 8 large wedges and brush each cut side with olive oil. Then plunge the oiled sides into the crushed crisps to coat them.

Sprinkle a hint of olive oil on a roasting tin and place the fennel wedges, uncoated side down, in the tin and roast in a hot oven (220C/430F/Gas 8) for 15 minutes. The fennel should be softened and the coating crispy.

Take 4 serving plates and strew each with the dressed mixed leaves. Then add the new potatoes and fennel wedges and season with salt and plenty of fresh black pepper.

VEGGIES LOVE IT TOO

In traditional beermaking a gelatin-like subject called isinglass (obtained from fish such as sturgeon) is used to clear cloudy particles from the brew. But this process takes place *after* the yeast extract has been removed, thus making Marmite a bona fide 100% veggie spread!

100% VEGETARIAN

Griddled Haddock Jacket with Marmite Cheese Sauce

SERVES 2

2 medium baking potatoes
a little olive oil
coarse sea salt
25ml milk
1 teaspoon Marmite
100g Emmental cheese, grated
freshly milled black and white
   pepper (black for flavour, white
   for strength)
150g natural smoked
   haddock fillets
fresh chopped parsley

Scrub the potatoes and coat with olive oil and a sprinkling of coarse sea salt – best to use your hands for this. A good tip is to bake the spuds on a metal kebab skewer; they will cook quicker and more evenly. Bake the spuds in the oven 210C/425F/Gas 7 for 45 minutes.

About ten minutes before the potatoes have baked, warm the milk gently in a small saucepan adding the Marmite. Fold in the grated Emmental stirring gently until the cheese is coated and only just beginning to melt. Season with a good grind of pepper – just imagine how delicious this is going to be on the potato, and remove from the heat.

Brush a griddle with a little olive oil and when hot, sear the skinned haddock for 3 minutes on each side to seal in the flavour.

Cut each hot jacket potato with a cross and pressing from the sides, open them up, cut the fish into chunks and spoon into the potato, then spoon over the Marmite cheesy mixture. Now pop it under a hot grill for a couple of minutes until the cheese starts to drizzle. Finally sprinkle this scrummy dish with lots of roughly chopped parsley – all the flavours will fuse together.

Indubitably for people of good taste. And certainly more than just a sandwich filler.

Deep-fried Eggs with Tomato Sauce

SERVES 4

oil for deep-frying
4 large free-range eggs
4 slices rustic bread
Marmite for spreading
ground black pepper
pinch cumin seeds
salt

For the tomato sauce

30ml olive oil
$1/2$ onion, chopped
1 clove garlic, chopped
400g tin of Italian chopped
    tomatoes
1 tablespoon of tomato puree
pinch cayenne pepper
squeeze lemon juice
salt
ground black pepper
$1/2$ teaspoon dried oregano
1 teaspoon caster sugar

First make the tomato sauce. Heat half the olive oil in a saucepan and sauté the chopped onion and garlic until soft. Add the tin of chopped tomatoes, and tomato purée and simmer for 20–25 minutes to reduce the sauce and create a deeper flavour. Add the cayenne, lemon juice, salt and pepper and blend until smooth. Stir in the oregano and the remaining olive oil and leave to one side.

Heat the frying oil until a cube of bread becomes brown and crisp in 60 seconds. Deep-fry the eggs one at a time: break each egg into an oiled ladle and lower the ladle into the hot oil.

As the oil begins to bubble around the egg, remove the ladle. Using a slotted spoon, gently roll the egg over once or twice to enfold the yolk in the white. Cook for 50–55 seconds until the white is fluffy and golden and the yolk still soft. Remove the egg, drain on kitchen paper and keep warm in a low oven while cooking the remaining eggs.

Toast the bread and spread with Marmite. Re-heat the tomato sauce and place each egg on a slice of Marmite toast on a warmed plate. Season with salt, pepper and cumin. Cover each egg with 2–3 tablespoons of the tomato sauce and serve immediately.

Pork Burgers with Fresh Salsa

MAKES 6 BURGERS

450g finely minced belly of pork
1 small onion, finely chopped
1 teaspoon chopped sage
$1/2$ teaspoon grated nutmeg
1 teaspoon Marmite

For the salsa
1 medium red onion, finely diced
5 tomatoes, skinned, seeded and
  diced
1 red chilli, seeded and finely
  chopped
1 teaspoon sugar
juice of 1 lime
2 tablespoons chopped fresh
  coriander leaves

Dunk the tomatoes in boiling water for 30 seconds to split their skins for easy removal.

Mix together all the salsa ingredients, add a pinch of salt and set aside. In a bowl mix together the minced pork, onion, sage, nutmeg and Marmite. Although it is a bit messy hands are definitely best for this. When all the ingredients are well combined, wet your hands and divide the mixture into 6 burgers. The water will prevent the mixture sticking to you. Put the burgers on greaseproof paper and chill for about 10 minutes to help them to set.

When ready, heat a lightly greased griddle and cook the burgers for 3–4 minutes on each side until they are thoroughly cooked through. Serve the hot burgers with the cool salsa for a mouth-watering combo.

~1912~

The word vitamin was created to describe chemicals necessary to diets. This was a major boost to Marmite when it was realised that yeast provided a good source of five types of B vitamin. This resulted in quantities of Marmite flooding into schools, hospitals and other public institutions.

Boston Baked Beans

SERVES 10

1kg dried haricot beans,
 soaked overnight
100ml molasses or black treacle
2 tablespoons brown sugar
2 teaspoons dry mustard powder
2 teaspoons Marmite
1 teaspoon ground black pepper
1 medium sized onion, peeled
500g belly of pork with rind

Cover the soaked beans with fresh water and bring to the boil skimming off any foam. Reduce the heat and simmer the beans until their skins begin to burst. Drain the beans and reserve the cooking liquid. Combine the molasses, brown sugar, mustard powder, Marmite and pepper with the cooking liquid.

Heat the oven to 100C/200F/Gas lowest. Place the onion in the bottom of a 2-litre ovenproof casserole and pour the beans on the top. Score the rind of the pork and push it down into the beans rind side up. Pour the seasoned liquid on top adding enough boiling water to cover the beans. Cover the casserole and bake in the oven for a mere nine hours!

Every hour add boiling water, if necessary, to keep the beans covered. Remove the cover for the last hour of baking so that the pork browns. Serve with the pork on top of the beans and accompany with chunks of the best sourdough bread available.

TAT-TOO GOOD .

When granting first-time tattooist and life-long friend Kev Smith free reign with inks upon his arm, Russell Tuck, from Ulverstone in Cumbria, could think of no more fitting an image than a jar of his beloved Marmite. Russell was chuffed with the result and his love for the spread is undiminished. Kev still sports a photo of Russell's arm in his tattoo shop window.

Spicy Sausage, Parsley and Caper Salad with Marmite Vinaigrette

SERVES 2

4 spicy sausages
   (merguez or similar)
$\frac{1}{2}$ small red onion,
   peeled and thinly sliced
1 tablespoon capers, rinsed
2 handfuls flat leaf parsley,
   chopped
freshly ground black pepper
1 freshly baked baguette,
   cut in half lengthways

For the vinaigrette
45ml olive oil
20ml white wine vinegar
$\frac{1}{2}$ teaspoon Dijon mustard
2 freshly chopped basil leaves
$\frac{1}{2}$ teaspoon runny honey
1 level teaspoon Marmite

To prepare the Marmite vinaigrette simply whizz together all the vinaigrette ingredients for about 30 seconds, until it emulsifies. This Marmite vinaigrette is great for all sorts of salads and can be kept in the fridge for 2–3 days.

Grill or fry the sausages until cooked, then slice thickly and keep them warm. Mix together the onion, capers and parsley. Combine the cooked sausage with the parsley salad and toss in the Marmite vinaigrette. Toast the cut side of the baguettes and pile the sausage salad mixture onto each half. Serve while still warm, seasoned with black pepper.

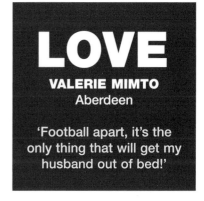

LOVE
VALERIE MIMTO
Aberdeen

'Football apart, it's the only thing that will get my husband out of bed!'

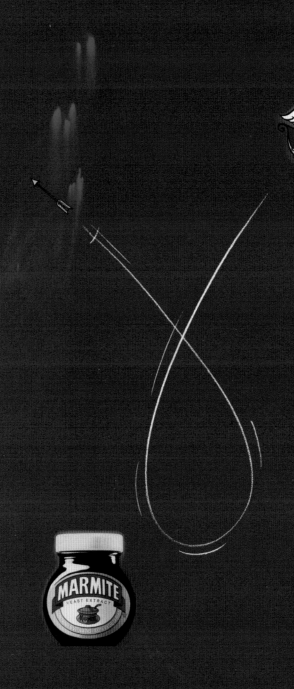

Marmite breath...
not the most romantic
Valentine's Day wake-up call!
But then there are those who
would disagree, of course....

Tuna and Sweetcorn Pancakes

MAKES 6–8

For the pancakes
1 egg
1 teaspoon Marmite
300ml milk
25g plain flour
vegetable oil

For the filling and topping
a small knob of butter
1 small tin sweetcorn, drained
2 tablespoons crème fraîche
1 small tin tuna
50g grated Emmental
handful of cashews
handful of crisps

First make the pancakes by whisking the egg, Marmite and milk together and then gradually blending in the flour until you have a smooth batter mixture. Leave to stand for 10 minutes.

Heat a lightly oiled non-stick frying pan and spoon a tablespoon of batter mixture into the pan. Swirl the batter around to coat the base of the pan and as soon as bubbles appear in the batter flip the pancake over. Repeat with the remaining mixture, keeping the cooked pancakes warm in a low oven.

In a saucepan melt the butter and over a gentle heat add the sweetcorn, followed by the crème fraîche and then the tuna. Turn the mixture gently to warm through. Take one pancake and spoon one sixth of the tuna mixture down the centre and roll it up. Follow with the other 5 pancakes and put them side-by-side in an ovenproof dish. Sprinkle with the grated cheese and pop the dish under a hot grill for a couple of minutes to melt the cheese. Serve the warm pancakes scattered with crushed crisps and chopped cashew nuts.

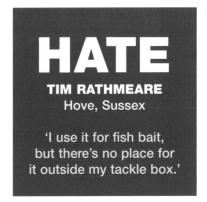

HATE
TIM RATHMEARE
Hove, Sussex

'I use it for fish bait, but there's no place for it outside my tackle box.'

Staffordshire Oatcakes with Goat's Cheese, Spinach and Walnuts

SERVES 2

100g frozen spinach, defrosted
1 teaspoon Marmite
1 pack Staffordshire oatcakes
(this is a pancake-like product
available from supermarkets)
100g soft goat's cheese
25g chopped walnuts
2 teaspoons snipped chives
freshly milled black pepper

Warm the spinach gently in a pan, adding a dash of water if needed, and then beat in the Marmite and cook gently for a couple of minutes. You can as an alternative mix the 2 together and heat in a microwave. Keep the mixture warm while you heat the oatcakes in a low oven,170C/325F/Gas 4.

When they are warm divide the goat's cheese between the 2 oatcakes and spread it right over. Drain the warm spinach thoroughly and then scatter it over the goat's cheese. Next strew the chopped walnuts over the spinach and season with fresh black pepper.

Roll up each oatcake and top with the snipped chives to garnish. For extra fun you can secure each roll with a cocktail stick, cut them in half at an angle and stand them up like chimneys.

LOVE

RAVI E. MOLMETI
Blackburn, Lancashire

'After the last scrape, I fill
the jar with warm water
and drink out the dregs.'

Quails' Eggs and Bockwurst Salad with Marmite Dressing

SERVES 2

8 baby new potatoes
2 Bockwurst sausages
6 quails' eggs
cos or little gem lettuce leaves, roughly chopped

For the salad dressing
45ml olive oil
1 level teaspoon Marmite
$\frac{1}{2}$ teaspoon Dijon mustard
25ml white wine vinegar
$\frac{1}{2}$ teaspoon runny honey
2 fresh basil leaves

Boil the baby new potatoes in salted water for about 15 minutes. Meanwhile gently grill the Bockwurst until cooked. Boil the quails' eggs for about 3 minutes. Plunge the eggs straight into cold water just until you can handle them and then remove the shells.

Make the salad dressing by placing all the ingredients into a blender and blitzing for about 30–50 seconds until they have emulsified.

Drain the new potatoes and allow them to cool a little. In a large bowl put the salad leaves, new potatoes and Bockwurst cut into thin slices on the diagonal. Add the dressing and toss them all very gently.

Place the coated leaves, Bockwurst and potatoes onto 2 plates then top with halved quails eggs. Season with a good grind of black pepper and enjoy while still warm with fresh crusty bread.

TAXI!

The livery of the London cab received a facelift during 2002, Marmite's centenary year. Thirty-three of them were decked out in distinctive eye-catching split-personality uniforms, with one side proclaiming '100 years of love', the other '100 years of hate'.

Pizza Milano de Chiviso

SERVES 2

1 pre-made pizza base
1 teaspoon Marmite
2 dessertspoons tomato purée
4 chestnut mushrooms, sliced
2 Italian plum tomatoes, sliced
2 slices (1cm thick) Milano salami,
   diced into cubes
8–10 separated rings of red onion
50g grated mozzarella
1 teaspoon fresh chopped oregano
   (or a good pinch of dried)
freshly ground black pepper
olive oil

Pre-heat the oven to medium hot 190C/375F/Gas 6. Spread the pizza base with Marmite and then the tomato purée. Next fan the mushroom slices followed by the tomato slices over the whole pizza. Top this with scattered salami cubes and the red onion rings and finally a flourish of grated mozzarella.

Season with oregano, fresh black pepper and drizzle with a little olive oil. Cook in the oven for 10–15 minutes or until the pizza is cooked through. Serve with a glass of chilled Pinot Grigio.

~1930~

Marmite stock cubes were launched in a distinctive green tin: easy to crumble straight into stews and soups. They were eventually dropped but were re-launched again 65 years later.

Indonesian Brunch

SERVES 4

groundnut oil for frying
6 shallots sliced lengthways
1 stick lemon grass, split open
    and finely diced
4oz peeled prawns
1 tablespoon fish sauce
3 mild red chillies, de-seeded
    and chopped
1 tablespoon sweet chilli sauce
1 teaspoon Marmite
100g button mushrooms
100g Shiitake mushrooms
250g long grain rice,
    cooked and cooled
4 medium free-range eggs

Heat two tablespoons of oil in a wok and fry the shallots, lemon grass and prawns for one minute. Then add the fish sauce and chilli and fry for a further 30 seconds. Next add the sweet chilli sauce and Marmite and toss together for 30 seconds. Finally add the mushrooms and the rice and stir-fry for about three minutes until it reaches a good deep colour.

Meanwhile fry the eggs keeping the yolks soft. Divide the rice mixture between warmed serving bowls. Top with a fried egg and accompany with a little informed and entertaining Oriental gossip.

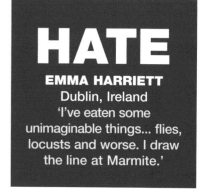

HATE
EMMA HARRIETT
Dublin, Ireland
'I've eaten some
unimaginable things... flies,
locusts and worse. I draw
the line at Marmite.'

Grange Asparagus Brunch

SERVES 1

4 stems fresh asparagus
3 cherry tomatoes
6 button mushrooms
a little olive oil
1 slice of good country bread
Marmite for spreading

Steam the fresh asparagus until its cooked but still has a crunch. Keep warm.

Brush the tomatoes and button mushrooms with olive oil and pop them under a medium grill for about 4 minutes. Do not over cook them or the tomato skins will split and the mushrooms will become crispy.

Toast the bread and then spread it with Marmite according to your taste.

Place the asparagus on the toast, 2 pieces horizontally and 2 vertically with equal gaps to form a 'chequer-board'.

Place a tomato in the top right hand corner, the central square and the bottom left hand corner, fill the remaining gaps with the button mushrooms and before devouring you can play noughts and crosses!

• This dish was influenced by Sarah from the Whatley Grange Cookery School, Somerset.

Back in the '30s, following the discovery that yeast extract was enriched with so many vitamins, GOOD became the buzz word, and GOOD could be found in both the spread and the newly launched stock cubes.

Baked Eggs with Marmite Mushrooms

SERVES 4

25g butter
2 shallots, peeled and finely
  chopped
300g flat mushrooms finely
 chopped (keeping a few
 slices for garnish)
$1/4$ of a whole nutmeg, grated
2 teaspoons Marmite
freshly ground black pepper
3 tablespoons of créme fraîche
  or Greek yoghurt
4 large free-range eggs
bunch of watercress

**You will need 4 ramekins and a
shallow roasting tin. This dish
looks really impressive when you
dunk your toasted soldiers into
the golden yolk.**

Heat half the butter in a small saucepan until it begins to sizzle. Add the shallots and cook on a low heat for five minutes until they have become transparent. Add the mushrooms, the nutmeg (warning – nutmeg is an aphrodisiac!), the remaining butter and the Marmite and season well with fresh pepper. Turn the heat right down and cook gently for a further 5–8 minutes until you have a lovely dark mixture.

Pre-heat the oven to 180C/350F/ Gas 4. Stir one tablespoon of the créme fraîche or yoghurt into the mushrooms, then divide the mixture between the ramekins. Make an indentation, break an egg into each one and season. Stir the rest of the créme fraîche or yoghurt to loosen it, divide it between the dishes and spread gently over the egg using the back of a spoon.

Put a slice of mushroom on the top of each ramekin and stand the ramekins in the roasting tin with $2/3$ cm of boiling water. Bake for 15–18 minutes. Serve with wholemeal toasted soldiers for dunking and garnish the plates with fresh watercress.

Haddock and Artichoke Chowder with Parsnip Crisps

SERVES 6

25g unsalted butter
1 small onion, finely chopped
400g Jerusalem artichokes,
   roughly chopped
700ml good fish stock
 (or fish bouillon and water)
1 teaspoon Marmite
200g natural smoked haddock,
   skinned and flaked
75ml double cream
cayenne pepper
vegetable oil for deep-frying
1 large parsnip
handful flat leaf parsley, chopped

Melt the butter and cook three quarters of the onion and half of the artichokes gently for 5 minutes in a covered saucepan making sure they don't brown. Add the fish stock and Marmite, bring to the boil and cover and simmer for about 15 minutes, until the vegetables are tender.

Begin to heat the vegetable oil ready for deep-frying the parsnip crisps. You should be able to make a sufficiently deep well of oil using a wok. Cool the mixture a little and then blitz in a liquidiser until puréed. Return the soup to a clean pan and add the remaining vegetables. Simmer gently for about 10 minutes until the vegetables are tender, then add the fish, cream and cayenne pepper, stirring gently for about 5 minutes.

When the chowder is nearly ready, peel the parsnip. Once peeled, continue to use the potato peeler to cut full-length shavings off the parsnip and deep-fry in oil pre-heated to 190C for about a minute until golden and crispy (like home-made crisps). Keep your eye on them as they will brown very quickly.

Serve the soup strewn with the parsnip crisps and flat-leaf parsley.

• It is best to use double cream rather than single as it won't split when over-heated.

Roquefort, Prawn and Pear Salad

SERVES 4

100ml olive oil
55ml lemon juice
1 teaspoon Marmite
freshly milled black pepper
pinch smoked paprika
4 ripe pears
mixed salad leaves
225g peeled prawns
100g Roquefort cheese
4 spring onions, diced

Put in a blender the olive oil and lemon juice, add the Marmite, pepper and smoked paprika and zap for 20–30 seconds.

Peel and core the pears and cut into 1cm slices and marinate in water and lemon juice to keep them from browning. (Lemon juice on its own will taint the natural flavour of the fruit).

On a plate, arrange a handful of mixed leaves into a nest. Lay in the sliced pear then the prawns and crumble the Roquefort over the top. Sprinkle on the spring onions and drizzle with the Marmite vinaigrette and serve.

NOT TO BE

CONFUSED WITH...

Margate
A seaside town on the south-east heel of England.
Marmoset
A small tropical American monkey with a long tail and a silky coat.
Araldite®
A brand of adhesives of fantastic use to people who like to glue things together. *Kitchen spread feasibility tests advised against (could possibly cement knife to bread).*

Lamb Kofte and Crispy Cabbage

SERVES 4

For the Kofte
450g minced lamb
1 teaspoon Marmite
1 teaspoon ground cumin seeds
(dry fried or roasted first)
2 tablespoons of chopped
fresh coriander
$\frac{1}{2}$ teaspoon garam masala
$\frac{1}{2}$ teaspoon cayenne pepper
3 tablespoons plain yoghurt
2 eggs, beaten

For the crispy cabbage
1 small white cabbage, shredded
(as you would for coleslaw)
2 pickled dill cucumbers, thinly
sliced
1 medium red chilli, finely diced
black pepper, freshly ground
white pepper, freshly ground
olive oil
lime juice

Put all the Kofte ingredients, except
the beaten egg, into a large bowl
and mix thoroughly with your hands
dipping your hands in water to
avoid the mixture sticking to you,
then shape into 20–24 equal-sized
meatballs.

Put the meatballs on greaseproof
paper in the fridge for 20 minutes
to set.

Mix the white cabbage, dill
cucumber and red chilli in a salad
bowl, season with freshly ground
black and white pepper and dress
with a little olive oil and lime juice.

Brush the Kofte with beaten egg
and deep fry in small batches.
Serve while still warm on the bed
of crispy cabbage.

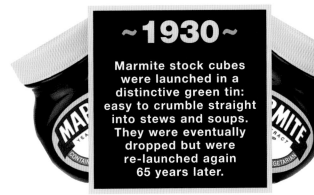

~1930~

Marmite stock cubes
were launched in a
distinctive green tin:
easy to crumble straight
into stews and soups.
They were eventually
dropped but were
re-launched again
65 years later.

HONK IF YOU EAT MARMITE

YOU'LL HONK IF YOU EAT MARMITE

Tuscan Picnic Loaf

SERVES 6

1 ciabatta loaf
250g sun-dried tomatoes, roughly
    chopped
250g mixed peppers in oil
1 dessertspoon Marmite
2 dessertspoons red pesto
100g pastrami
2 Italian plum tomatoes, sliced
100g mozzarella, sliced
handful fresh basil leaves
freshly ground black pepper

Cut the ciabatta in half lengthways and remove a little of the soft bread in the centre to make way for the filling. Drizzle a tablespoon of oil from the sun-dried tomatoes and peppers over one half of the ciabatta and then spread the Marmite. Over the other half spread the red pesto.

Taking the base of the loaf layer the sun-dried tomatoes and then the peppers, then the pastrami. Pile the tomatoes and the mozzarella on top and finish with a dozen fresh basil leaves and some freshly ground black pepper. Replace the lid of the loaf and press down firmly.

You can now slice the loaf into portions and enjoy, or wrap in greaseproof paper and pack in the picnic hamper. This loaf is perfect made the night before, kept in the fridge and sliced off for all the family to enjoy for lunch.

CARRYING THE TORCH

Marmite sponsored the 1956 British Olympic team. The Games of this twenty-sixth Olympiad were held in Melbourne, Australia, except for the equestrian events, which, due to Australia's strict six-month quarantine regulations, were switched, late, and at some inconvenience, to Stockholm in Sweden. This was (and remains) thonly occasion that events of the same Olympics had been held in different countries. Great Britain managed to bag a haul of 24 medals, six of them gold. Part of the legacy of the Melbourne Games was that it firmly established television sets in the homes and hearts of the Australian people. Prior to the Games, there had been a widely-held perception that television was American and 'cheap'. Every Aussie wanted to watch the Games, though, and this made ownership of televisions respectable and popular, resulting in rocketing sales of television sets for the duration of the Olympics.

Manhattan Bagel

SERVES 1

1 bagel
butter for spreading
Marmite for spreading
good dollop of peanut butter
50g sliced pastrami
handful of rocket leaves

Split and toast the cut sides of the bagel. Spread with a little butter and then a good layer of Marmite.

Next add the peanut butter, then the pastrami and finally pack the rocket on top and replace the lid of the bagel. Ready to go!

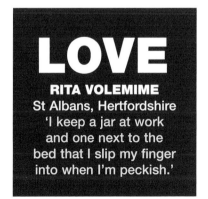

LOVE
RITA VOLEMIME
St Albans, Hertfordshire
'I keep a jar at work
and one next to the
bed that I slip my finger
into when I'm peckish.'

Creamy Garlic Mushrooms on Toasted Brioche

SERVES 2

200g chestnut mushrooms
25g unsalted butter
1 clove garlic, crushed
100g crème fraîche
2 teaspoons Marmite
2 medium brioche rolls
1 dessertspoon chopped parsley

Wipe the mushrooms with a clean damp cloth and then cut each one into quarters. Melt the butter in a frying pan and add the garlic and mushrooms and sauté them until just cooked. Season generously with fresh black pepper and add the crème fraîche and the Marmite. Cook on a medium heat, stirring well, until the sauce has thickened to coat the mushrooms.

Split and toast the cut sides of the brioche rolls and place them on 2 warmed plates. Pile the creamy mushrooms over the brioche and garnish with a drift of parsley.

Prawn and Marmite Sesame Toasts

SERVES 4

100g cooked peeled prawns
1 teaspoon cornflour
1 egg white, lightly beaten
4 slices white bread
Marmite for spreading
2 tablespoons sesame seeds
2 tablespoons vegetable oil

Finely mince the prawns to form a paste (a pestle and mortar will do the trick) and then add the cornflour and egg white to bind the mixture. Take the bread slices, cut off the crusts and spread with a thin layer of Marmite and then the minced prawns. Put the sesame seeds on a flat plate then press he bread slices, prawn side down, onto the sesame seeds until thickly coated.

Heat half the oil and gently fry each slice, prawn side down first, for 2–3 minutes, turning after 1–1$\frac{1}{2}$ minutes, until just golden. Add a little more oil as needed and cook the remaining slices in the same way. Serve while still warm, cut into triangles for an ideal munchie or a scummy starter.

POWERING ROCKET MAN

'I always take Marmite with me...'. So says Elton John of one of the 'stock essentials' he just can't do without whilst away on tour. In 1979, so the story goes, Elton played a series of concerts in Moscow and Leningrad, in the former Soviet Union. During the tour, Elton developed a hankering for the tastes of home, so an urgent request was sent back to his London office for Marmite and a few other store cupboard ingredients. Incredibly, these delights were sent out to Elton via the British Embassy's 'diplomatic bag', taking it outside the jurisdiction of customs officials, and ensuring its speedy delivery to the craving popstar. It was this same diplomatic bag that kept Winston Churchill in Cuban cigars during World War Two, courtesy of a well-wishing American.

Toasted Rye Bread with Goat's Cheese and Rocket

SERVES 4

1 German country-style rye bread
  (Landbrot)
50g sunblush tomatoes
Marmite
100g goat's cheese
small bunch of rocket
freshly milled black pepper

Cut and toast four slices of rye bread. The bread needs to be about 1cm thick.

While this is toasting, chop up the sunblush tomatoes, setting aside some of their delicious oil. Spread a teaspoon of Marmite on each piece of toast. Then lay enough slices of goat's cheese on top of the Marmite to cover the toast. Return the toast to the grill until the cheese just starts to melt.

Sprinkle the sunblush tomatoes over the goat's cheese and finally add a flourish of rocket leaves over the top. Season generously with pepper and drizzle a little of the remaining oil from the tomatoes over the top.

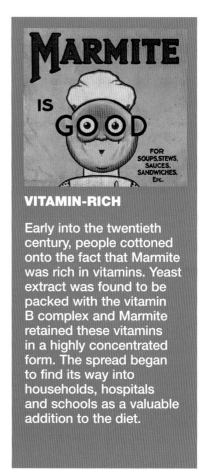

VITAMIN-RICH

Early into the twentieth century, people cottoned onto the fact that Marmite was rich in vitamins. Yeast extract was found to be packed with the vitamin B complex and Marmite retained these vitamins in a highly concentrated form. The spread began to find its way into households, hospitals and schools as a valuable addition to the diet.

Pasta al Penne

SERVES 4

200g pasta al penne
1 tablespoon olive oil
100g dried wild mushrooms,
   pre-soaked in water for
   30 minutes and drained
1 teaspoon Marmite
150ml double cream
black pepper
1 tablespoon of pitted black
   olives, roughly chopped
freshly grated vintage Parmesan
fresh parsley, chopped

Boil the pasta in plenty of salted water for about 8–10 minutes or until it is just al dente. While the pasta is cooking heat the olive oil in a frying pan and gently sauté the mushrooms for a couple of minutes. Add the Marmite to the mushrooms and toss them until well coated and then add the cream and some fresh pepper. Toss the mushrooms in the sauce for 2–3 minutes until the cream reduces down just a little and add the black olives.

Drain the cooked pasta and divide it between two warmed plates, then pile the mushrooms and sauce over the pasta. Finish with a good sprinkling of Parmesan and chopped parsley.

~1956~

Carrying the torch! Some 20 years after the restoratitive wonders of Marmite were hailed in the pamphlet *Invalid Dishes*, Marmite were installed as sponsors of the British Olympic team in Melbourne.

Potato Wedges with Minted Yogurt Dip

SERVES 2

2 large baking potatoes, washed
2 level teaspoons Marmite
2 tablespoons olive oil
small tub of Greek yogurt
2 teaspoons ready-made mint jelly

Put the potatoes in their skins into a large pan of water and boil gently for about 20 minutes until the potatoes are 'half cooked'. Drain the potatoes and allow to cool sufficiently to handle.

Pre-heat the oven to medium hot 190C/375F/Gas 6. Whisk together the Marmite and olive oil. Cut each potato in half lengthways and then still working lengthways cut the potato into wedges about 2cm thick at the skin edge. Lay the wedges on a baking tray and douse each one with plenty of the Marmite oil. Roast in the oven for about 20 minutes until crispy and golden.

In a small dish mix together the yogurt and mint jelly, place it in the centre of a large plate and serve the golden wedges fanned all around the dip.

Chicken Club Sandwich

MAKES 2 SANDWICHES

6 rashers of rindless back bacon
3 large free-range eggs
knob of butter for frying
6 slices good brown bread,
    toasted
3 dessertspoons mayonnaise
6 large Iceberg or webb's lettuce
    leaves
1 chicken breast fillet,
    cooked and thinly sliced
2 tomatoes, sliced
freshly ground black pepper
Marmite for spreading
crisps or chips to serve (optional)

Prepare the fillings first. Grill the bacon until crispy. Whisk the eggs and then lightly scramble them in a knob of butter until just set.

Build each sandwich in this order. Lay a piece of toast on a chopping board, spread with mayonnaise, then cover it with a layer of lettuce leaves and half the sliced chicken breast. Cover this with a layer of sliced tomato and season with freshly milled black pepper. Take another piece of toast and spread with Marmite and put it Marmite side down on the tomatoes.

Spread the top side of the same piece of toast with Marmite, pour half the scrambled egg over this piece of toast and then cover it with half the crispy bacon rashers. Finish with another layer of lettuce leaves and the final piece of toast, spread with mayonnaise.

Secure each half of the sandwich with a cocktail stick and slice the sandwich diagonally. Serve while still warm for a delicious brunch with a few potato chips or home-made crisps.

~1974~

This year brought a shortage of the traditional glass jar. There was a brief, but worrying, interlude in which Marmite was sold in more conventionally shaped jars.

Spinach, Marmite and Mozzarella Muffins

SERVES 1

1 English muffin
butter for spreading
Marmite
2 tablespoons of wilted
    baby leaf spinach
50g mozzarella, thinly sliced
freshly milled black pepper
1 medium free-range egg

Pre-heat the grill to medium-high. Split and toast the muffins and spread each half with a little butter and then a good layer of Marmite. Pile the spinach onto each muffin half and top with the slices of mozzarella. Season well with fresh black pepper.

Pop the stack back under the grill and cook for about 3–4 minutes or until the mozzarella is just melting down the side. In the meantime poach the egg and serve the hot muffin topped with the poached egg.

SIMPLE IS BEST

Rigorous academic research has shown that the most pleasurable way to eat Marmite is thus:
a) use white bread (toasted to avoid dampness);
b) butter whilst still warm;
c) apply Marmite thinly, and leave small gaps;
d) cram it in your mouth as quickly as possible. What could be easier?

Marmite celebrated its centenary year in style. 2002 saw a frenzy of activity around Marmite – commemorative jars, limited-edition designer T-shirts, brightly branded London taxis, and a trio of memorable TV adverts.

And one of those adverts, of course, featured Zippy. He revealed his dislike to a shocked nation by zipping up and taking cover under the table!

Marmite Popovers with Turkey and Tomato

MAKES 18

Popovers
2 large free-range eggs,
   plus one egg yolk
250ml milk
   (or milk and water mixed)
2 teaspoons Marmite
1 tablespoon melted butter
125g self-raising flour
vegetable oil for greasing

To serve
36 cherry tomatoes
   (2 per popover)
18 turkey rashers (1 rasher per
   popover, each cut into 4 pieces)

Heat the oven to 230C/450F/Gas 8. In a large bowl beat the whole eggs plus the one egg yolk, then blend in the milk, Marmite and melted butter. Now sift in the flour and beat well until you have a creamy smooth consistency. Strain the mixture into a jug, then chill in the refrigerator for 10 minutes or until required. Batter is always better when made a little in advance.

Meanwhile lightly oil a 12-bun tray and place in the oven for 2–3 minutes to heat the oil. Remove from the oven and three-quarter-fill the hollows of the tin with the batter mixture – a bit like making Yorkshire puddings.

Bake in the oven for 15 minutes, then reduce the oven temperature to 200C/400F/Gas 6 and bake the popovers for a further 15 minutes until well risen and crisp. Avoid opening the oven door until cooked because the change in temperature may cause them to sink – and that would be a real shame. Serve the popovers piled with grilled cherry tomatoes and crispy turkey rashers.

Once made and cooled you can freeze the popovers for another day. Turkey rashers are available from most supermarkets and make a fun alternative to bacon.

Pancetta and Gruyère Frittata

SERVES 3–4

250g diced pancetta
1 medium red chilli,
   de-seeded and finely chopped
6 large free-range eggs
150g Gruyère cheese,
   roughly grated
1 level teaspoon Marmite
1 teaspoon fresh chives,
   finely chopped
freshly ground black pepper
1 tablespoon flat-leaf parsley,
   roughly chopped

You will need a non-stick frying pan, 30cm in diameter and about 5cm deep.

Cook the Pancetta in it's own fat for 5 minutes over a medium heat until lightly browned. Add the chilli and cook for 30 seconds.

Beat the eggs lightly in a large jug and mix in the grated cheese, Marmite and chopped chives. Season lightly with pepper.

Pre-heat the grill to it's highest setting. Pour the egg mixture into the frying pan and cook over a low heat for 5–8 minutes or until the egg has set. Put the pan under the grill about 10cm from the heat. Let it cook for a few minutes or until golden on top – but do keep an eye on it. Sprinkle the parsley over, cut into thick wedges and serve.

~1980~

An army marched across our television screens to herald the beginning of the 'My Mate Marmite' campaign. The 'Love it, Hate it' campaign would hit our screens 16 years later with just as big a punch.

Sicilian Scramble

SERVES 4

2 slices of focaccia bread
  (garlic and rosemary focaccia
  is sensational)
1 teaspoon Marmite
2 large slices of Prosciutto ham
  (enough to cover the bread)
butter for scrambling
1 small green chilli, finely diced
4 free-range eggs
celery salt
freshly milled black pepper
dash of Tabasco sauce
1 tablespoon chopped
  sunblush tomatoes
chopped fresh parsley

Lightly toast the focaccia bread
and then spread with the Marmite.
Lay the slices of ham on the hot
Marmite toast.

Melt a little butter in a pan. Add the
chilli, whisked eggs and season
with the celery salt and pepper and
then add a dash of Tabasco Sauce
to taste. When the eggs are just
beginning to set, add in the
sunblush tomatoes and stir well.

Pile the scrambled eggs on top of
the toast, garnish with fresh parsley
and serve immediately.

FIGHTING FIT

The word vitamin was
only coined in 1912,
to define chemicals
that were found to be
necessary in our diets.
Marmite was packed with
B vitamins... and still is.

Cream Cheese, Pistachio and Watercress Crumpets

SERVES 2

4 crumpets
unsalted butter
Marmite for spreading
75g cream cheese
50g chopped pistachio nuts
a bunch of watercress

Toast and butter the crumpets. Spread the Marmite on next, according to taste, and then the cream cheese.

Sprinkle the chopped pistachios over the top and finally pile on some good sprigs of watercress. The combination of the 'salty' Marmite, creamy cheese and peppery watercress is divine – hence two per person!

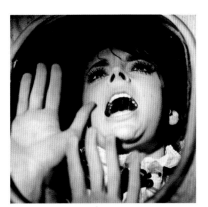

HATE

MARTIE THAME
London
'When I was young, my older brother told me it was chocolate spread. I've not forgiven him to this day.'

Panini with Marmite Tapenade, Taleggio and Sweet Peppers

SERVES 4

1 red pepper, deseeded
2 tablespoons olive oil
pinch sugar
225g black olives, stoned
1 teaspoon Marmite
25g capers, drained
1 teaspoon lemon juice
freshly ground black pepper
1 dessertspoon breadcrumbs
  (optional)
1 small ciabatta loaf
50g Taleggio cheese
  (or similar Italian hard cheese)
few basil leaves, torn

Set the grill to medium-high. Cut the pepper in half and brush with a little olive oil, add a pinch of sugar, and grill skin side up until charred. Remove the peppers leaving the grill on. Put the seared peppers in a plastic bag and leave to cool – this will help lift the skin from the flesh easily.

In the meantime make the tapenade by blitzing the olives, Marmite and capers in a food processor until you have a purée. Then gradually add the olive oil followed by the lemon juice and pepper. If at this stage the tapenade is not like a firm paste, mix in a dessertspoon of breadcrumbs. This tapenade will keep for a week in the fridge, so if you have some left over keep it ready for your next feast.

Cut the ciabatta in half lengthways, toast and then spread with the tapenade, followed by the roughly chopped peppers. Using a potato peeler cut shavings off the Taleggio and sprinkle over the peppers. Serve at once with the torn basil leaves scattered on top.

Another of Marmite's centenary-commissioned TV adverts. This time, the unveiling of the freak called 'Marmite Man'. Audiences gasped as he spooned the notorious spread straight from the jar into his mouth!

Red Onion Marmalade and Goat's Cheese Tartlet

SERVES 4

1 pack puff pastry
flour for dusting
Marmite
4 dessertspoons red onion marmalade (available from most good food stores)
150g soft goat's cheese
1 medium egg yolk plus tablespoon of water, beaten together

few sprigs of freshly torn flat-leaf parsley
black pepper

Pre-heat the oven to 200C/400F/Gas 6. Roll the pastry out on a lightly floured board to form a large square and then cut the pastry into 8 smaller squares about 8–10cm square.

Spread a layer of Marmite over each square and then turn up the edges to make a border. Now add a tablespoon of onion marmalade to each tartlet, spreading it evenly with the back of a spoon. Add a slice of goat's cheese on top and put the tartlets onto a floured baking tray.

Brush the borders of the tartlets with the egg and water wash and chill for at least 15 minutes before baking in the centre of the oven for 15 minutes.

Allow the finished tartlets to cool a little and serve strewn with the torn parsley leaves and some fresh black pepper.

*Puff pastry rises better when cold from the refrigerator, so make these tartlets in advance and cook when ready.

~2002~

Marmite's centenary year: the year of Marmite-flavoured Walkers Crisps; children's TV favourite Zippy zipping up in disgust at Marmite; 33 London taxis painted with the Love-It-Hate-It slogan; and a visit to the Marmite factory in Burton-on-Trent from HRH The Duke of Edinburgh.

Marmite Corn Fritters

SERVES 4

1 egg
2 level tablespoons
   self-raising flour
$1/4$ teaspoon cayenne pepper
$1/2$ teaspoon Worcestershire sauce
1 teaspoon Marmite
326g tin of sweetcorn, drained
vegetable oil for frying
bacon and maple syrup,
   to accompany

Make a stiff batter by mixing together the beaten egg, sieved flour and Cayenne pepper. Beat well and then add the Worcestershire sauce and Marmite and beat for a further minute. Fold in the sweetcorn so that it is well mixed with the batter and refrigerate for 20 minutes.

Oil a griddle or heavy frying pan over a medium-high heat and spoon on tablespoons of the mixture. Cook for 4–5 minutes, turning once, until golden brown. Kids love this dish, which is great served with grilled bacon and maple syrup.

LOVE
VIOLET MAMRIE
Loughborough
'On toast morning and night, on roast potatoes, in stews, in soups... when and wherever I can get it.'

Basil French Toast with Dolcelatte and Pimento

SERVES 2

3 medium free-range eggs
100ml milk
level tablespoon of freshly
  chopped basil leaves
freshly ground black pepper
Marmite for spreading
4 slices firm rustic bread
150g Dolcelatte, cut into 4 slices
1–2 large red peppers, sliced
2 tablespoons olive oil

In a shallow bowl mix together the egg, milk, chopped basil and pepper. Spread the bread with Marmite and dip each slice into the mixture until well soaked and transfer to a large plate. Add the Dolcelatte and the slices of pepper. Season well with fresh pepper and then sandwich together the remaining slices of bread, gently pressing together to seal them.

Heat half the olive oil on a griddle or in a large non-stick frying pan and fry the sandwiches over a low heat for about 3–4 minutes on each side until golden, adding the remaining oil as needed. Check that the bread has cooked through and is not soggy inside and then drain on kitchen paper to remove any excess oil.

Serve immediately on warmed plates.

OLD TIMER

Among the younger kids on the block:

Teabags (invented by Thomas Sullivan, 1904)
The cornflake (invented by William Kellog, 1906)
Plastic (discovered 1907)
Crossword puzzle (first published New York, 1912)

Traffic lights (first installed outside the British House of Commons, 1914)
Zip fasteners (invented 1914)
The band-aid bandage (launched by Johnson & Johnson, 1921)
London red double-decker bus (1925)
McDonalds (founded 1959)

Roasted Vegetable Filo Parcels

SERVES 2

ready-made filo pastry
1 small aubergine
1 small courgette
$\frac{1}{2}$ red pepper, deseeded
4 shallots, peeled
2 tablespoons olive oil
1 teaspoon Marmite
1 teaspoon white sugar
melted butter
50g Philadelphia Lite
bunch watercress

Heat the oven to190C/375F/Gas 6. Cut the different vegetables into 2–3cm dice and put them onto a baking tray. Mix the olive oil with the Marmite and drizzle it over the cut vegetables, tossing them to make sure they are well coated. Sprinkle with the sugar and roast for about 20 minutes until still crunchy but seared around the edges. Remove from the oven and leave to cool just a little.

Cut the filo pastry sheet into 20cm squares. Brush with melted butter and lay one square on top of another each time rotating 15 degrees to form a star shape with 3 squares of filo. (Easy to think of the degrees as 5, 10, 15 minutes past the hour and so on).

Put a teaspoon of cream cheese in the centre of each star plus a tablespoon of mixed vegetables. Gather up the outer points of the pastry star, pinch together and twist at the neck to form a little parcel. Repeat with the remaining cream cheese and vegetables tomake four parcels (you will have vegetables left over). Put all of the parcels on a greased baking sheet, brush them all over with melted butter and cook in the centre of a medium oven 180C/350F/Gas 5 for 5–8 minutes until the pastry turns golden brown at the edges.

Allow the parcels to cool a little and serve with any remaining vegetables around the base of the parcels and a big bunch of fresh peppery watercress.

Mushroom, Ham and Honey Stack

SERVES 4

For the pancakes
280g plain flour
1 teaspoon salt
2 teaspoons baking powder
2 tablespoons caster sugar
225ml milk
1 teaspoon Marmite
3 free-range eggs, beaten
50g melted unsalted butter

For the topping
200g button mushrooms
1 tablespoon olive oil
100g diced smoked ham
runny chestnut honey for pouring

Sift the flour, salt, baking powder and sugar into a bowl, then whisk in the milk, Marmite, beaten eggs and butter mixing to form a thick batter. If it isn't very smooth don't worry and don't be tempted to over-mix.

Heat a lightly buttered griddle or frying pan and add 2 tablespoons of the batter for each pancake, cooking in batches of 3–4 at a time. As soon as you see bubbles forming on the surface of the pancakes flip them over. They will need about a minute on each side. Keep the pancakes warm while you repeat, using up all the mixture.

Slice 3/4 of the mushrooms, leaving a few whole for topping the stacks. Heat the olive oil in a pan and sauté the whole ones first adding the sliced ones later until they are just golden. Toss in the diced ham and cook with the mushrooms for no more than a minute. For each serving, layer some sliced mushrooms and ham between four pancakes in a stack on a warmed plate and then some whole mushrooms on the top. Finish with a good drizzle of chestnut honey.

Roasted Onion Soup with Cheddar Croûtons

SERVES 4–6

4 medium onions
40g unsalted butter
sea salt and fresh black pepper
1 dessertspoon Demerara sugar
175ml of dry white wine
1.5 litres good vegetable stock
1 teaspoon Marmite
1 small French stick
100g grated Cheddar
fresh thyme

Peel the onions and quarter them from the top to the bottom. Lay them on a roasting tray and scatter them with pieces of the butter. Season with a little salt and lots of black pepper. Roast for about 30–40 minutes until they begin to darken.

Allow the onion quarters to cool a little and then slice them into half moons. Put them in a large heavy based saucepan, add the sugar and wine and bring to the boil, bubbling until the wine has almost disappeared. Add the stock and Marmite, bring back to the boil and then cook gently for about 20 minutes.

To make the croûtons, slice the French bread to allow 2 per person and toast on one side under the grill. Turn them over and sprinkle with a little grated cheese and return to the grill long enough to melt the cheese. Serve the hot soup with the melted cheese croûtons floating temptingly on the surface and scattered with fresh thyme.

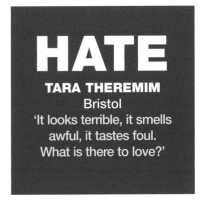

HATE
TARA THEREMIM
Bristol
'It looks terrible, it smells awful, it tastes foul. What is there to love?'

THE COLMAN'S MUSTARD
RECIPE COLLECTION

Butterfly Lamb with Honey and Mustard

SERVES 6–8

3kg leg of lamb, gross weight
(ask your butcher to prepare
a butterflied leg of lamb)

For the marinade
150ml soy sauce
8 cm fresh ginger, grated
2 tablespoons runny honey
4 cloves of garlic, finely chopped
1 level tablespoon Colman's
English mustard powder
freshly ground black pepper
25ml olive oil

Place the lamb in a suitable big dish or roasting tray. Mix together all the other ingredients. Spoon the mixture evenly over the lamb and leave overnight in the fridge. It is even better if left for up to two days.

Remove the lamb from the fridge one hour before cooking. Set the oven on high (200C/400F/Gas 6). Take the lamb out of the marinade and dry it with some kitchen paper. Open it out fully and flatten with the palm of your hand. Now place the lamb in a roasting dish and put it into the very hot oven for 20–30 minutes until the fat just begins to crisp. Remove from the oven, cover with foil and leave to rest for 10 minutes.

Now for the good bit. Heat the remaining marinade slowly, do not allow it to boil. Thickly slice the lamb and ladle the marinade over. Perfect served with crispy potato wedges cooked in goose fat, a dish of fresh green beans or mixed green salad. This makes a great dinner party, Sunday lunch or barbecue dish.

In the beginning...

■■■ The origins of mustard date back to the sixth century BC: Pythagoras is said to have used it as an antidote to scorpion stings. A hundred years later, the pioneering Greek physician Hippocrates used the seed for making a variety of medicines and poultices.

■■■ The potent nature of the mustard seed was attested to in an exchange between King Darius of Persia and the young Alexander the Great. Darius gifted Alexander a sack of sesame seed to represent the number of his army. Alexander returned the compliment, with a sack of mustard seeds to symbolise both the

Tequila Prawns with Mustard and Lime

SERVES 4

500g large cooked prawns
1 yellow pepper cut into 1.5cm
   pieces
8 salad onions (white bulb part only)
16 cherry tomatoes

For the marinade
30ml Tequila
juice 1 lime
1 teaspoon Colman's English
   mustard

1 whole lime, cut into 8 wedges

You will need 8 wooden kebab
skewers.

Soak the kebab skewers in water to prevent the ends burning during cooking. Spear the prawns, peppers, onions and tomatoes alternately onto the skewers. Place the kebabs in a shallow dish.

To make the marinade, blend the Tequila, lime juice and mustard and pour it over the prawn kebabs. Cover and chill for 30 minutes, turning the kebabs from time to time to take up the juices.

Fire up the barbie and cook the kebabs for 3–4 minutes on each side, basting with the juices of the marinade. Serve each kebab with a wedge of lime, leaving the cook to enjoy the rest of the Tequila accompanied, in time honoured tradition, with a little lime and salt.

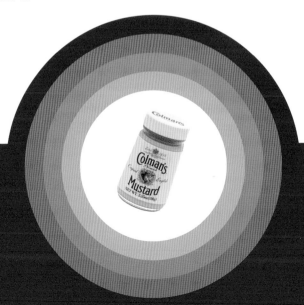

■■■ The word 'mustard' is thought to derive from the Latin words 'must' (much) and 'ardens' (burning).

Crispy Pork with Pink Champagne and Passionfruit

SERVES 6

6 trimmed pieces pork belly, about 200–250g, preferably square and scored by your butcher

12 banana shallots, peeled and halved

6 cloves garlic, peeled and sliced

2 dessertspoons Colman's English mustard powder

25g flour

1 stock cube, dissolved in 1 litre water

37.5cl pink Champagne (or sparkling rosé)

1 tablespoon sea salt

3 passionfruit, halved and flesh removed

Heat a deep frying pan on the hob and place the belly pork fat-side down for about 5 minutes to tease out the fat. Turn the pork belly pieces once there is enough juice for them to sit in. Add the halved banana shallots and the garlic to the frying pan and continue to cook on a medium heat for a further 8–10 minutes until the shallots begin to caramelise.

Meanwhile, mix the mustard, flour and half the stock in a separate jug, whisking until no lumps remain. Pour the mixture over the pork belly with the remaining stock and the Champagne. Transfer everything to a roasting tin, cover with foil and place in a pre-heated oven at 180C/350F/Gas 5 for $1^1/_2$ hours. Remove the roasting tray from the oven and take out the belly pork and place on a new oven tray. Pour all the remaining juices into a sauce pan and set aside. Sprinkle the pork belly with sea salt and return to a hot oven 230C/450F/Gas 8 for 15–20 minutes to crisp up the pork.

Meanwhile, heat the pan of Champagne juices adding the passion fruit flesh, mix together well and continue to simmer until the sauce has reduced enough to be able to coat the back of a spoon. Place the pork on a warmed serving plate and serve the Champagne sauce around the pork.

Fennel Coleslaw with Colman's Mustard Mayonnaise

SERVES 4

750g fresh fennel, greenery removed and finely sliced
1 large onion, finely sliced
2 large carrots, peeled and grated
1 tablespoon small capers
1 tablespoon diced dill pickle
4 tablespoons mayonnaise (preferably home-made)
1 tablespoon Colman's English mustard
1 teaspoon lemon juice
olive oil
salt and freshly ground black pepper
1 dessertspoon vermouth
1 teaspoon sesame seeds, toasted
50g fresh coriander, chopped

Place the sliced fennel, onion and grated carrots into a big mixing bowl, add the capers and diced dill pickle.

In a separate dish mix together the mayonnaise, mustard, lemon juice, 2 teaspoons of olive oil, a pinch or two of salt and some freshly ground black pepper. Finally add the vermouth and mix all together with a wooden spoon until you have a smooth, creamy dressing.

Spoon the dressing over the salad and mix together thoroughly. Place the dressed salad into a clean dish and sprinkle with the sesame seeds and the coriander.

This makes a great accompaniment to fish, barbecued pork or bangers and mash.

HOT FACT

The town of Al Aziziyah in Libya, 20 miles inland of the country's capital, Tripoli, is the place where the hottest world temperature in history was recorded. On September 13th, 1922, thermometers in the town peaked at a blistering 136 Fahrenheit (57.8 Celsius). A road runs from the town into the Sahara Desert, where a burning wind called the 'ghibli' – one intensely hot and strewn with sand – can soar temperatures up to between 40 and 50C within the space of sixty minutes.

Orange-spiced Chocolate Cookies

MAKES 20 COOKIES

100g dark cooking chocolate
50g salted butter, softened
100g soft brown sugar
1/2 teaspoon ground cinnamon
1 teaspoon Colman's English
mustard powder
150g plain flour
2 teaspoons baking powder
1 medium free-range egg, beaten
1 tablespoon Grand Marnier
liqueur
zest 1 medium orange

Melt the chocolate in a bowl over a pan of boiling water and then set aside. Into a food mixer, put the softened butter, sugar, cinnamon and mustard powder. Sieve in the flour and baking powder and add the egg. Mix together and, after about 30 seconds, slowly add the melted chocolate. Finally, add the Grand Marnier liqueur and the orange zest and again mix together at the slowest speed until you have a dough like consistency.

Place a large piece of greaseproof paper onto the worktop and gently roll out the dough to about 3cm thick. Using a biscuit cutter begin to cut out the biscuits, re-rolling until all the dough has been used. Leaving the biscuits on the greaseproof paper, transfer them to the fridge to chill for about 2 hours. Once chilled, place in a pre-heated oven at 190C/375F/Gas 5 for 8 minutes. Leave to cool before serving.

Surprisingly good on cold winter days or with tea in the garden. The mustard gives the whole recipe a real lift.

COLD TRUTH

When the woodland frog stumbles upon cold times, he's not one to worry. He calls home a place just north of the Arctic Circle, and when the cold winds come blowing, can survive for weeks in a frozen state. The glucose in his blood acts like a kind of antifreeze that centres on his vital organs, protecting them from damage, but which allows the rest of his body to freeze solid. So, whilst up to 65% of his body water can become frozen, his cells don't – only the water outside the cells. As soon as the outside temperature rises, his body begins to thaw and he's on the move once more.

Kidneys Devilled with Colman's Mustard

SERVES 2

500g lambs' kidneys
12g butter
1 dessertspoon vegetable oil
1 medium onion, finely diced
Worcestershire sauce
100g button mushrooms
55ml Madeira wine
2 heaped teaspoons Colman's
  English mustard powder
salt and freshly ground black
  pepper
120ml double cream

Cut the kidneys in half and with scissors carefully remove the white centre. Put the butter and oil into a large frying pan and heat until hot (butter for flavour, oil to withstand higher heat).

Sauté the onions until transparent, add the kidneys and a dash of Worcestershire sauce and sauté for another 3–4 minutes. Now add the mushrooms and the Madeira and let it all bubble and reduce by about one third.

Meanwhile, in a separate bowl mix the cream with the mustard and season with salt and pepper. Remove the kidneys from the heat and allow to cool for about 1 minute. Add the mustard cream and allow to bubble and thicken. Serve on thick granary toast with a sprinkle of chopped parsley, accompanied by a glass of chilled Somerset cider.

TV, music... the Vatican...

■■■ In 1996, the J Walter Thompson creative agency developed the now-famous 'Farmyard campaign' featuring animatronic farmyard animals, among whom the indubitable star was the pig. The campaign reached its climax with the 1998 installment which saw our funky pig strutting his stuff and singing lines to the ironic tune of 'Staying Alive'. Pig sang:

'Well you can tell by the way I'm made of pork / I'm not a Colman's fan. I think we should talk.'

The advert was a huge success.

Cream of Cauliflower & Mustard Soup

SERVES 2

50g unsalted butter
1 kg cauliflower (I try to use Romanesque for this, as it has a lovely nutty flavour)
300g good firm shallots (try and locate the purple tinted banana shallots)
100g celery
1 heaped dessertspoon garlic, finely diced
25g Colman's English mustard powder, freshly made
100ml single cream
20g brown sugar

salt and freshly ground black pepper
1 dessertspoon chopped French parsley

Melt the butter gently in a pan. When melted, add all the other ingredients apart from 4 small cauliflower florets and the parsley. When the shallots have become transparent and the other vegetables have begun to soften, add 1 litre of cold water and bring the mixture to the boil.

Simmer gently for 30 minutes. Allow to cool a little and then blitz in a liquidiser, adding the cream until smooth. Season to taste.

Next, take the reserved florets and blanch for about 5 minutes. Serve the soup in deep round bowls placing 2 florets in the centre of each bowl. Garnish with the parsley. This is excellent served piping hot in the cold winter months, or chilled during the summer.

■■■ 'Mustard's no good without roast beef.'
Chico Marx, *Funny Business*.
■■■ 'Mean Mister Mustard sleeps in the park /
Shaves in the dark trying to save paper'
From the Beatles' 'Mean Mr Mustard'.
■■■ Pope John XXII was said to be fond of mustard.

Somerset-style Pork Chops

SERVES 2

oil
2 pork chops
1 wine glass medium Somerset
   cider
55ml thick double cream
1 teaspoon onion marmalade,
   home-made or bought
1 teaspoon Colman's English
   mustard

Heat a heavy-based frying pan over a high heat, add the oil and seal the pork chops. Now lower the heat and continue until the meat is cooked just right.

Remove the chops from the pan and keep warm. De-glaze the pan with half of the cider and simmer to reduce the liquid to a quarter. Now add the cream, the onion marmalade and the mustard and heat through until the sauce begins to just tremble.

Carefully place the pork chops onto serving plates and pour over the sauce. Garnish with halved cherry tomatoes and watercress and serve with baby new potatoes and baked apples, and your remaining half-glass of cider.

HOT FACT

The long, hot UK summer of 1976 culminated in the biggest drought and highest temperatures since records began in 1727. A hose pipe ban was enforced in late spring and the Government even went so far as to appoint a Minister of Drought, in a desperate effort to alleviate the problem. Temporary taps – standpipes – had to be erected in badly affected areas to continue the supply of water. From the 23rd of June, in various parts of the UK, temperatures exceeded 32°C (90°F) for 15 consecutive days.

Ham & Mustard Pasties

MAKES 4 LARGE OR 8 SMALL PASTIES

200g potatoes, diced into
  1 cm cubes
150g swede, diced
150g carrot, diced
1 medium onion, diced
450g puff pastry
200g off-cut ham (trimmings
  – see your friendly butcher)
good dollop Colman's English
  mustard
good sized sprig parsley,
  finely chopped
pepper, according to taste
1 egg, beaten

In a large saucepan of boiling water, place the potatoes, swede, carrot and onion and boil until al dente. Drain and leave in a colander to cool slightly.

Meanwhile, divide the puff pastry into 4 or 8 even squares (depending on the number of pasties required) and roll out to approximately 3–4 mm deep.

Trim off any excess fat from the ham, and cut into rustic shaped pieces. Combine the ham with the potato mixture and add the mustard, parsley and pepper. Pre-heat the oven to 190C/375F/ Gas 5. Divide the mixture equally between the puff pastry squares. Wet the edges of the pastry and fold the diagonal corners together. Crimp the edge of the pastry to resemble a pasty shape, brush with the beaten egg and refrigerate for 15 minutes. Place on a baking tray and bake in the centre of the oven for approximately 15–20 minutes, (or until an even golden brown).

Serve immediately. Perfect with a glass of chilled Somerset farmhouse cider.

Right Every minute, 45 jars of Colman's Mustard are bought all over the world.

COLMAN'S

MUSTARD

ALL OVER THE WORLD.

Roasted Parsnips with Mustard and Herbs

SERVES 4

4 large parsnips, peeled, quartered lengthways and cores removed
2 level tablespoons plain flour
1 level tablespoon Colman's English mustard powder
1 level teaspoon Parmesan, finely grated
salt and freshly ground black pepper
1 dessertspoon mixed fresh sage, rosemary and thyme, stalks removed and finely chopped
2 tablespoons vegetable oil or goose fat

Pre-heat the oven to 180C/350F/ Gas 4. In an oblong dish, mix together the flour, mustard, Parmesan, salt and pepper and herbs. Set aside.

In a large saucepan par-boil the parsnips for 4–5 minutes, drain, and roll them in the herby, mustard mixture until completely coated. (The coating sticks to the parsnips much better if they are still warm.) Pour about 2 tablespoons of vegetable oil or goose fat into a roasting dish and place in the hot oven for 5 minutes.

Remove the pan from the oven and carefully add the seasoned parsnips and baste with the hot fat. Roast for 10–20 minutes until golden brown and scrummy.

Wonderful with sliced beef, wild boar or venison as a main course. Also good as a starter, sprinkled with a little lemon zest and served on thin toasted rye bread, spread with a slither of Colman's English mustard. This is a dish best served after the first frost of the year, when parsnips are at their best.

Sowing the seeds...

■■■ Mustard comes from the seeds of the mustard plant; the brown mustard plant (Brassica Juncea) produces the flour which provides the heat, whilst the white mustard plant (Sinapis Alba) produces the flour which provides the flavour. The two flours are mixed into a special Colman's recipe.

■■■ For many centuries, mustard seeds were used widely as a condiment at meal times. Before the eighteenth century, however, diners were expected to crush the seeds for themselves (in similar fashion to the way we grind pepper at the table today), some choosing to mix them with vinegar and water before flavouring their food.

Venison Sausage Potato Puff

SERVES 4

8 venison sausages
4 large potatoes
25g butter
3 eggs, separated
salt and freshly ground black
  pepper
1 level tablespoon freshly chopped
  parsley
4 tablespoons of Colman's English
  mustard
50ml double cream

Turn the grill to medium and lightly grill the venison sausages until cooked. Meanwhile, peel the potatoes, cut them into quarters and boil in lightly salted water until cooked. Drain and return them to the pan, adding the butter, egg yolks, salt and pepper, the parsley and the mustard. Whisk thoroughly with an electric beater, slowly adding the cream. Set aside.

In a separate bowl, whisk the egg whites into soft peaks and

carefully fold in the mashed potato. Grease an ovenproof dish, spread half of the potato mixture onto the bottom of the dish, cover with the grilled sausages and top with the rest of the potato. Bake in a moderate oven (180C/350F/Gas 4) for about 20–25 minutes until the potato has become brown. Serve hot with Countryman's Piccalilli (see page 89) and a tomato and basil salad.

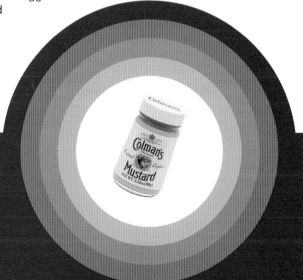

■■■ In 1720, Mrs Clements of Durham spotted that she could take the strain out of all this meal-time pestle-and-mortar action, deciding that she would grind and sift the seed before it reached the table. This new mustard 'flour' was sold as Durham Mustard and became a favourite condiment of King George I.

Cheese Soufflé

SERVES 6

50g fresh breadcrumbs
40g butter (you will need extra
    butter to grease the cooking
    dishes)
25g flour
300ml hot milk
4 eggs, separated
400g good tasty crumbled cheese
    like Shropshire blue or
    Montgomery Cheddar
cracked black pepper
6 grates fresh nutmeg
3 to 4 dashes Tabasco sauce
pinch cayenne
4 spring onions, finely chopped
2 tablespoons Colman's English
    mustard
Parmesan, grated, for sprinkling

You will need 6 individual
ramekins or one 25cm
soufflé dish.

Pre-heat the oven 200C/400F/Gas 6. Butter the soufflé dish and sprinkle the bottom and sides with some of the fresh breadcrumbs (these help the soufflé to 'climb up').

To make the roux, melt the butter in a small pan over a low heat. Remove the pan from the heat and add the flour and beat until smooth and lump free. Return to the heat for about 3 minutes. Remove the pan from the heat and stir in half the milk and beat until smooth. Add the remaining milk and simmer for 10 minutes until thick and smooth. Take off the stove and allow to cool.

Beat the egg yolks lightly and add them to the pan. Stir in the crumbled cheese, pepper, nutmeg, Tabasco, cayenne, spring onions and mustard.

Whisk the 4 egg whites with a pinch of salt to form soft peaks and then fold the egg whites into the sauce. Pour this into the ramekins or the soufflé dish and sprinkle with the remaining breadcrumbs and the Parmesan. Bake the soufflé for 30–40 minutes until it looks like a chef's hat. Serve immediately, either on it's own as a starter or with a bowl of garden-fresh green vegetables as a main course. Please note that a good soufflé should be runny and soft in the centre and firm on the outside.

Baked Field Mushrooms with Mustard & Tarragon Butter

SERVES 6

6 large field mushrooms, skins
 peeled

For the tarragon butter
200g unsalted butter
2 heaped tablespoons of ready-
 made Colman's English mustard
1 clove garlic, peeled and mashed
1 heaped tablespoon picked
 leaves tarragon, roughly
 chopped
juice 1 lime
olive oil
salt and freshly ground pepper

To make the tarragon butter, gently soften the butter and place in a bowl with the well-mashed garlic. Add the tarragon and the mustard, salt and pepper (but not too much as it will drown the sweet tarragon flavour). Finally, add the lime juice and mix carefully into a thick paste.

Pre-heat the oven to 200C/400F/ Gas 6.

Remove the stalks from the mushrooms and place in a roasting tray. Fill the centre of each mushroom with the tarragon mustard butter. To help the cooking process its worth brushing the filled mushrooms with a little olive oil. Place the mushrooms in the oven and bake for 30 minutes. Serve on a bed of diced crispy lettuce or fresh spinach leaves drizzled with a little chilli oil.

COLD TRUTH

Whilst doctors will tell you that there is no cure for the viral common cold, it hasn't stopped people trying to ward it away with a bizzare concoction of passed-down remedies. Old wives' tales include numerous strange remedies for fighting off symptoms, from wrapping up in a red blanket to tying sweaty socks around the neck! All to little avail, though. Colds can come about as a result of the nose becoming infected by any one of 200 different individual viruses. The average cough can unleash a charge of air at 60mph; a sneeze can top the 100mph mark!

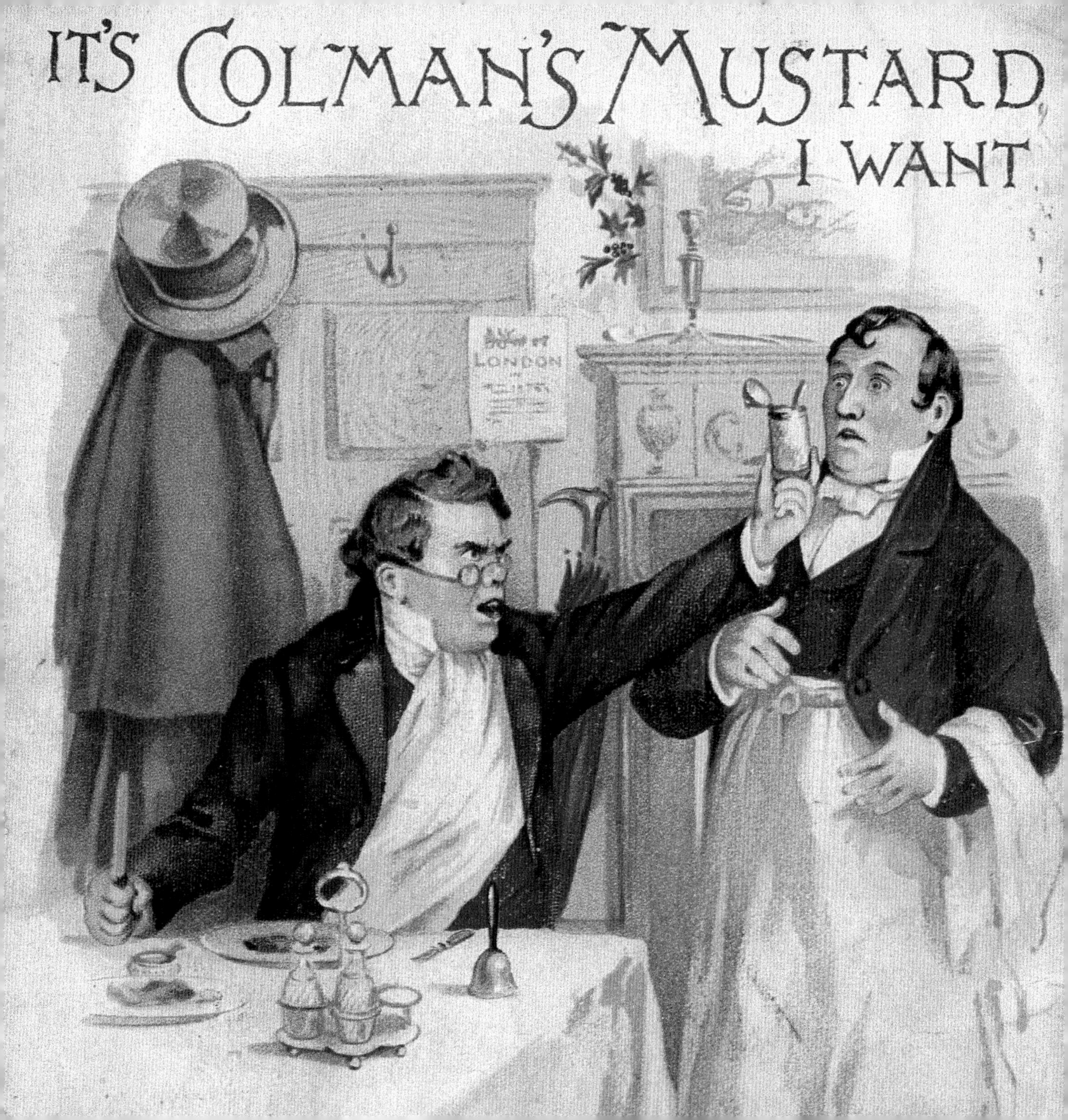
IT'S COLMAN'S MUSTARD
I WANT
LONDON

The Countryman's Piccalilli

**MAKES APPROX.
4KG OF PICCALILLI**

3kg prepared vegetables,
  as follows
1 cucumber – leave skin on and
  cut ends off, cut into quarters
  and then into 2.5cm lengths
1 kg cauliflower, broken into
  florets, halved or quartered
  according to size
1 kg small shallots
500g runner beans, cut into 2.5cm
  slices
2 tablespoons salt
1$^1/_2$ litres malt vinegar
1 tablespoon turmeric
1 tablespoon ground ginger
1 tablespoon Colman's English
  mustard
2 cloves garlic, crushed
200g sugar
3 tablespoons cornflour
salt and freshly ground black
  pepper

This recipe comes from Tony,
a man with a passion for the
countryside equal to my passion
for food.

Place all the vegetables into a large
pan, sprinkle with the salt, cover
and leave overnight. The next day,
drain the vegetables and rinse with
cold water.

Put most of the vinegar into a large
pan, add the spices, mustard, garlic
and sugar and bring to the boil.

Add the vegetables, and simmer
for a maximum of 3 minutes. Blend
the cornflour with the remaining
vinegar and stir into the mix. Boil for
2 minutes, stirring gently. Ladle into
sterilised kilner jars.

Cod with Mustard Crust

SERVES 4

4 teaspoons Colman's English
  mustard powder
1 dessertspoon white wine
pinch soft brown sugar
pinch nutmeg
1 sprig rosemary, finely chopped
  with all the stalks removed
1 dessertspoon cold water
8 chicken drumsticks, preferably
  free-range

Mix together in a bowl the mustard, the wine, brown sugar, nutmeg and chopped rosemary, adding the water until you have a thick workable smooth paste.

Take each drumstick in turn and make 2 or 3 incisions into the fleshly part. Prize them open and stuff with the fiery yellow paste. Pull the skin or flesh together on the outside and tightly wrap in kitchen foil.

Cook on a baking tray or in a roasting dish in a pre-heated oven at 180C/350F/Gas 4 for 20 minutes. Then open up the foil parcels for a further 10 minutes to brown. Then lift each one out of the dish and unwrap the kitchen foil. Now prepare a big round plate with a covering of diced lettuce, and place the drumsticks with the narrow end at the centre in a circle (like the face of a clock). Serve with freshly made parsnip crisps.

Right The bull's head of the Colman's logo was adopted as the firm's trademark in 1855. Royal approval came about ten years later vis-a-vis a warrant as manufacturers to Her Majesty Queen Victoria.

Quick tips...

■■■ To remove odours such as fish or garlic from dishes and utensils, add a tablespoon of Colman's English mustard to your washing-up water to help remove the whiff! Similarly, if your hands smell of onions or spice, try rubbing some Colman's English mustard onto them, before rinsing with warm water, and this should diminish the odour.

■■■ Blocked nose or sore throat? Try smearing a bit of Colman's English mustard over a slice of bread or savoury biscuit. Research has shown that hot or spicy foodstuffs stimulate the secretion of mucus in the airway, which helps to soothe and relieve the congestion of the nose and throat.

TAKE NOTICE

COLMAN'S BEST QUALITY MUSTARD IS PACKED IN 1lb. ½lb. & ¼lb. TINS OF THIS SHAPE ONLY.

TRADE MARK—BULL'S HEAD.

J. COLMAN

RD MANUFACTURERS

TO THE

QUEEN.

108, CANNON STREET, LONDON.

Broccoli & Stilton Quiche

SERVES 6–8

250g short crust pastry
small knob butter
200g finely chopped onions
1 red pepper
1 dessertspoon Demerara sugar
2 dessertspoons Colman's English
   mustard powder
200g broccoli florets, blanched
200g Stilton, crumbled
6 large eggs, beaten

You will need a 10-inch flan dish.

Pre-heat the oven 220C/425F/Gas 7. Roll out the pastry, and line the flan dish with it. Place in the fridge for 30 minutes. Prick the base with a fork then line with baking parchment, fill with baking beans and bake blind in the pre-heated oven for 10 minutes.

Remove the flan dish and reduce the oven temperature to 180C/350F/Gas 4.

Melt the butter in a frying pan and add the onions.

Gently fry the onions until they start to colour. Add the red pepper, sugar and mustard and continue to fry gently for a couple of minutes more. Spread the onion mixture over the baked flan base and arrange the broccoli florets on top. Add the Stilton and the beaten eggs. Carefully return the flan dish to the oven, and bake for a further 20 minutes. To test if your quiche is cooked, pierce with a fork – it should come out clean.

Mustard most odd...

■■■ The Mount Horeb Mustard Museum in Wisconsin, USA is home to the world's largest individual collection of mustards and mustard memorabilia – more than 4,000 different pots and jars. Curator Barry Levenson has been collecting mustard since 1986, and his range just keeps growing!

■■■ What links mustard with billiard rooms and candlesticks? Why the board game, Cluedo! Colonel Mustard is one of the six characters from the boardgame that was dreamed up by Birmingham solicitor's clerk Anthony Pratt and his wife, and released by Waddingtons in 1948.

Parma Ham and Asparagus with Fig & Port Mustard

SERVES 2 AS A STARTER

8 slices Parma ham
8 spears freshly cooked asparagus
250g fresh figs, peeled and
    quartered
150ml port
1 dessertspoon Colman's English
    mustard
$\frac{1}{2}$ teaspoon caster sugar

Take 4 wafer thin slices of Parma ham per person and lay them out flat. Place one piece of asparagus at one end and roll up into a cylinder making sure that the asparagus spear peeps out of one end. Repeat for all 8 slices.

Drop the fresh figs, port, Colman's mustard and sugar into a blender and blitz for 20 seconds.

Place the rolled Parma ham and asparagus on a plate and drizzle with the sauce.

■■■ A 'mustard-chucker' is an archaic term for a pickpocket. It was used to describe street criminals who would temporarily blind their victims by throwing (mustard) powder into their faces, before looting their pockets.

Cheddar Scones with Trout Pâté

**MAKES ABOUT
16 SMALL SCONES**

225g self-raising flour
1 heaped teaspoon Colman's
   English mustard powder
pinch salt
$\frac{1}{2}$ teaspoon of baking powder
40g unsalted butter
60g Cheddar cheese, grated
2 medium free-range eggs
milk, for the glaze
150ml sour cream
pinch cayenne pepper
100g smoked trout paté
   (either best shop-bought or
   home-made)
lemon mayonnaise, to serve
parsley, chopped, to serve

Sift the flour, mustard powder, salt and baking powder into a bowl. Using the back of a wooden spoon rub in the butter until the mixture resembles breadcrumbs. Stir in the cheese and break in one of the eggs, adding enough sour cream to form a light dough.

On a lightly floured surface, roll out the dough to a thickness of about 2cm and, using a traditional pastry cutter, cut out as many scones as you can, reforming the dough and rolling out again, disregarding the last bits. Place the scones onto a greased baking sheet. Beat the remaining egg with a little milk and brush the tops of the scones, finishing with a sprinkle of cayenne pepper.

Bake at 220C/425F/Gas 7 for about 10 minutes until golden brown. Allow to cool slightly before cutting in half, on the bias, and filling with the trout paté. Serve warm with the lemon mayonnaise and a flourish of chopped parsley.

Spinach, Mushroom and Chorizo Salad

SERVES 2

300g freshly washed raw spinach,
    torn into bite-size pieces
100g button mushrooms, sliced
25g butter
1 clove garlic, finely chopped
2 Spanish chorizo sausages,
    sliced into 1.5cm rings

For the dressing
9 teaspoons good olive oil
5 teaspoons tarragon vinegar
pinch salt
freshly ground black pepper
1 teaspoon Colman's English
    mustard powder

Toss the spinach into a salad bowl and sprinkle with the raw sliced mushroom and set aside.

In a frying pan, melt the butter and gently fry the garlic for about 4–5 minutes. Add the chorizo, and fry for about 3 minutes to warm through.

Meanwhile, place all the dressing ingredients into a blender and blitz for 20 seconds. Take the chorizo from the frying pan and drain on kitchen paper before sprinkling it over the salad.

Drizzle with the dressing and serve with chunks of bread.

Right This intrepid explorer is headed for Klondike, the hostile and remote Alaskan town to where, in 1897 and 1898, 100,000 'stampeders' were said to have set off for, after the discovery of gold in 1896. San Francisco and Seattle newspapers carried headlines of 'GOLD! GOLD! GOLD! GOLD!' when they got wind of the story the following year (the news took this long to reach the US due to the dividing Yukon River freezing over, thus preventing communication.) As with Scott's Antarctica trip, Colman's seemed to be a warming staple to take for such a cruel journey. Only four in ten men returned alive (most without having found a speck of gold.)

Sherried Rabbit with Rustic Vegetables

SERVES 2

1 tablespoon olive oil
1 large onion, roughly chopped
1 large carrot, roughly chopped
2 sticks celery, sliced
1 large clove garlic, finely sliced
1 whole rabbit
3–4 peppercorns
good pinch salt
1 tablespoon plain flour
1 tablespoon Colman's English
   mustard powder
500ml dry sherry
2 tablespoons parsley, freshly
   chopped
2 bay leaves

Pre-heat the oven to 170C/325F/ Gas 3. Place a deep frying pan on a medium to high hob, pour in the olive oil and add the onions, carrots, celery and garlic and fry gently until starting to colour.

Now place the rabbit on top of the vegetables and continue to fry for approximately 5–10 minutes, turning the rabbit regularly to get a good colouring all over. Add the peppercorns and season with salt. Blend the flour, mustard powder and sherry until you have a paste, then gradually stir it into the juices in the pan.

Transfer to a baking dish, adding the parsley and bay leaves, and cook for a couple of hours until the meat separates easily from the carcass.

Giant's Canapés

SERVES 4

2 tablespoons runny honey
1 tablespoon Colman's English
mustard powder
juice $\frac{1}{2}$ a lemon
6 best-quality sausages

Mix together the honey, mustard powder and lemon juice and with a pastry brush coat the sausages all over and then bake them in a pre-heated oven at 200C/400F/Gas 6 for 20 minutes.

When the sausages are cooked, display on a big round white plate with a white (yes it must be white) bowl in the centre.

While the sausages were cooking, prepare some standard mashed potato and using the handle of a wooden spoon swirl in 3 teaspoons of green pesto. Your guests can then dip the mustardy bangers into the pesto mash.

HOT FACT

Löyly (pronounced *leuw-luw*) is a Finnish word used to describe the steam that rises from hot stones. The Finns began their hot-stone-water-vaporising antics back in ancient times, when they lived in dwellings little short of mud bunkers covered over with turf. Hot stones would surround the hearth of their fireplaces, storing heat during the day, enabling the abode to stay warm through the night, without the need to tend a fire. A freaky splish-splash of water later and the Finns discovered that the stones let off even more heat when they came into contact with liquid. Voila! The sauna was invented.

Colman's Scotch Eggs

MAKES 8 EGGS

400g sausage meat
150g prepared sage and onion
    stuffing mix
1 tablespoon Colman's English
    mustard
salt and ground black pepper
8 large free-range eggs,
    hard-boiled
2 medium free-range eggs
1/2 teaspoon Colman's English
    mustard
200g fresh breadcrumbs
vegetable oil for deep-frying

Mix together the sausage meat, the sage and onion stuffing mix (made as per the instructions on the packet) and the mustard. Season with salt and pepper and then divide the mixture into 8 equal portions.

Cut 8 pieces of clingfilm, each approximately 15cm square. Spread out the sausage meat mix on each piece, lay the egg in the centre and gather up the clingfilm, moulding the sausage meat inside around the egg until it is completely covered, leaving the clingfilm on. Repeat until all the eggs are coated and chill in the fridge for 2–3 hours. Remove clingfilm.

In a small bowl beat the raw egg and the mustard powder. In a second dish, lay out the breadcrumbs. Now roll the sausage-meat-covered eggs firstly in the egg and mustard mix and then in the breadcrumbs, taking care to completely coat them during both actions. When all the eggs have been covered, place them in the fridge for 2–3 hours. This will set the coating and ensure that it doesn't fall off during cooking.

If you have a deep fat fryer, set it to 190C/375F, or alternatively pour about 7.5cm of vegetable oil into a heavy-based saucepan and heat until just smoking. Fry 2–3 eggs in the hot fat at the same time. When the coating has turned golden brown, remove from the hot oil and drain on kitchen paper. Serve cut in half, with chunks of cheese and fresh tomatoes and a good dollop of Colman's English mustard!

Fillet of Beef Romanoff

SERVES 4

1 tablespoon olive oil
1 medium-sized onion, finely
    chopped
750g fillet of beef cut into
    5cm x 1cm strips (ask your
    butcher for tail end of fillets)
1 large pickled dill, roughly
    chopped
100g closed-cup mushrooms,
    sliced
3 heaped teaspoons Colman's
    English mustard
salt and ground black pepper
1 large glass red wine

Heat the wok on the stove with the olive oil in it. Drop in the onions and cook for 2 minutes, then add the sliced mushrooms and cook for a further 2 minutes

Next add the cracked pepper, mustard, chopped dill and the wine and stir well. Turn up the heat to reduce the liquid and then add the beef to the sizzling juices. Cook for a further 2–3 minutes until the beef is glossy but still rare and ready to be devoured.

Right Another member for The Mustard Club!

Great Scott!...

■■■ *'I have much pleasure in informing you that the flour, cornflour and mustard supplied by you to this expedition has proven entirely satisfactory. I have to especially thank you for the careful manner in which your food was packed.'*
Letter from Captain Scott, on his second Antarctica trek, to J.J. Colman, Carrow Works, Norwich.

Mustard Cheese Straws

MAKES 16

100g ready-made puff pastry
2 heaped teaspoons Colman's
   English mustard
50g mature farmhouse Cheddar,
   grated
1 teaspoon fresh parsley, finely
   chopped

Pre-heat the oven to 190C/ 375F/ Gas 5. Roll the pastry on a floured board until 3–4mm thick. Spread the mustard over the pastry, then sprinkle the cheese over evenly and scatter the parsley on top. Cover with clingfilm, press down firmly and chill for 30 minutes. This will make it easier to cut as well as producing good pastry.

Remove the pastry from the fridge and cut into 7.5 x 1cm strips. Place the strips on a greased baking tray with space between to expand during cooking.

Place the tray in the top of the oven for 10–15 minutes or until the cheese straws have risen and the cheese looks crisp on the outside. Leave to cool slightly, and then arrange on a plate ready for cocktails at 6.

Mustard and the Bard...

■■■ Mustard-Seed was one of the fairies who beckoned to the calls of Titiana, the Fairy Queen in *A Midsummer Night's Dream*.

■■■ 'What say you to a piece of beef and mustard?' Grumio to Katharina, *The Taming of the Shrew*

■■■ 'Of a certain knight that swore by his honour they were good pancakes and swore by his honour the mustard was naught[...]' Touchstone to Celia, *As You Like It*

■■■ 'His wits as thick as Tewkesbury Mustard.' *Henry IV Part II*

Stir-fried Monkfish

SERVES 2

25g butter
1 small onion, finely diced
1 tablespoon prepared Colman's
  English mustard
500g trimmed and filleted
  monkfish, diced into 3cm chunks
50ml Scotch whisky
2 tomatoes, skinned, de-seeded
  and diced
juice 1 lemon
salt and pepper, to season
1 small wine glass cream sherry
150ml double cream
1 teaspoon tomato purée

Place a wok over a medium heat and add the butter and finely diced onion and stir-fry until softened – do not let the onions colour. Add the mustard, mix well and cook gently for 2–3 minutes. With lighter in hand, pour in the whisky and ignite it, being careful to ensure eyebrows and hair are well out of the way.

Add the tomato, lemon juice a sprinkling of salt and the sherry. Mix well, and now reduce the liquid over a high heat for 3–4 minutes. Turn down the heat, add the cream and the tomato purée and simmer gently for 10 minutes. Finally, add the monkfish and cook for a further 3–4 minutes so that it is just cooked. Serve with a crispy, lightly dressed endive salad.

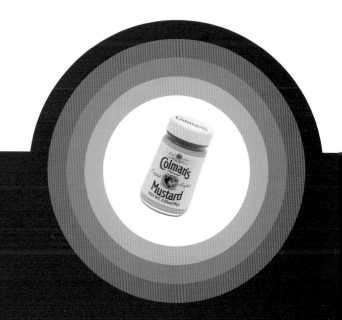

■■■ Other notable literary mentions include appearances in the writings of Anton Chekhov, Alexandre Dumas, Jerome K. Jerome and Hans Christian-Anderson.

Mussel Power

SERVES 4–6

1kg frozen green-lip mussels
  in their half shell
Colman's English mustard
1 tube tomato purée
2 large cloves garlic, finely
  chopped
fresh white breadcrumbs
olive oil
parsley, to garnish

Defrost the mussels in their shells, then drain and pat dry. Coat the flesh of each mussel with a thin spread of Colman's English mustard followed by a small dollop of tomato purée straight from the tube and spread over.

Sprinkle all the chopped garlic over the coated mussels and then cover with breadcrumbs. Lay out the mussels in a shallow roasting tin and drizzle lightly with olive oil.

Place under a medium hot grill for 3–4 minutes until the breadcrumbs are toasted to golden. Scatter with fresh parsley and a good grind of black pepper. Serve as tapas with chilled Cava or other decent-quality fizz, or just as a great lunch with plenty of warm crusty bread.

Packing punch...

■■■ The heat of mustard emanates from the oils which are released when the seeds are crushed. These oils contain chemicals and enzymes which, when mixed with water, react to free compounds known as *isothiocyanates*. When mixing mustard flour with water, it can take up to about 15 minutes for the mustard to reach its most potent heat.

■■■ Chilli peppers, on the other hand, are measured in Scoville heat units. In 1912, the US pharmacist, Wilbur Scoville, devised a test which determined the amount of capsicum (the active heat element) within chillies. His scale ranges from the humble bell pepper, which rates a '0', to the fiery jalapeño pepper, which registers at about the 3,000 mark, up to the scorching habañero pepper, which clocks in at an incredible 500,000 units! Pure capsicum measures an incredible 16,000,000 units, but a chilli would never contain anywhere near this concentration. The ribs of the chilli contain the highest level, followed by the seeds and then the flesh and skin. Colman's is hot, but not that hot!

THE ADVENTURES OF THE MUSTARD CLUB

Being a selection of the famous advertisements of the MUSTARD CLUB, together with many interesting cartoons and hitherto unpublished documents.

PRICE 6^D

Stuffed Mushrooms

SERVES 6 AS A STARTER

450g medium-sized cup
mushrooms
100g butter
1 medium onion, roughly chopped
3 gloves garlic, roughly chopped
1 tablespoons Colman's English
mustard powder
2 tablespoons chopped chives
salt and pepper
1 lemon (half for juice and half for
the garnish)
3 slices wholemeal bread

*Left 'The Mustard Club' was a
famous advertising campaign that
ran from 1926 to 1933. The club
comprised a playfully quaint
coterie of individuals, such as
Master Mustard, Signor de
Spaghetti and the club's president,
Baron de Beef. Artists William
Brearley and John Gilroy, and
copywriters Dorothy L. Sayers and
Oswald Green were the geniuses
who created the cartoons that
decorated magazines and many
billboards of the day.*

Remove the stalks from the
mushrooms carefully, so that you
don't split them. A little pressure
on the stalk from side to side
should suffice. Chop the stalks
and set aside.

Melt the butter in a saucepan over
a low to medium heat and add the
whole de-stalked mushrooms, stir,
coating the mushrooms with the
butter. Remove and set aside.
In the same pan place the onion,
garlic, mushroom stalks and gently
cook for 4–5 minutes until the
onions have softened. Add the
mustard, chives and season with
salt and pepper and the juice from
half the lemon. Stir and remove
from the heat.

In a blender, place the bread and
the onion and mustard mixture
and zap the lot together. With a
teaspoon, fill the mushroom cups
and place filled side up on a
baking tray. Before serving, bake
in a pre-heated oven at 180C/350F/
Gas 4 for about 10 minutes.
Serve the mushrooms on a bed
of shredded lettuce with a dollop
of garlic mayonnaise.

Colman's-style Baked Chicken Kiev

SERVES 4

For the filling
125g ricotta cheese
100g butter, softened
zest and juice 1 lime
2 cloves garlic, finely chopped
1 heaped teaspoon Colman's
   mustard powder
1 dessertspoon finely chopped
   parsley
salt and pepper
4 chicken breasts

For the coating
250g breadcrumbs
1 medium free-range egg whisked
   with 100ml milk
about 50g plain flour

Ask your butcher to remove the skin off the chicken breasts, trim the wing bone and leave in, and cut the chicken to make it easy for stuffing.

In a small bowl, mix together all the ingredients for the filling. Place the chicken breasts on a board and open them out. Divide the mixture from the small bowl into 4 equal parts. Place a spoon of mixture just under the knuckle of the bone so as to sit it in the centre of the chicken breast. Fold all the sides of the chicken breast over the mixture to ensure the mixture is completely wrapped. Repeat with the remaining chicken breasts.

Take each filled breast and dust lightly with the flour and dip each one into the beaten egg and milk. Finally, roll carefully in the breadcrumbs, then back into the egg and milk and again roll in the breadcrumbs.

Pre-heat the oven to 180C/350F/ Gas 4. Place the chicken breasts on a greased baking tray and bake for 30 minutes. Remove and rest the chicken for 5 minutes. Serve with sauté potatoes or Fennel Coleslaw with Mustard Mayo (see page 73).

Right 'Returned from Klondyke': One of the lucky few who did!

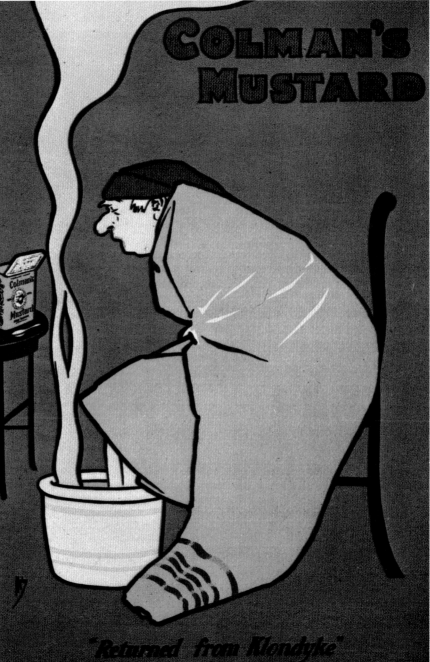

Stuffed Peppers with Brie and Mustard

SERVES 2

4 red peppers
25g butter
1 medium-sized red onion, roughly chopped
2 small leeks, sliced
150g cup mushrooms, sliced
1 dessertspoon Colman's English mustard
small glass white wine
100g Somerset Brie, cut into small pieces, rind on
salt and black pepper

Halve the peppers lengthways and remove the seeds – you may leave the stalk in for decoration. Place the peppers in boiling water for about $1\frac{1}{2}$ minutes, remove and chill quickly in cold water (preferably iced). Place the pepper on some kitchen paper to dry whilst you are preparing the filling.

Melt the butter in a pan and add the onions and leeks and cook on a low heat for about 3–4 minutes. Add the mushrooms, mustard, wine and bring to the boil. Cook until the liquid has reduced by half. Remove from the heat, stir in the Brie and then fill the peppers with the mixture. The peppers can be served warm or cold. To serve warm, simply place on an oven tray and gently warm in the oven at 150C/300F/Gas 2 for about 10 minutes. Great with salad, vegetables or sauté potatoes.

COLD TRUTH

Stories of yetis are linked with the snow-capped mountains of the Himalayas, but this myth exists in various forms in places far and wide across the world. The Himalayan-named yeti was dubbed as such by the native Sherpa people, with yeti translating as 'dweller among the rocks'. The Chinese, though, have their very own yeti: the 'Chi-Chi' or 'Chang Mi' (wild man), whilst natives of Canada and the United States tell stories of 'Sasquatch', (or 'hairy man of the forest' – but better know as 'Bigfoot').

MUSTERING OF THE MUSTARD CLUB

Smoked Salmon with Sweet Mustard Sauce

SERVES 4

12 slices Scottish smoked salmon

For the sauce
1 large free-range egg (yolk only)
2 tablespoons Colman's English
  mustard
1 tablespoon soft brown sugar
1 tablespoon Mascarpone cheese
6 tablespoons olive oil
2 tablespoons cider vinegar
2 tablespoons fresh dill. finely
  chopped
4 pieces fresh dill left whole,
  for the garnish
1 lime cut into 8 segments
toasted fingers of brown bread,
  to accompany

In a food processor or blender drop in the egg yolk, mustard, sugar and Mascarpone and blitz for about 10 seconds. Leaving the machine running, gently add the olive oil, the vinegar and chopped dill and within 30 seconds you should have a delicious thick sauce.

On each plate, place three rolls of smoked salmon (like a propeller blade). Between each roll put first the lime, second the throng of fresh dill and lastly a good dollop of the sweet mustard sauce. Serve with lightly toasted fingers of brown bread.

Left and right
The club's President, Baron de Beef.

ALL OVER THE WORLD
COLMAN'S
D.S.F.
MUSTARD
Colman's
MUSTARD
BULL'S
HEAD
BY SPECIAL APPOINTMENT TO THE KING
Colman's
BULL'S
HEAD
Mustard
DOUBLE SUPERFINE

Roast Rib of Beef with Malayan Mustard

SERVES 4

2 kg rib of beef

For the Malayan Mustard
1 dessertspoon Colman's English
   mustard powder
3 teaspoons finely chopped
   galangal or fresh ginger
2 teaspoons crushed dried chillies
4 cloves garlic, finely chopped
vinegar, to blend

Pre-heat the oven to 200C/400F/
Gas 6.

Using a hand blender or a pestle
and mortar, mix all the mustard
ingredients together, gradually
adding enough vinegar to create a
paste. Spread this paste all over
the meat and leave the rib to stand
in a roasting tin for 30 minutes so
that the flavours seep in.

Put the beef into the oven for
15 minutes and then reduce the
temperature to 150C/300F/Gas 2
and cook for a further 1 hour.
This will give you a crispy but rare
meat in the centre. For medium
beef add 15 minutes to the final
cooking time and for well-done
beef add a further 15 minutes.

When cooked to your liking, allow
the beef to stand for a good
10 minutes for the meat to relax
and the juices to settle back before
carving. Wonderful served hot with
your favourite roast vegetables or
cold with salad and pickles.

*Left Colman's English mustard:
exported far and wide, all over
the world.*

Three Fish Pie with Peas, Cheese and Mustard

SERVES 6

Make up 600g of fish with
200g natural smoked haddock
200g white cod
200g raw prawns

5 large potatoes, peeled and
    quartered
30g butter
240ml double cream
2 medium free-range eggs
1 large onion, finely chopped
olive oil for frying
100g frozen petit pois
2 large handfuls fresh spinach,
    chopped
3 tablespoons strong mature
    Cheddar, grated
2 heaped teaspoons Colman's
    English mustard
1 heaped tablespoon of flat-leaf
    parsley, finely chopped
salt and freshly ground black
    pepper

Ask your fishmonger to fillet and
pin-bone the haddock and cod.

Slice the fish into 2.5cm strips,
leaving the prawns whole.

In a large saucepan of boiling salted
water, cook the potatoes until soft.
Drain and mash with the butter, half
the cream and season to taste.
While the spuds are cooking, boil
the eggs for 8 minutes, then cool
them and peel and quarter.

Fry the onion in a little olive oil until
just transparent. Remove from the
heat and add the remainder of the
double cream, peas, spinach,
cheese, mustard and parsley, allow
to cool to room temperature. When
cool, pour into an ovenproof dish.
Finally, drop in the fish and season,
then layer the eggs and top with
the mashed potato.

Place in a pre-heated oven at 180C/
350F/Gas 4 for 25–30 minutes
until the potato is golden brown.
Serve with a shower of parsley.

Spiced Rarebit

SERVES 6

50ml pineapple juice
50ml coconut milk
1 teaspoon rum essence
2 level teaspoons Colman's
   English mustard powder
$1/_2$ teaspoon cayenne pepper
400g mature Cheddar, grated
6 slices of thick, toasted bread
6 good sprigs of fresh watercress
a pinch of smoked paprika
spicy mango chutney,
   to accompany

In a bowl, mix the pineapple juice, coconut milk and rum essence with the mustard powder and cayenne pepper and set aside for 30 minutes. Place the mixture in a saucepan and slowly bring to the boil, adding the grated cheese a little at a time.

When all the cheese has melted, remove the pan from the heat and allow to cool. Toast the bread and pour the cheese mixture over the slices of toast. Place them all under a medium hot grill until the cheese begins to bubble and turn golden.

Place on bright white plates with a sprig of watercress and a final pinch of smoked paprika. Accompany with mango chutney.

Right What better reminder of home?

HOT FACT

Our fascination with flame began over $1^1/_2$ million years ago. The evolution of the humble matchstick begins in pre-history, when cavemen rubbed two pieces of wood together. This basic concept – one surface abrading against another – took focused form in the 17th century with the discovery of phosphorous. A few years later saw Robert Boyle experimenting with phosphorous-coated paper and sulphur-coated wooden splints. It was in 1826 that John Walker chanced upon the matchstick proper (scraping a mixture-coated stick across his floor). But it was Samuel Jones who sprang to patent the idea and, in no time at all, 'Lucifer's' matches hit the shops!

Cider-glazed Gammon Steaks

SERVES 4

4 gammon steaks
275ml Somerset cider
1 tablespoon honey
1 dessertspoon Colman's English
   mustard
2–3 slices fresh pineapple, about
   1cm thick, cubed

Cut incisions into the gammon steaks around the fat side, about 5cm apart. Place them in a fairly deep baking tray. Pour over most of the cider. Drizzle with the honey. Coat the gammon steaks with the mustard by placing the mustard in a sieve and gently tapping the sides to coat evenly. Place the tray under a very hot grill and cook till everything is sizzling nicely (about 10 minutes). Remove the steaks from the tray.

Arrange the cooked gammons on plates and keep warm.

Place the cooking tray back on a high heat, adding a little more cider, and the finely cubed pineapple. Whisk the mixture together and pour back over the gammon. Serve with braised fennel and sauté potatoes.

Right Used and loved by all kinds of folk!

Strange sayings...

■■■ *To cut the mustard.*
To succeed, to have the ability to do what's necessary. 'He didn't cut much mustard' is an American phrase that dates back to about 1900. Mustard was a slang variant for 'real thing' or 'genuine article', and this may have contributed to the idiom.

■■■ But, also, mustard is a very difficult crop to harvest, so not being able to 'cut it' could similarly suggest that you don't have what's required. To *cut the muster*, meanwhile, means to be 'well turned out'. It's conceivable that 'cut the mustard' could have come about as a botched translation of this saying.

■■■ *Keen as mustard.*
To be very sharp, extremely keen. Thomas Keen's company made mustard from 1742 until 1903, when the business was acquired by Colman's. Keen is often associated with the origins of the phrase, but the phrase 'the keenest mustard' pre-dates Keen by almost 100 years.

Spiced Dough Balls

**MAKES 12–18
DOUGH BALLS**

100g butter, softened
150g mature Cheddar, grated
150g self-raising flour
1 rounded teaspoon Colman's
   mustard powder
freshly ground black pepper
pinch sea salt
2 medium free-range eggs, beaten

Beat together the softened butter and the grated cheese until well blended. Add all the dry ingredients and mix well.

Gradually add the eggs to form a dough and roll into marble-sized balls using floured hands. If the dough seems too wet, just add a little more flour.

Place on greased baking trays and bake for 10–15 minutes at 180C/ 350F/Gas 4.

Salad of Smoked Duck with Mild Chilli Vinaigrette

SERVES 4

1 oakleaf or frisée lettuce, washed
   and leaves torn
50g sliced fresh radish
50g finely sliced red onion

For the Chilli Vinaigrette
4 tablespoons olive oil
1 tablespoon white wine vinegar
1 teaspoon Colman's English
   mustard
4 good dashes mild green
   Tabasco sauce
juice $\frac{1}{2}$ lemon
2 teaspoons runny honey

2 smoked duck breasts
freshly ground black pepper

Put the lettuce leaves, radish and onions into a bowl and combine well. In a blender, blitz the oil, vinegar, mustard, honey, Tabasco and lemon juice and pour over the salad. Toss the salad well to coat all the leaves. Pile the tossed salad onto 4 plates.

Slice the duck breasts very thinly and arrange over the top of each salad portion. Pour any remaining juices from the salad bowl over the duck slices and finish with a good grind of black pepper. Serve with crusty bread.

HOT FACT

When we overheat, we cool ourselves down by perspiring, but did you know that this simple process we take for granted can call upon the resources of over two million individual sweat glands? These sudoriferous glands secrete a mixture of water, fatty acids and minerals, and any odour is determined by the amount of bacteria that mix with these secretions. About one-eighth of these can be found in the feet, which release about eight ounces of moisture a day! The average adult loses 500-plus calories with every litre of sweat. And the sweatier sex? Men: they sweat about 40% more than women.

Lord Kitchener's Mackerel

SERVES 2

2 whole large mackerel – ask your fishmonger to butterfly fillet them
butter to grease the cooking tray
salt and ground black pepper
1 bunch watercress, stalks removed
1 tablespoon prepared Colman's English mustard
125ml medium white wine – a Chardonnay would be good
$\frac{1}{2}$ fish stock cube
150ml double cream
juice 1 lemon

Place the mackerel fillets skin-side down on a well-greased baking tray, sprinkle with salt and black pepper. Place under a low grill for 8–10 minutes, keeping an eye on them to ensure that the butter doesn't burn.

Roughly chop half of the watercress and set aside. In a pan, place the mustard and the white wine with the stock cube added. Bring to the boil. Add the chopped watercress and the double cream. Boil gently to reduce the sauce by about half (this should take 3–4 minutes). Remove the mackerel fillets from the cooking tray and keep warm. Add the juice of 1 lemon to the cooking juices and add the rest of the watercress, just long enough to let it wilt. Pour some of the watercress sauce onto each plate, place the mackerel on top and drizzle with the remaining sauce. Makes a perfect light lunch served with parsnip crisps and a rocket salad.

COLD TRUTH

Did you know that eskimos have more than thirty common ways of describing snow? These account for the myriad nuances of snow and the way that it falls and spreads. *Apun* is simply 'snow' and *kannik* is 'snowflake'; but there are words and word-units for drifting snow, for newly drifted snow, for the rippled surface of snow, even for snow which settles on clothes. *Sisuuk* means 'avalanche'.

Colman's Mustard

Sausage & Cider Hotpot

SERVES 4

2 tablespoons olive oil
1 large red onion, roughly chopped
2 cloves garlic, finely chopped
8 pork and herb sausages
450g pork belly, rind removed and
   diced
500ml medium cider
1 vegetable bouillon cube
1 heaped teaspoon Colman's
   English mustard powder
1 teaspoon roughly picked thyme
1 teaspoon fresh sage leaves, torn
3 bay leaves
black pepper
200g broad beans, preferably
   fresh, but frozen will be OK

Heat the oil in a large heavy-based frying pan and gently fry the onions and garlic for 3–4 minutes. Add the sausages and pork belly and continue cooking until just browned.

Transfer the sausage mixture to a large casserole dish and add the cider, crumbled stock cube, mustard and herbs. Season with black pepper. Cook in a pre-heated oven 200C/400F/Gas 6 for 30 minutes, uncovered.

Remove the casserole from the oven, add the broad beans and stir. Return the casserole to the oven for a further 30 minutes. When cooked remove from the oven and allow to stand for at least 5 minutes before serving. Great with basmati rice or sweet potato chips.

Right Ahh! The perfect setting.

Leek & Mustard Crumble

SERVES 4

1kg baby leeks, trimmed and cut
  into 5cm lengths
25g butter
50g plain flour
200ml warm milk
150g Cheddar cheese, grated
25g Parmesan cheese, grated
2 teaspoons Colman's English
  mustard
salt and black pepper

For the crumble
4 tablespoons fresh white
  breadcrumbs
25g Cheddar cheese, grated
1 tablespoon parsley, chopped

Pre-heat the oven to 200C/400F/ Gas 6. Bring the leeks to the boil in a pan of salted water and simmer for 3 minutes. Remove from the heat, drain and plunge into cold water. Set aside.

In a small saucepan, melt the butter and then add the flour, stirring constantly for 2 minutes. Gradually add the warm milk until the mixture re-heats and thickens. Reduce the heat and add the grated Cheddar and Parmesan, stirring as you add. Lastly add the mustard and season with a little salt and freshly ground black pepper.

Put the leeks into a shallow ovenproof dish and pour the cheese sauce over the top. Sprinkle with the breadcrumbs and top with grated Cheddar cheese and parsley. Bake in the oven for about 20 minutes until the crumbs on top have turned to a golden brown. Leave to cool a little before serving.

Right In its glory indeed!

BY SPECIAL APPOINTMENT
TO THE KING

Colman's

BULL'S   HEAD.

Mustard

DOUBLE SUPERFINE

MANUFACTURED IN ENGLAND

BY APPOINTMENT
TO THE
QUEEN of NORWAY
MUSTARD

PURVEYORS
BY APPOINTMENT
TO THE
KING.
MANUFACTURERS

"IN ITS GLORY"

THE LEA & PERRINS' WORCESTERSHIRE SAUCE RECIPE COLLECTION

Cheese & Worcestershire Muffins

MAKES 12 MUFFINS

150g self raising flour
40g rye flour
$1^1/_2$ teaspoons baking powder
1 teaspoon salt
1 teaspoon English mustard
   powder
100g strong Cheddar, grated
5 tablespoons vegetable oil
120ml yogurt
100ml milk
1 free-range egg
2 tablespoons Lea & Perrins
   Worcestershire Sauce

For the topping
50g strong Cheddar cheese,
   grated
Lea & Perrins Worcestershire
   Sauce

You will need a non-stick muffin tray or a baking tray with 12 paper muffin cases. Pre-heat the oven to 210C/400F/Gas 6.

In a large bowl mix the flours, baking powder, salt and mustard powder together with a fork. In a separate bowl beat together the cheese, oil, yogurt, milk, egg and Worcestershire sauce. Gradually add the liquid to the dry ingredients and mix with a fork. Don't be over zealous as good muffins tend to be made with a lumpy mixture.

Pour the mixture equally into the muffin cases and place in the hot oven for 20 minutes. Then quickly take the muffins out of the oven, sprinkle with the topping cheese, a few dashes of Worcestershire sauce and return them to the hot oven for a further 5 minutes.

Allow to cool a little and then devour while still just warm.

Chicken Salad Loaf

SERVES 4

200g soft cream cheese
2 tablespoon mayonnaise
2 tablespoons lemon juice
1 tablespoon Lea & Perrins
   Worcestershire Sauce
$^1/_2$ teaspoon ground ginger
sea salt and freshly ground black
   pepper
450g cooked chicken, diced
2 hard boiled eggs, roughly
   mashed
1 small red onion, finely diced
handful of rocket
100g black olives, finely diced
1 small sweet red pepper, finely
   diced

Mix together the cream cheese, mayonnaise, lemon juice, Worcestershire sauce and ginger and season with salt and pepper.

Next add in the chicken, eggs and onion and form a loaf shape with the mixture on a piece of clingfilm. Wrap it up and refrigerate for 3–4 hours.

Remove the chilled loaf and lay on a bed of rocket on a suitable serving dish. Gently press in a mixture of the olives and pepper all over the surface of the loaf. Serve with crispy toasted rounds of French bread, perfect for a summer brunch party.

WORCESTERSHIRE SOURCE

Worcestershire is the birthplace of Edward Elgar, the composer who will forever be associated with 'Land of Hope and Glory', the song which is sung so lustily at every Last Night of the Proms. Whilst the tune belongs to Elgar – Pomp and Circumstance March No. 1 – the actual lyrics were added by the poet A.C. Benson, and an extra note had to be added to Elgar's piece to make the lyrics fit!

Bloody Mary Sorbet

1 litre tomato juice
juice of 2 lemons
1 dessertspoon Lea & Perrins
   Worcestershire Sauce
few drops Tabasco Sauce
$1/2$ teaspoon celery salt
good grind of black pepper
1 teaspoon caster sugar
150ml vodka
2 egg whites
few sprigs of fresh mint

Blitz together all the ingredients except the egg whites and mint in a liquidiser. In a separate bowl whisk up the egg whites to stiff peaks and then fold them into the tomato mixture. If you have an ice cream maker it can be used at this stage, otherwise pour the mixture into a suitable sized plastic container and place in the freezer.

Remove from the freezer every hour or so and give the mixture a good stir. You will need to do this 3 or 4 times during the process to achieve a light and fluffy consistency.

Serve in wine glasses garnished with sprigs of fresh mint as a great starter for breakfast, lunch or dinner. Also superb with a fillet of smoked trout.

WORCESTERSHIRE SAUCED

Bartender Fernand Petiot of Harry's New York Bar in Paris claims to have invented the Bloody Mary, then a simple mix of vodka and tomato juice, sometime during the 1920s. By 1934, Petiot had moved to the King Cole Bar at the St Regis Hotel in New York. To suit New Yorker tastes, Petiot refined his recipe, adding various spices and the all-important kick of a few drops of Worcestershire Sauce. The drink is said to have got its name when one of Petiot's colleagues suggested naming it after the Bucket of Blood Club in Chicago, and a girl who frequented the joint, called Mary. The same drink less the vodka is called a Virgin Mary (or a Bloody Shame). When Tequila replaces the vodka, it's known as a Bloody Maria.

Smoked Chicken Caesar

SERVES 4

For the salad
1 oakleaf lettuce
1 cos lettuce
1 clove garlic, finely chopped
1 teaspoon Dijon mustard
1 teaspoon Lea & Perrins
　Worcestershire Sauce
$1/2$ teaspoon anchovy paste
1 tablespoon freshly squeezed
　lemon juice
freshly ground black pepper
2 tablespoons olive oil
50g Parmesan cheese
4 smoked chicken breasts

For the croûtons
2 slices good white bread, crusts
　removed
2 cloves garlic, finely diced
good drizzle of olive oil

Pre-heat the oven to 200C/400F/ Gas 6. Wash and dry the lettuce leaves and tear them into bite-sized pieces.

In a large bowl put the garlic, mustard, Worcestershire sauce, anchovy paste, lemon juice and pepper and whisk the ingredients together. Slowly add the olive oil (must be at room temperature) whisking all the time until the dressing begins to thicken.

Add the torn lettuce leaves and toss the whole lot together to coat the leaves. Grate the Parmesan cheese over the salad, reserving a few slivers shaven off with a potato peeler for the finishing touch. Toss the salad once more.

Pile the salad equally onto four serving plates. Cut each chicken breast into 6 or 8 diagonal slices and arrange on top of the dressed salad leaves.

To make the croûtons, cut the bread into 2cm cubes and scatter on a baking tray with the garlic. Drizzle with the olive oil and turn the whole lot a few times to mix. Put the baking tray in the hot oven for 4–5 minutes until crisp and golden – do keep an eye on them as they can turn quite quickly.

Finish the salad by topping with the crispy croûtons and reserved Parmesan shavings.

Summer Strawberry Salad

SERVES 2

1 punnet of strawberries
150g baby leaf spinach
100g lambs tongue lettuce
1 teaspoon Lea & Perrins
  Worcestershire Sauce
50g caster sugar
pinch sweet smoked paprika
60ml olive oil
50ml balsamic vinegar
1 shallot, finely sliced

Rinse and dry the strawberries, removing the hulls of all but 4 of them. Wash the spinach and lettuce, drain and pat dry on kitchen paper.

Whisk together the Worcestershire sauce, sugar, paprika, olive oil and vinegar and set aside until ready.

In a large bowl put the spinach, lettuce and shallots and then slice or quarter the hulled strawberries according to size. Drizzle the vinaigrette all over the leafy mixture and then gently toss the salad. Serve a plateful of salad each with the 2 leaf-topped strawberries perched on top – a perfect summer salad.

LEA & PERRINS

Chemists AND Druggists

No 68, Broad Street,

Worcester.

Honey-Glazed Butternut Squash

1 butternut squash
  (about 1kg)
salt and freshly ground black
  pepper
60ml honey
25g unsalted butter, melted
2 tablespoons pine nuts, chopped
2 tablespoons raisins, chopped
1 tablespoon Lea & Perrins
  Worcestershire Sauce

Left An early label from Lea & Perrins' shop at No. 68 Broad Street, Worcester.

Pre-heat the oven to 200C/400F/ Gas 6.

Cut the squash into quarters lengthways without removing the seeds or fibres and season with salt and pepper. Place on a baking tray, cut sides up, and bake in the hot oven for 40 minutes, or until soft.

Put the honey, butter, nuts, raisins and Worcestershire sauce into a bowl and mix together well.

When cooked, take the squash out of the oven and carefully scoop out the seeds and fibres from each quarter and discard. Spoon the honey nut mixture over the flesh of the squash and return it to the oven for a further 15 minutes until the squash is beautifully glazed. It's ready to serve for lunch with some warm briôche or as an accompaniment to a Moroccan lamb tagine.

IT TAKES TIME!

The ingredients that make up a bottle of Lea & Perrins Worcestershire sauce are left to work their magic together for more than three years. During this time it goes through a pin-point accurate process of ageing, mixing, straining and maturing. The sauce begins with onions, garlic, anchovies and shallots being aged in barrels of malt vinegar. After they have matured sufficiently they are transferred to huge vats where they are mixed with tamarinds from India, red hot chillies from China and India, cloves and finally black strap molasses from the Caribbean. Then it's over to a rigorous routine of mixing, stirring and pumping which lasts for several months, before the final sauce is strained and bottled. Worth the wait though.

Chilled Gazpacho with Celeriac Crisps

SERVES 6

2 cloves garlic, peeled and roughly
   chopped
1 red pepper, deseeded and
   roughly chopped
1/2 cucumber, roughly chopped
390g tin chopped tomatoes
500ml tomato juice
1 tablespoon sherry vinegar
1 dessertspoon Lea & Perrins
   Worcestershire Sauce
50ml olive oil
1 teaspoon ground cumin
1 teaspoon fresh tarragon
salt and freshly ground black pepper
500ml still mineral water, chilled
few torn basil leaves
few ice cubes

For the garnish
3 firm tomatoes, diced
1 red onion, peeled and diced
1 green pepper, deseeded and
   diced
50g pitted black olives, chopped

For the crisps
1 small celeriac, peeled
oil for deep-frying

Put the garlic, pepper and cucumber into a food processor and blitz to a chunky pulp. Then add the tinned tomatoes and the tomato juice and whiz once more. Pour the contents out into a large bowl.

Stir in the sherry vinegar, the Worcestershire sauce and then the oil and finally the cumin, tarragon, salt and pepper, stirring all the time. Chill the soup.

To make the crisps, cut the celeriac into 4 chunks and with a potato peeler, or fine mandolin, shave off thin slices. Deep fry in batches until you have used all the celeriac, draining the crisps each time on kitchen paper.

Put the chilled soup into a deep bowl and stir in the mineral water. Float the ice cubes in the soup with the torn basil leaves and ladle into individual bowls at the table together with a platter of garnishes and a basket of celeriac crisps for all to help themselves.

Welsh Lamb Noisettes

SERVES 4

8 lamb noisettes
1 tablespoon olive oil
200g chestnut mushrooms
4 dessertspoons redcurrant jelly
2 tablespoons Lea & Perrins
  Worcestershire Sauce
juice of 1 lemon
250ml good meat stock
salt and freshly ground black
  pepper
good grate of nutmeg

Pre-heat the oven to 170C/325F/ Gas 3.

Heat the oil in a frying pan and brown the noisettes on both sides. Remove from the pan and layer in a casserole dish together with the sliced button mushrooms.

Put the redcurrant jelly, Worcestershire sauce and lemon juice into a saucepan and whisk over a low heat until the jelly has dissolved. Add the stock, turn up the heat and reduce all the liquid by about one third.

Taste and season the sauce with salt and pepper, add the nutmeg and then pour over the noisettes and mushrooms in the casserole dish. Cover and cook in the medium oven for $1^1/_2$ hours.

This is a perfect dish to herald the arrival of those wonderful Jersey Royals at the start of the English summer.

WORLD SUPERPOWER!

On September 29th, 1938, leaders of the four European superpowers met in Munich to sign the 'Munich Agreement'. Leaders Neville Chamberlain, Edouard Daladier and Benito Mussolini met with Adolf Hitler. The day after the paperwork was out of the way the leaders dined together and a photograph reveals that on the table in front of them rested a bottle of Lea & Perrins Worcestershire Sauce!

Oriental Slow Cook Pork

SERVES 4–6

2 litres water
2kg belly pork (in one piece with
   rind and bones in)
170ml rice wine (or dry sherry)
small cinnamon stick
10cm chunk of fresh ginger,
   peeled and finely sliced
1 level teaspoon dried chilli flakes
150ml Lea & Perrins
   Worcestershire Sauce
150ml dark soy sauce
1 tablespoon redcurrant jelly
5 tablespoons balsamic vinegar
20 garlic cloves

For the garnish
bunch of spring onions, trimmed
   and shredded
1 sweet red pepper, thinly sliced
handful of fresh coriander leaves

In a large pan bring the water to the boil and then add the piece of pork. Bring it back up to the boil for a few minutes and remove any residue that comes to the surface. Add the rice wine, reduce to a simmer, cover and cook for 30 minutes.

Add all the remaining ingredients and bring back to the boil. Reduce to a simmer, cover and cook for a further 3 hours either on top of the cooker or in a very low oven at 150C/300F/Gas 2.

When cooked the pork should be meltingly tender. Gently lift the pork from the pan onto a serving dish and keep warm, together with any ginger and garlic pieces. Reduce the sauce over a high heat until you have a rich, syrupy consistency. Spoon this over the piece of pork.

Finally strew the garnish all over the pork and serve. This is delicious with steamed pak choi, Chinese leaves or noodles.

Sardinian Baked Seafood Pasta

SERVES 4

4 shallots, chopped
2 cloves garlic, finely chopped
1 tablespoon olive oil
400g tinned chopped plum
  tomatoes
1 tablespoon Lea & Perrins
  Worcestershire Sauce
150ml fish stock
1 teaspoon dried Italian herbs
800g frozen seafood cocktail,
  defrosted
200g spaghetti
4 giant shell-on prawns
8–10 fresh mussels, cleaned
  (frozen greenlip mussels can
  be used)

Prepare an ovenproof serving dish (ideally oval and shallow) by lining it with double layered foil and leaving a good 20cm of foil all round the outside to wrap up the whole pasta dish. Pre-heat the oven to 200C/400F/Gas 6.

Sauté the shallots and garlic in the olive oil until soft and then add the tinned tomatoes, Worcestershire sauce, fish stock and herbs. Cook the sauce gently for 10 minutes, remove from the heat and add in the mixed seafood.

Cook the spaghetti in plenty of salted water until only just al dente – no more. Drain and pour into the foil-lined dish.

Pour the tomato and seafood mixture over the spaghetti and lay the shell-on prawns on the top. Bed the mussels, hinge end down, into the pasta and then seal up with the foil. Bake in the oven for 15–20 minutes.

This dish is best served in the centre of the table, where you can then undo the foil and release the wonderful aroma.

As an alternative you can prepare it in 4 individual ovenproof serving dishes so that each person can unwrap their own delicious pasta. Serve with a crispy green salad and warm ciabatta bread.

Spinach and Stilton Bake

SERVES 6

250g spinach
1 tablespoon olive oil
350g button mushrooms, sliced
1 large onion, chopped
2 cloves of garlic
250ml béchamel sauce
2 teaspoons Lea & Perrins
   Worcestershire Sauce
large pinch ground nutmeg
freshly ground black pepper
50g Stilton
1 tablespoon fresh breadcrumbs
50g Cheddar, grated

Wash the spinach and wilt in a saucepan with a small amount of water. Drain completely.

Heat the olive oil in a saucepan and add the mushrooms, onion and garlic and cook until softened. Add the wilted spinach, béchamel sauce, Worcestershire sauce, nutmeg and black pepper, turn down the heat and simmer for 5 minutes.

Crumble in the Stilton and allow it to melt a little. Transfer to a serving dish and scatter with breadcrumbs and grated Cheddar. Place the dish under a hot grill until bubbling and golden.

Serve with garlic bread and a tomato and watercress salad but also comes highly recommended with grilled pork chops.

Cincinnati Chilli

SERVES 4

2 tablespoons olive oil
2 large onions
1kg lean minced beef
1 litre good beef stock
2 tablespoons tomato purée
4 large chillies, finely chopped
2 cloves garlic, chopped
1 tablespoon Lea & Perrins
    Worcestershire Sauce
4 bay leaves
1 teaspoon ground cinnamon
1 teaspoon allspice
1 teaspoon cayenne pepper
1 teaspoon cocoa powder
salt and freshly ground black
    pepper
245g tin red kidney beans, drained
    and rinsed

Heat the oil in a heavy based pan and fry the onions until just transparent. Add the beef, cook until browned and then add in the stock. Bring up to the boil and then reduce down to a simmer.

Add all the other ingredients, except for the kidney beans, and simmer away for 1 hour. Check the seasoning after this time and add salt and freshly ground black pepper as needed.

Lastly add in the kidney beans and continue simmering for a further 1 hour. Then it's red hot and ready. You can always make this the day before and re-heat when ready, as chilli always improves the next day. Serve with wedges of sourdough bread warm from the oven.

RIDLEY CULE PROMOTIONS

LEACH & HERRING SAUCE

A BLOOD-RED SAUCE
FOR DISCERNING GOURMANDS TO
SPLASH ALL OVER THEIR CATCH.

AUDACIOUS IMPOSTERS!

Kitchen Recipes

WITH

Lea & Perrins' Sauce

THE ORIGINAL WORCESTERSHIRE

Copyright.

Basque Breakfast

SERVES 2–4

1 tablespoon olive oil
150g smoked streaky bacon,
 diced
1 large onion peeled and chopped
3 red peppers, halved,
 de-seeded and diced
2 large tomatoes, diced
2 teaspoons Lea & Perrins
 Worcestershire Sauce
handful basil leaves, torn
salt and freshly ground black
 pepper
4 medium free-range eggs

Heat the oil in a large heavy frying pan and fry the bacon for 3–4 minutes and then add the onion. Fry for a further 5 minutes adding the pepper, tomatoes and Worcestershire sauce. Continue cooking for about 15 minutes finally adding the basil, plenty of sea salt and freshly ground black pepper.

Make four small nests in the mixture with the back of a large spoon and crack in the eggs. Season and cook for about 5 minutes or until the egg whites are firm but the yolks still runny.

Put a board in the centre of the table and present breakfast straight from the pan with a warm baguette to tear and dip with.

Chianti Calves' Liver

SERVES 4

4 large slices calves' liver, about
   150–200g each
salt and freshly ground pepper
flour to coat
1 tablespoon olive oil
25g butter
150g rindless back bacon, cut into
   strips
1 onion, cut in half moons
1 clove garlic, crushed
150ml Chianti (or gutsy red wine)
150ml beef stock
1 tablespoon Lea & Perrins
   Worcestershire Sauce
good grate of nutmeg
4 sage leaves, roughly torn

Pat the liver dry with some kitchen paper, season it with salt and pepper and lightly coat in flour, shaking off any excess. Heat the oil and butter in a pan and flash fry the liver for a couple of minutes on each side. Take out the liver, cover with foil and leave aside keeping it warm.

Add the bacon, onion and garlic to the same pan and fry gently until soft. Then add the wine, beef stock, Worcestershire sauce, nutmeg and sage and bring the whole lot up to the boil. Simmer for 5 minutes until the sauce is rich and thick.

Arrange the liver on warmed serving plates and spoon over the delicious sauce. Serve with new season fresh broad beans and sauté potatoes.

Worcester Seared Rib-eyes

SERVES 4

4 tablespoons tomato sauce
2 tablespoons Lea & Perrins
  Worcestershire Sauce
2 tablespoons runny honey
freshly ground black pepper
4 rib-eye steaks

Mix together the sauces, honey and black pepper.

Lay the steaks side by side in a shallow dish and pour the sauce over them, turning the steaks to coat. Leave to marinate for 3–4 hours.

Lift out the steaks and chuck them on the hot barbecue. It's as easy as 1-2-3.

A couple of shakes is all it takes

to quicken the heart
and tickle the palate. The tickly
touch of Lea & Perrins
Worcestershire sauce awakens
and enlivens the flavour
of soups, stews, sauces
– all the savoury dishes that
ever came out of a
cheerful kitchen.

The milkshake was invented on one exceptionally hot day in 1922, when Ivar 'Pop' Coulson, an employee at a branch of the Chicago drugstore chain, Walgreens, took an old-fashioned malted milk drink and dolloped in two scoops of ice cream. Coulson looked after the soda fountain at his store, but his creativity with the tools under his charge led to one of the most significant growth spurts in the chain's history. Coulson's milkshake came with two complimentary vanilla cookies and cost 20 cents.

The most convincing theory on how the handshake came to be our common form of greeting goes back to ancient times. An open right hand was a sign that you were not carrying a weapon. Therefore, for two men to display an open right hand meant that each could presume a certain level of trust (basically, that neither would injure the other). It's been suggested that the shaking motion ensured that weapons that might have been concealed in the sleeve would become dislodged. A variation on the handshake, where the the part of the forearm towards the elbow was grasped was also a way of checking for weaponry all the way down the sleeve. Just prey that your enemy isn't left-handed!

Creamed Lobster Toasties

SERVES 4

300g lobster meat
100ml hollandaise sauce
1 teaspoon Lea & Perrins
   Worcestershire Sauce
freshly ground black pepper
4 English muffins
100g Emmental cheese, grated
2 tablespoons fresh white
   breadcrumbs

Flake the lobster meat into a bowl, add the hollandaise and Worcestershire sauce, season with black pepper and fold gently to mix.

Pre-heat the oven to 200C/400F/ Gas 6. Split and toast the muffins and spread with a little butter. Spoon the lobster mixture equally onto the toasted muffin halves and sprinkle each with the grated cheese, followed by the breadcrumbs.

Put the loaded muffins onto a baking tray and cook in the top of the hot oven for 10–15 minutes or until the breadcrumbs are lightly browned and the cheese has melted. Serve with swathes of fresh peppery watercress.

Right The discerning gourmand of the 1930s was interested in receiving only the original Worcestershire Sauce at his table!

FIRESTARTER?

On 10 June 1886, Mount Tarawera let rip with a volcanic eruption that destroyed and engulfed the Maori village of Te Wairoa in New Zealand, a small settlement close to the shore of Lake Tarawera. Over 150 people died. It became known as the Buried Village. During excavations in the 1970s a bottle of Lea & Perrins Worcestershire Sauce was found buried in the rubble.

Mushroom & Lentil Meatloaf

SERVES 4

225g white rice
1 onion, finely chopped
1 clove garlic, finely chopped
1 green pepper, de-seeded and
   finely chopped
50g mixed dried wild mushrooms,
   soaked in hot water then finely
   chopped
2 tablespoons vegetable oil
1 tomato, finely chopped
200g cooked red lentils
2 tablespoons pine nuts
1 tablespoon Lea & Perrins
   Worcestershire Sauce
1 medium free-range egg, beaten
1 tablespoon mixed dried herbs
1 tablespoon chopped fresh
   parsley

Pre-heat the oven to 180C/350F/ Gas 4.

In a saucepan bring 450ml of water to the boil, add the rice, reduce the heat, cover and simmer for 15 minutes. Drain and leave until ready to use.

Whilst this is cooking sauté the onions, garlic, pepper and mushrooms in the oil until they are all softened, add the tomato and cook for a few minutes longer.

In a large bowl put the rice, sautéed vegetables, lentils, pine nuts, Worcestershire sauce, egg and herbs and combine all the ingredients well. Season with salt and pepper.

Transfer the mixture into a lightly greased loaf tin or similar shaped ovenproof dish and press it all down firmly. Cover with foil and bake in the centre of the pre-heated oven for 45 minutes. Allow to cool a little then turn out and serve.

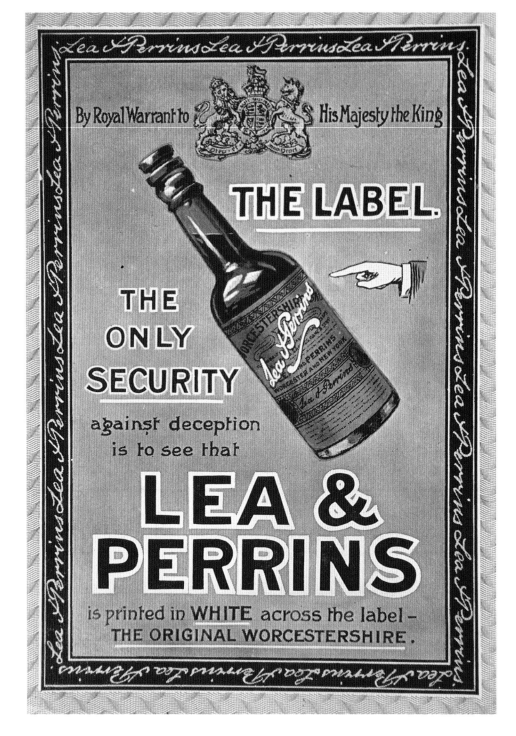

Burgundy Beef

SERVES 4

For the marinade
1 large onion, chopped
1 carrot, sliced
1 stick celery, sliced
2 bay leaves
8 peppercorns, lightly crushed
2 tablespoons olive oil
1 bottle Burgundy wine
1kg braising steak, cut into 5cm
   cubes

1 tablespoon olive oil
knob of butter
200g button mushrooms
150g button onions
3 tablespoons plain flour
2 tablespoons brandy
2 garlic cloves, crushed
few sprigs fresh thyme
1 tablespoon Lea & Perrins
   Worcestershire Sauce
salt and freshly ground black
   pepper

Mix together all the ingredients for the marinade in a large bowl. Add the beef and leave in the fridge overnight – or for at least 4 hours.

Pre-heat the oven to 180C/350F/ Gas 4. Remove the beef from the marinade with a slotted spoon and pat dry with kitchen paper. Keep the marinade. Heat the oil and butter in a large frying pan and sauté the mushrooms and onions for a few minutes. Add the beef, brown it all over and then sprinkle with the flour, keeping the beef moving round the pan. Add the brandy, garlic, thyme, Worcestershire sauce and seasoning and stir well.

Transfer the lot to an ovenproof casserole dish and pour over the reserved marinade. You may need to add a little water to cover the meat with liquid. Put the casserole in the oven and cook for 2 hours.

Serve piping hot with roasted sweet potatoes.

Turkey Jerky

SERVES 4–6 AS A SNACK

500g raw turkey meat, sliced into
thin strips
2 tablespoons hickory smoked
BBQ marinade
2 tablespoons soy sauce
2 tablespoons Lea & Perrins
Worcestershire Sauce
6 dashes Tabasco sauce
2 teaspoons jerk seasoning

Mix all the ingredients together in a dish, cover with clingfilm and pop into the fridge for 24 hours, turning the mixture 2 or 3 times during the chilling.

With a slotted spoon lift out the turkey, place on kitchen paper and pat lightly to remove any excess liquid. Lay out the strips of turkey on a baking sheet and place in the oven at the lowest possible setting to de-hydrate the meat.

Leave in the oven for at least 12 hours! Probably best to do this overnight – but don't forget it in the morning. The end result, similar to the South African version called biltong, is a tough yet crisp healthy snack for all the family to enjoy.

THE ORANGE LABEL

Lea & Perrins Worcestershire Sauce is unmistakably Lea & Perrins Worcestershire Sauce. It's become one of the most instantly recognisable store-cupboard icons in the world, which owes much to its distinctive orange label and signature. Orange is a high-visibility colour. The colour of the Golden Gate Bridge is International Orange. In English heraldry, orange denotes strength, honour and generosity. Orange is also the national colour of the Netherlands.

Breakfast Kebabs with Seville Orange Sauce

SERVES 4

1 tablespoon olive oil
2 tablespoons Lea & Perrins
   Worcestershire Sauce
juice and the rind of one large
   orange
sea salt and freshly ground black
   pepper
450g shoulder bacon joint, cut into
   2.5cm cubes
4 thin skinless pork sausages,
   halved
8 small onions, par boiled
12 button mushrooms

For the sauce
3 tablespoons chunky Seville
   orange marmalade
150ml water (if needed)

First make a marinade by mixing the oil, Worcestershire sauce, orange rind and juice, salt and pepper in a large shallow dish. Thread alternately onto each skewer the bacon, sausages, onions and mushrooms, place in the marinade and leave for at least one hour, turning occasionally.

Remove the kebabs from the marinade and place on a well-oiled grill grid. Brush with more of the marinade and cook on medium hot for 12–15 minutes, turning frequently.

While the kebabs are grilling, make the sauce by placing the remaining marinade in a saucepan and then stir in the marmalade. Bring to the boil stirring, then reduce the heat and simmer gently for two minutes, adding a little water if the sauce is too thick for drizzling. Serve the kebabs on warmed breakfast plates drenched with the marmalade sauce.

Satay Duck

SERVES 4

2 boneless duck breasts
1 teaspoon finely chopped fresh
   ginger
1 tablespoon soy sauce
1 tablespoon Lea & Perrins
   Worcestershire Sauce
finely grated zest and juice of
   2 oranges
salt and freshly ground black
   pepper
50g unsalted peanuts
1 bird's-eye chilli, deseeded and
   finely chopped
Orange wedges

You will also need 8 bamboo
skewers, pre-soaked in water to
stop them burning.

Slice the duck breasts diagonally
into 1cm thick strips. In a bowl,
mix the ginger, soy sauce,
Worcestershire sauce, orange zest
and juice and season with pepper.
Add the sliced duck, cover and
refrigerate for 2 hours.

Heat the grill to medium hot.
Thread the thin slices of duck onto
the skewers and place them in the
grill pan. Spoon over the marinade
and grill for 3–4 minutes, or until
the duck is just cooked.

Meanwhile, spread the nuts on a
baking tray and roast in the oven
for 5 minutes, until golden brown.
Set aside.

When the duck is cooked, lift the
skewers onto a heated serving
dish, cover and keep hot. Put the
nuts into a food processor together
with the cooking juices from the
duck and the chilli and blitz until
smooth. Place in a small saucepan
and gently reheat.

To present – put the skewered duck
onto serving plates with the orange
wedges together with little side
dishes of warm peanut sauce for
dipping.

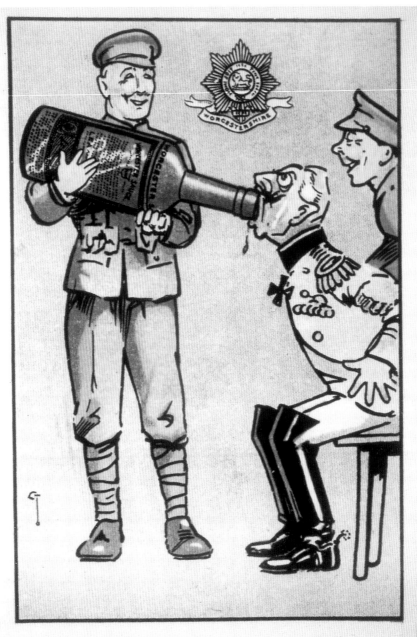

THE OLD BOLD' WORCESTERS

Worcester Roasties

SERVES 4

12–16 medium sized new potatoes
4 tablespoons olive oil
1 tablespoon Lea & Perrins
   Worcestershire Sauce
50g butter
sea salt to sprinkle

Right A First World War cartoon, showing boys from the Worcester regiment indicating to the Kaiser where they've gleaned their strength from. Many soldiers relied upon the Lea & Perrins Worcestershire Sauce to liven up their tins of bully beef.

Pre-heat the oven to 200C/400F/ Gas 6. Put each potato in the bowl of a wooden spoon and rest the spoon on your chopping board. Cut down through the potato at 3mm intervals all the way along the potato. You do not want to slice all the way through the potato – the bowl of the spoon will prevent this happening.

Whisk the olive oil and Worcestershire sauce in a small bowl. It does not need to perfectly amalgamate. Heat the butter and Worcestershire oil until sizzling in a baking tin on top of the cooker and then add the potatoes, turning them a few times and spooning over the oil.

Return all the potatoes to cut side up, sprinkle with a little sea salt and roast in the oven for 45 minutes, or until the potatoes are soft centred and crispy on the outside.

PROBLEMS OF PRONUNCIATION

Three syllables, not four, is the aide memoire to keep in mind. Lea & Perrins Worcestershire Sauce is sold in more than 130 different countries, and, inevitably, some countries find it more difficult to wrap their tongues around the name than others. Outside of the UK, many people pronounce the word phonetically. It should be pronounced 'woos-ter-sher'. Still, Yosemite Sam got the message across, managing to land some for his steaks despite garbling his delivery as 'Warchestershershire Sauce'.

LEA & PERRINS
SAUCE

THE ORIGINAL
AND GENUINE
WORCESTERSHIRE
SAUCE

Printed in England

Hungarian Cabbage Parcels

SERVES 4

1 large savoy cabbage
150g cooked white rice
1 medium onion, chopped
1 teaspoon chopped garlic
1 teaspoon oregano, roughly
 chopped
1 free-range egg, beaten
1 tablespoon Lea & Perrins
 Worcestershire Sauce
450g minced pork
salt and freshly ground pepper
150g rindless streaky bacon
1 tin condensed tomato soup
fresh soured cream

Pre-heat the oven to 180C/350F/ Gas 4. Bring a large pan of salted water to the boil. Remove any damaged outer leaves from the cabbage and plunge the whole thing into the water to blanch. Bring the water back to the boil for 2 minutes and then drain the cabbage and refresh with cold water to keep the colour. Blanching will make it easy to separate the cabbage leaves.

To make the stuffing mix together in a large bowl the rice, onions, garlic, oregano, egg, Worcestershire sauce and pork. Season with salt and pepper and shape the mixture into balls using a dessertspoonful for each.

Cut off the larger cabbage leaves and spread each in turn on the work surface, trimming off any larger stalks. Place a stuffing ball in the centre of each leaf, wrap up in a parcel and place in a shallow ovenproof serving dish. Continue until you have used all the stuffing mixture and pack the parcels tightly into the dish.

Stretch the bacon with the back of a knife, cut each rasher in half and use to criss-cross over each parcel. Pour over the tomato soup and cook in the oven for 45 minutes. Serve with good dollops of soured cream.

Left
Keep it near for cooking!

Spiced Meatballs

SERVES 4–6

1kg minced steak
50g fresh breadcrumbs
1 teaspoon curry powder
salt and freshly ground black
    pepper
2 medium free-range eggs, beaten

For the gravy
knob of unsalted butter
1 tablespoon olive oil
1 onion, chopped
1 clove of garlic
2 tablespoons flour
500ml good beef stock
1 tablespoon Lea & Perrins
    Worcestershire Sauce
2 tablespoons fruit chutney

Pre-heat the oven to 180C/350F/
Gas 4. In a large bowl mix together
all the meatball ingredients.
When the mixture is well blended
form into balls slightly larger than
a golf ball.

Add the butter and oil to a frying
pan and over a medium heat fry the
meatballs for 5 minutes. Add the
onion and garlic and cook for a
further 4–5 minutes, or until the
meatballs are nutty and golden
and the onions softened.

Using a slotted spoon lift out the
meatballs and onions and put them
into a shallow ovenproof dish. Add
the flour to the remaining juices in
the pan, stirring all the time, and
cook for a further minute. Pour in
the beef stock, a little at a time,
and lastly add the Worcestershire
sauce and fruit chutney.

Pour the gravy mixture over the
meatballs and put the dish,
uncovered, into the hot oven for a
further 20 minutes. Serve with fluffy
Basmati rice or ribbon pasta.

RIDLEY CULE PROMOTIONS

PEA & LEMMING SAUCE

MADE FROM
MISS BETTY BOIS'
FINEST PEA HARVEST

INGREDIENTS HERDED TOGETHER,
COAXED FROM AN EXTREMELY
HIGH LEDGE AND MATURED FOR
SIX YEARS AND THREE MONTHS

AUDACIOUS IMPOSTERS!

Cheddar, Chicken & Spinach Pancakes

MAKES 6 FILLED PANCAKES

40g unsalted butter
40g plain flour
500ml milk
150g mature Cheddar cheese, grated
salt and freshly ground pepper
few shakes of sesame oil
400g baby leaf spinach, washed
1 tablespoon Lea & Perrins Worcestershire Sauce
300g cooked chicken breast, cut into strips
handful flatleaf parsley leaves, chopped
6 ready made pancakes

Pre-heat the oven to 200C/400F/ Gas 6.

First make the sauce by melting the butter in a saucepan, add the flour and stir rapidly for 1 minute. Gradually add the milk, still stirring constantly and bring to the boil to thicken. Remove from the heat and stir in three quarters of the cheese until melted. Season with salt and pepper and leave aside.

Heat the sesame oil in a pan (a wok is ideal) and add the spinach and Worcestershire sauce and toss until wilted.

Take one pancake and put one sixth of the chicken and spinach down the centre of it. Spoon over some of the cheesy sauce, roll up the pancake and place in a lightly greased ovenproof dish. Repeat with the other pancakes and then pour the remaining sauce over the 6 filled pancakes.

Sprinkle the rest of the grated cheese over the top of the pancakes and bake in the oven for 20–25 minutes until golden. Serve strewn with the chopped parsley and a mixed leaf salad.

Far Left Lea & Perrins were forced to issue a temporary label after their printers had been damaged by enemy action during the Second World War.
Left Back to something more familiar in 1945.

Crab Louisiana

SERVES 4

For the sauce
150ml light mayonnaise
2 tablespoons tomato ketchup
1 tablespoon Lea & Perrins
   Worcestershire Sauce
3 tablespoons olive oil
1 tablespoon white wine vinegar
1 small onion, finely chopped
2 tablespoons chopped flatleaf
   parsley
4 tablespoons crème fraîche
100g pimento stuffed olives
salt and freshly ground pepper

2 ripe avocados
lemon juice
mixed salad leaves
450g fresh crabmeat
sweet smoked paprika

Blend together all the sauce ingredients, except the olives, and season with salt and pepper. Chop the stuffed olives and add them into the mixture. Chill for 1 hour.

Halve and stone the avocados and then remove the skin. Lay each avocado half flat side down and cut lengthways into 6–8 long slices. Drizzle each with a little lemon juice to hold the fresh green colour. Scatter some salad leaves on each plate and transfer the avocado halves on top. Press down gently on the avocado until the slices fan out.

Add the crabmeat to the chilled mayo mixture and fold in gently. Pile the crab salad on top of the avocado and sprinkle a little paprika over the top. Serve with hot crusty ciabatta bread.

Malt Vinegar

Molasses

Spirit Vinegar

Garlic

Anchovies

Shallots

Sugar

Tamarinds

Spices

Salt

IT TAKES US THREE YEARS TO ——— TURN THEM INTO ——— A BOTTLE OF LEA & PERRINS.

It only took Mr Lea and Mr Perrins a few days to make the first batch of Worcestershire Sauce in 1835. They prepared it for Lord Sandys, who'd discovered the recipe when he was governor of Bengal.

Everything went fine until the tasting. The sauce turned out to be throat-grippingly foul. Even Lord Sandys, who'd swallowed many a raging Vindaloo in Bengal, turned a ghastly shade of green.

With apologetic shrugs and a large dose of bicarbonate of soda for the queasy ex-governor, the sauce was consigned to the cellar in stone jars and quickly forgotten.

There was no time to dwell on failures. Lea & Perrins Chemist Shop was doing a roaring trade in everything from Taraxacum (dandelion coffee), to Dr Locock's Lotion For The Hair.

Some years later, during a general clearout, they came across the stone jars again. Scientific curiosity forced the two chemists to sample the contents once more.

They stared at each other in astonishment. The sauce tasted superb. It had matured.

They had stumbled across the vital missing ingredient: time.

What could be better for business than naming the sauce after their home town? The only question was what on earth you used it on. The answer was simple: everything.

People used it to enrich lamb hot-pots, steak and kidney pies, casseroles, fish, salads.

Others went further with dishes like Veal en Croûte, and Mushrooms à la Grecque.

By the time the Chinese got hold of it the list was as long as the Great Wall itself. (For a few suggestions try the L&P Cookbook advertised on our bottles.)

People are still finding new ways to use Lea & Perrins.

For instance, brushing it on white meat before microwaving improves both flavour and appearance. Talking of microwaves, surely we could devise a quicker way to make our sauce?

Perhaps we could. But even after 152 years, we can't quite forget the effect on Lord Sandys of our first attempt at high speed production.

ADD a LITTLE DASH to YOUR COOKING

Beef Carpaccio

SERVES 6–8 GUESTS AS A STARTER

500g fillet of beef
freshly ground black pepper
75g Pecorino cheese
   (or Parmesan)

For the marinade
5 tablespoons Lea & Perrins
   Worcestershire Sauce
5 tablespoons dark soy sauce
10 tablespoons balsamic vinegar
500ml olive oil
300ml dry white wine
5 garlic cloves, finely chopped
1 tablespoon fresh thyme leaves
handful fresh basil leaves, roughly
   torn
sea salt and freshly ground black
   pepper

Remove any fat from around the piece of beef and discard.

In a bowl, large enough to hold the beef, put all the liquid ingredients of the marinade and mix well with a whisk. Add the garlic, herbs (all but a few basil leaves for the finishing touch), plenty of black pepper and the sea salt and then immerse the beef in the marinade.

Cover the bowl with clingfilm and refrigerate for 5 days, turning the beef in the delicious juices at least once every day.

Remove the beef from the marinade, wrap in clingfilm and chill for a further few hours. It can also be wholly or partly frozen at this stage depending on how much you need to use.

Cut the beef into 1cm thick slices. Put a slice at a time between 2 sheets of clingfilm and with a rolling pin and a little pressure gently roll out each slice until you have a wafer thin piece of meat. Repeat with the remaining slices.

To serve, divide the beef between your serving plates, drizzle with a few teaspoons of the marinade, scatter a few basil leaves over and finally, using a potato peeler, add shavings of Pecorino cheese to finish.

Ruby Coleslaw

SERVES 6–8

$1/_2$ red cabbage, shredded
2 carrots, grated
1 red pepper, deseeded and finely
sliced
1 yellow pepper, deseeded and
finely sliced
1 onion, finely sliced
200g fresh peas (tinned as second
best)

For the dressing
75ml peanut oil
50ml rice wine vinegar
2 tablespoons Lea & Perrins
Worcestershire Sauce
1 tablespoon honey

Mix together all the vegetables in a large bowl – best to use your hands for this job.

In a separate bowl, whisk together all the dressing ingredients and then pour over the vegetables. Toss well so that everything is well coated. Cover and chill.

When ready to serve, bring back to room temperature. Great with barbecues, roast chicken and cold meats.

FIRE!

Fire has threatened our beloved sauce twice. In 1882, on the 15th December, a fire began in the packing room at the Bank Street factory. Fortunately, it was discovered early and was extinguished. Damages were later valued at £17.11.6d. Then, in 1964, a large and very serious fire broke out in the Midland Road factory. Reports from the time confirm that twelve appliances and 50 men were needed to fight the fire. It required fourteen jets to quell the giant blaze. A huge amount of damage was caused, although, amazingly, full productiion was back underway just ten days later.

Deskfast Pizza

SERVES 2–4

1 ready-made pizza base
2 tablespoons tomato purée mixed
   with 1 teaspoon Lea & Perrins
   Worcestershire Sauce
2 pork and herb sausages cooked
   and thinly sliced
2 tomatoes, roughly chopped
2 sliced mushrooms
4 rashers of streaky bacon, grilled
   and diced
drizzle of olive oil
1 handful rocket leaves

Pre-heat the oven to 200C/400F/
Gas 6.

Take the pizza base and spread it
with the tomato and Worcestershire
sauce mixture. Place the sliced
sausages over the pizza and top
with the tomatoes and sliced
mushrooms. Finally sprinkle the
whole pizza with diced streaky
bacon and drizzle with olive oil.

Pop the pizza onto a baking tray
and into the hot oven for about
10–15 minutes or until the bacon
is crispy. Cut into sections and top
each wedge with a handful of
rocket leaves.

Wrap up and take it to work for
the perfect breakfast on the go or
sneak it into the kids' lunchbox and
they'll love you all day!

RIDLEY CULE PROMOTIONS

PLEA & PORRIDGE SAUCE

**FROM MR. OLIVER T. WIST'S
ORIGINAL MOOREISH RECIPE.**

THE TWO-STEP SAUCE FOR ALL
WHO REQUIRE THAT LITTLE BIT MORE
FOR THEIR SUPPER.
IDEAL WITH GRUEL
AND OTHER MEAL DISHES.

AUDACIOUS IMPOSTERS!

Seared Beef Salad with Dates & Pistachios

SERVES 2

400g rump steak
2 tablespoons Lea & Perrins
  Worcestershire Sauce
1 tablespoon olive oil
3 tablespoons walnut oil
1 tablespoon white wine vinegar
salt and freshly ground black
  pepper
handful flatleaf parsley leaves,
  roughly chopped
100g dates, stoned and sliced
40g shelled pistachio nuts
25g dried cranberries
mixed salad leaves

Place the rump steak in a shallow dish and spoon over the Worcestershire sauce. Leave to marinate for at least an hour, turning the steak occasionally.

Heat the olive oil in a heavy based frying pan until just smoking. Remove the steak from the marinade and pat dry. Carefully put the steak into the hot oil and sear the beef for 2 minutes on each side so that it is crusty brown on the outside and rare on the inside. Take out the steak and leave to one side.

Whisk together the walnut oil and vinegar in a bowl and season with salt and pepper. In a separate bowl mix together the parsley leaves, dates, pistachios and cranberries then add the steak cut into thin slices.

Dress the salad leaves with the vinaigrette and scatter on 2 plates. Pile the steak mixture on top and season well with freshly milled black pepper. Serve with warm flatbreads or naan bread.

SSHHH! DON'T SPILL THE SECRET

In 1911, the secret ingredient was nearly revealed when one of the new partners died, and his papers and documents were being decided over. The directors of Lea & Perrins, fearfully realising that a copy of the recipe might be found, swiftly gave instructions to seal the envelope containing the information. The secret has remained safe ever since.

Red Lentil, Tomato & Stilton Soup

SERVES 4

25g unsalted butter
1 medium onion, finely chopped
100g red lentils, washed
400g tin tomatoes
500ml semi-skimmed milk
250ml chicken stock
2 teaspoons Lea & Perrins
   Worcestershire Sauce
150g Stilton
salt and freshly ground black
   pepper

Melt the butter in a heavy based saucepan and sauté the onion until soft. Add the red lentils and stir for a few minutes.

Add the tomatoes, milk, stock and Worcestershire sauce and keep stirring until it comes to the boil. Turn down the heat and simmer for 45 minutes, stirring occasionally.

Remove from the heat and crumble in the Stilton, stirring gently to melt it. Taste and season with salt and pepper as required. Serve with crusty French bread.

Creole Prawns with Fettuccine

SERVES 4

25g unsalted butter
2 cloves garlic, minced
handful basil leaves, torn
small handful oregano leaves,
   roughly chopped
good sprig of thyme, leaves only
$1/_2$ teaspoon salt
freshly ground black pepper
level teaspoon cayenne pepper
3–4 plum tomatoes, skins removed
   after plunging into boiling water
150ml chicken stock
1 tablespoon Lea & Perrins
   Worcestershire Sauce
1 tablespoon hot chilli sauce
400g fettuccine
800g–1kg raw tiger prawns
   (according to budget!)

Melt the butter in a pan and add in the minced garlic, herbs, salt and peppers. Allow these to infuse over a gentle heat for a couple of minutes. Then add the tomatoes, stock, Worcestershire and chilli sauces and simmer gently for 10 minutes until you have a rich, fiery sauce.

Place the fettuccine in plenty of boiling salted water and cook for 10–12 minutes until the pasta is tender but still firm. Drain the pasta and return it to the pan to keep warm.

Add the prawns to the tomato sauce, turn up the heat and cook for 3–5 minutes or until the prawns have turned pink. Pour the sauce over the cooked fettuccine, toss the whole lot together and then serve on hot plates with plenty of ice-cold beer.

Gascony Lamb Shanks

SERVES 2

2 tablespoons olive oil
2 lamb shanks
1 onion, sliced
1 carrot, sliced
1 small leek, sliced
1 tablespoon flour
1 tablespoon tomato purée
1 tablespoon Lea & Perrins
    Worcestershire Sauce
2 glasses red wine
4 cloves garlic, peeled
8 cherry tomatoes, halved
1 tablespoon dried mixed herbs

Pre-heat the oven to 160C/325F/ Gas 3.

Heat the oil in a heavy based casserole and brown the lamb shanks all over and then remove them from the pan. Pour out all but a little of the fat from the pan, add the onion, carrot and leek and cook them for a few minutes until softened.

Stir in the flour, tomato purée, Worcestershire sauce and cook for a couple of minutes. Add in the wine, bring to the boil and then simmer for 10 minutes. Add the remaining ingredients and put back the lamb shanks together with enough water to just cover the meat.

Replace the casserole lid and cook in the oven for 2–3 hours. Check and stir the casserole from time to time and add a little more water if it looks too dry. The sauce should be thick and rich and the meat should just fall away from the bone.

Right
A turn-of-the-century triptych of reasons to trust Lea & Perrins.

LEA & PERRINS' SAUCE

Was introduced over sixty years ago and never varies in excellence of quality.

LEA & PERRINS' SAUCE

MANUFACTORY, WORCESTER, ENGLAND.

Beware of ⅔ of it cheap imitations

(The original & only genuine Worcestershire)

THE SIGNATURE IN WHITE ACROSS THE RED LABEL DISTINGUISHES THE ORIGINAL AND GENUINE WORCESTERSHIRE SAUCE.

LEA & PERRINS' SAUCE

Is made only from the choicest ingredients and keeps perfectly in every climate.

Globe Artichokes with Sesame Tarragon Dip

SERVES 4

4 globe artichokes
juice of 1 lemon
1 teaspoon salt

For the dip
200ml mayonnaise
2 tablespoons Lea & Perrins
   Worcestershire Sauce
1 tablespoon olive oil
1 tablespoon sesame oil
1 tablespoon runny honey
1 tablespoon lemon juice
1 teaspoon finely chopped
   tarragon
sea salt and freshly ground black
   pepper

Prepare the dip in advance by whisking together all the dipping ingredients. Cover and refrigerate.

Cut the artichoke stems down to the base of the globe so that they will stand up. Put the 4 globes side by side in a large pan and add water until it comes two thirds of the way up the artichokes. Add the lemon juice and salt and bring to the boil. Reduce to a simmer, cover and leave cooking for 30–35 minutes.

After this time lift out one of the artichokes with a slotted spoon. When cooked the bottom 'petals' should fall away from the globe. Drain and serve on a large plate with a small bowl of dipping sauce each.

To eat, simply pull off each petal, dip in the sauce and bite off the fleshy base, discarding the rest of the petal. When you reach the centre of the artichoke, remove the hairy leaves on the top and eat the heart – it's the best of all!

Cumberland Venison Steaks

SERVES 2

For the sauce
2 tablespoons cranberry sauce
zest and juice of $1/2$ lime
zest and juice of $1/2$ orange
2 teaspoons Lea & Perrins
　Worcestershire Sauce
$1/2$ teaspoon grated ginger
$1/2$ teaspoon mustard powder
100ml port

2 venison steaks
1 teaspoon crushed mixed
　peppercorns
1 tablespoon vegetable oil
1 large shallot, finely chopped

You can make the sauce in advance to make life easier. Put the cranberry sauce, fruit juice and zest, Worcestershire sauce, ginger and mustard powder into a pan and bring up to a simmer whisking to combine all the ingredients. Remove from the heat, stir in the port and keep until ready to use.

Pat the venison steaks dry with some kitchen paper and then press in the crushed peppercorns on both sides of the steaks. Heat the oil in a heavy based pan until smoking and then add the venison. The steaks will need to cook for 4–5 minutes each side for medium. You can reduce or increase the time for rare or well done by 1 minute. Halfway through cooking, add the shallots to the pan tucking them in around the steaks and not on top.

Just before the steaks are cooked to your liking add the sauce and let it bubble in the hot pan for 30 seconds. Serve the steaks with the shallots and sauce poured over accompanied by crispy jacket potatoes and a good leafy salad.

LEA & PERRINS' SAUCE

DONALDSON BROTHERS, N.Y.

L&P Liptauer Cheese

SERVES 4–6

250g cream cheese
1 tablespoon capers, rinsed and
  drained
1 tablespoon Lea & Perrins
  Worcestershire Sauce
1 tablespoon mild mustard
1 tablespoon sweet smoked
  paprika
salt and freshly ground black
  pepper

Mash the cream cheese in a bowl.
Pound the capers into a paste and
mix them into the cheese. Stir in
the Worcestershire sauce, mustard
and paprika.

Blend the whole mixture well.
Taste and add salt and pepper if
required.

Serve with sliced dill pickles and
good dark rye bread.

Left Fit for a monarch's table.
King Edward VII granted the rare
Royal Warrant to Lea & Perrins
in 1904.

RIDLEY CULE PROMOTIONS

EEL & FERRET SAUCE

A FINE SAUCE FOR SLIPPERY FILLETS
OF FISH AND MEAT.

BE SURE TO GET

AUDACIOUS IMPOSTERS!

Sticky Honey Ribs

SERVES 4

For the marinade
4 tablespoons white wine vinegar
2 tablespoons soy sauce
2 tablespoons Lea & Perrins
  Worcestershire Sauce
2 red chillies, deseeded and
  chopped
1 teaspoon chopped fresh ginger
$\frac{1}{2}$ teaspoon ground cinnamon
1 tablespoon sesame oil
1 tablespoon groundnut oil

16 good meaty pork spare ribs
2 tablespoons runny honey
2 spring onions, chopped
small bunch coriander, chopped

Mix together all the marinade ingredients in a jug. Put the ribs into a large, strong plastic bag and pour in the marinade. Seal or knot the bag and squidge the whole lot round so that all the ribs are coated with the gooey mixture. Leave in a cool place for a couple of hours or ideally in the fridge overnight.

Pre-heat the oven to 200C/400F/ Gas 6. Empty the contents of the bag into a suitable roasting tin, cover with foil and pop into the oven for 1 hour.

Remove the foil and drizzle the runny honey over the ribs. Put them back in the oven, uncovered for a further 20–25 minutes, turning once during this time.

Pile the ribs onto a warmed serving plate and scatter with spring onions and coriander.

Lamb Chops with Worcestershire Mint Sauce

SERVES 4

2 red peppers, deseeded and
   quartered
2 tablespoons olive oil
good pinch of sugar
sea salt and freshly ground black
   pepper
1 aubergine, sliced
8 lamb chops

Combine the following to make
the mint sauce
2 tablespoons Lea & Perrins
   Worcestershire Sauce
handful fresh mint leaves, finely
   chopped
good pinch caster sugar

Pre-heat the oven to 200C/400F/ Gas 6. Put the quartered peppers in a roasting dish and drizzle them with the olive oil. Sprinkle the sugar over them and then season with plenty of salt and pepper. Roast for 30 minutes.

While the peppers cook, cut the aubergine into 1cm slices, brush with olive oil and season. Heat a griddle pan or large non-stick frying pan over a fairly high heat and sear the slices in batches until golden on both sides. Put them aside on a plate.

In the same pan brown the chops on both sides. Take the roasting dish of cooked peppers and lay the aubergine slices on top. Next add the chops and put the whole lot back in the oven for 15–20 minutes.

To serve, divide the chops, peppers and aubergines between 4 warmed serving plates and spoon over the Worcestershire mint sauce.

My good friend Ken, without any vinegar to make his mint sauce one day, reached for the Lea & Perrins and created this brilliant variation. He's been making it this way ever since!

BOTTLE IT

Most sauces in 1837 – the time when Lea and Perrins Worcestershire Sauce began to be commercially produced – were sold in square bottles. The origin of the round Lea & Perrins bottle lies in the fact that the sauce had originally been decanted into the standard trade medicine bottles that Lea & Perrins – who, let us not forget, were chemists – poured all of their mixtures. The design stuck!

Corned Beef Hash

SERVES 2

200g corned beef
2 tablespoons Lea & Perrins
   Worcestershire sauce
1 teaspoon whole grain mustard
1 large onion
275g potatoes
   (Desirée or King Edward)
2–3 tablespoons olive oil
salt and freshly ground black
   pepper
2 large free-range eggs

Dice the corned beef into 1cm cubes and scoop into a bowl. Mix together the Worcestershire sauce and mustard in a cup, pour over the corned beef and mix well. Peel and halve the onion, cut into half moons. Scrub, but do not peel the potatoes and cut into 1cm cubes.

Place the potatoes in a saucepan and pour enough boiling water from the kettle to almost cover them, add salt, a lid and simmer for 5 minutes. Drain in a colander and leave aside.

Heat the oil in a large heavy based frying pan until smoking hot, add the onions and toss in the oil for three minutes until well browned. Add the potatoes and toss until browned then season with a little salt and a good grind of pepper. Finally add the corned beef mixture and continue to toss everything in the pan for about three minutes.

In a separate pan fry the eggs. Serve the hash divided onto two warm plates with a fried egg on top of each.

Scallop & Bacon Brochettes

SERVES 2

4 rashers rindless streaky bacon
8 large king scallops
freshly ground black pepper
50g soft almost melted butter
1 tablespoon Lea & Perrins
    Worcestershire Sauce
1 lemon, half for zest and half for
    wedges
few fronds of fresh dill

You will also need 8 cocktail
sticks and a griddle or heavy
based frying pan.

Cut each rasher of bacon in half, and holding one end of each rasher, run the knife blade along its length to stretch the rasher. Season each scallop with a little black pepper. Wrap each one in a length of bacon and fix in place by pushing a cocktail stick through the centre.

Melt the butter in the griddle pan and when sizzling add the scallop parcels. Cook for 3–4 minutes, turning once, until the bacon fat is starting to turn golden.

Then add the Worcestershire sauce, taking care it doesn't spit and make sure the parcels are well coated.

Cook for a further 2–3 minutes and serve hot from the pan scattered with the lemon zest, dill and a good grind of pepper. Add some wedges of lemon, hot buttered granary toast and devour.

SAUCY HABIT
Lieutenant Colonel Sir Francis Edward Young made a pioneering visit to Tibet, arriving at the forbidden city of Lhasa on 3 August 1904. Weary after his long journey, the monks offered him a quick refreshment. To his amazement, he saw sitting in the middle of the refectory table, a bottle of Lea & Perrins Worcestershire Sauce. It had got there first!

THE LYLE'S GOLDEN SYRUP
RECIPE COLLECTION

Baked Apples with Prunes in Cinnamon Syrup

SERVES 4

100g semi-dried prunes, stoned
2 tablespoons Armagnac
   (or brandy)
$1/_2$ teaspoon ground cinnamon
40g pecan nuts, finely chopped
50g dark muscovado sugar
4 tablespoons Lyle's Golden
   Syrup, plus extra for coating
4 apples, approx. 175g each
   (Cox's or Golden Delicious are
   good)

Preheat the oven to 150C/300F/ Gas 2.

Chop up the prunes and put them into a bowl with the Armagnac, cinnamon, nuts, sugar and golden syrup and leave aside to infuse.

Wash, dry and core the apples but do not peel. The easy way to core the apples is using a long thin knife or a potato peeler to make a circular hole about 3cm diameter right through the centre of the apple. Chop up the flesh, rejecting the pips and core you have just removed, and add it to the prune stuffing mixture.

Coat the apples with golden syrup by pouring the syrup and twirling the apples as you go. Then sit them in a greased ovenproof baking dish making sure they don't touch. Pack each one with the syrupy prune stuffing – don't worry about any overflow as it all adds to the rustic charm of the dish. Drizzle with any of the remaining juices.

Bake in the oven for 40–45 minutes, basting once or twice while they cook. Allow to cool a little before serving with good hot thick creamy custard.

Salmon Kebabs with Lime & Syrup

SERVES 4

800g salmon fillet, skinned and cubed

For the marinade
zest of 1 lime and juice of 2 limes
1 stalk of fresh lemongrass, finely sliced
1 tablespoon light soy sauce
1 tablespoon fish sauce
2 tablespoons Lyle's Golden Syrup

4 sheets of medium egg noodles
chopped chives to garnish

Put the cubes of salmon fillet into a large, shallow dish. In a bowl mix together the ingredients for the marinade until well blended and then pour over the salmon. Cover with clingfilm and leave in the fridge for at least 2 hours, turning the fish once during this time. Soak some wooden skewers in water to prevent them burning later.

Bring a pan of water to the boil. Add the noodles and then remove from the heat and cover with a lid. After a couple of minutes swizzle the noodles about with a fork to loosen them then cover again and leave for 5 minutes. Drain, return them to the pan and add a couple of tablespoons of the marinade to the noodles. Keep them warm while you finish the salmon.

Line a grill pan with foil and lightly oil the grill rack. Thread the salmon cubes onto the skewers and grill under a medium heat for 3–4 minutes on each side basting with some of the marinade. Serve the kebabs on top of the noodles scattered with chopped chives.

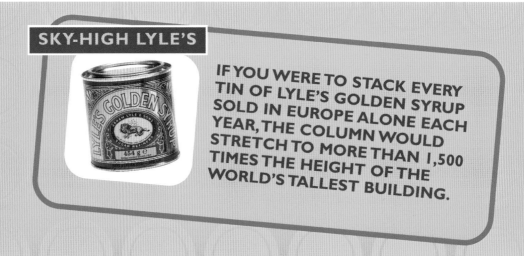

SKY-HIGH LYLE'S

IF YOU WERE TO STACK EVERY TIN OF LYLE'S GOLDEN SYRUP SOLD IN EUROPE ALONE EACH YEAR, THE COLUMN WOULD STRETCH TO MORE THAN 1,500 TIMES THE HEIGHT OF THE WORLD'S TALLEST BUILDING.

Oaty Mixed Berry crumble

SERVES 4

450g mixed berries (such as
 blackcurrants, redcurrants,
 blueberries, raspberries)
2 tablespoons Lyle's Golden Syrup
75g butter (from the fridge)
100g plain flour
50g Demerara sugar
50g porridge oats
25g flaked almonds or mixed nuts
 (well crushed)
pinch ground cinnamon

Preheat the oven to 200C/400F/
Gas 6. Lightly grease the inside of
a 23cm/9" round ovenproof dish.

If you are using berries from the
freezer they can be used from
frozen. Simply put them in the dish
and drizzle with the golden syrup,
they will release their own juice. If
you are using fresh berries in
season it is worth adding a couple
of tablespoons of fruit juice as well
as the syrup. Spread the berries in
the dish and press down gently and
evenly.

Cut the butter into small cubes and
put in a large bowl with the flour.
Gently rub the two together with
your fingertips. When you arrive at
a texture like breadcrumbs add the
sugar, oats, almonds and cinnamon
and blend in well. Spread the
crumble mix loosely over the
berries – a little higher in the centre
as it may sink a little when cooking.
You can sprinkle a little more sugar
on top for extra crunch if you wish.
Bake in the oven for 30–35 minutes,
until golden brown. Great served
with dollops of fruit sorbet.

LYLE'S LEGEND & LORE

TREACLE MINES

TREACLE MINES have been a standing British joke for many, many years. It's a story that has been passed down from one generation to the next, just like the exotic myth of the Spaghetti Tree. What helps to make the story plausible to children is that treacle is darker than syrup and its extraction in this darkened raw state seems to bear some resemblance to the mining for coal. As for the science behind this sticky underground story, well, explanations range from claims that the treacle got there when Cromwell's army buried leaking barrels of molasses, to the fib of fossilised prehistoric sugar cane beds!

Glazed Sausage Toad in the Hole

SERVES 4–6

150g plain flour
salt and freshly milled black
  pepper
2 medium free-range eggs
150ml semi-skimmed milk mixed
  with 150ml cold water
6 free-range pork sausages
2 tablespoons Lyle's Golden Syrup
2 tablespoons lard

You will need a 23cm x 30cm
(12 x 9-inch) roasting tin.

Preheat the oven to 220C/425F/
Gas 7.

Sieve the flour into a large bowl
and season with salt and pepper.
Make a well in the centre and crack
in the eggs. Using an electric whisk
slowly mix the flour with the eggs
then gradually add the milk and
water. Whisk until you have a
smooth batter and then leave aside
until ready to use.

Line a grill pan with foil, put the
sausages on the rack and brush
generously with the golden syrup.
Grill them very gently, basting
frequently with the syrup until they
are golden and cooked through.

Heat the lard in a roasting tin in the
top of the oven for 5 minutes until
its shimmering hot. Lard has a
higher smoking point than
vegetable oil, which is crucial for
good Yorkshire pudding – puffy and
crispy. The hotter the fat is when
the batter first hits it the better the
end result. Take the tin out of the
oven and put it over a medium heat

on top of the cooker while you
quickly and carefully (taking care
of any spitting fat) arrange the
sausages and immediately pour
in the batter around the sausages.
Put the tin straight into the top of
the hot oven.

Bake for 30 minutes until the batter
is puffed up, crispy edged and
golden brown. Serve with good rich
onion gravy and creamy mash.

Treacle Tart

SERVES 4–6

150g ready made shortcrust
  pastry
butter for greasing
150g fine fresh white breadcrumbs
zest of 1 lemon
454g tin of Lyle's Golden Syrup
lemon wedges to serve

**You will need a lightly buttered
20cm/8" diameter flan dish.**

Preheat the oven to 180C/350F/
Gas 4.

Roll out the pastry fairly thin and
line the flan dish. Make sure the
pastry is gently pushed in around
the edge to fully fit the dish and
trim the excess pastry from the rim.
Chill in the fridge for 15 minutes.

Mix together the breadcrumbs and
the lemon zest and tip them into
the flan, spreading them evenly
over the base. Starting at the

outside, in a circular motion
working inwards, pour the contents
of the golden syrup tin over the
breadcrumbs – simple as that!

Put the treacle tart into the oven
and cook for 10 minutes. Remove
it from the oven and leave, as the
treacle tart will continue cooking for
a further 10 minutes all on its own.

Serve warm or cold with wedges of
lemon and thick cream.

LYLE'S LEGEND & LORE

SCOTT'S SWEET TOOTH

**IN 1912 a larder was set up in the frozen
wastelands of Antarctica as part of the
preparations for Captain Scott's epic
journey to the South Pole. This store of
food contained many provisions, including
several large tins of Lyle's Golden Syrup.
Tragically, Scott's expedition team died
just ten miles short of the hut's salvation
on their return from the Pole. Five months
earlier, writing from his Cape Evans base,
Scott wrote a letter to Lyle & Sons
thanking them for the provisions of syrup:
'I have pleasure in informing you that
your "Golden Syrup" has been in daily
use in this Hut throughout the winter
and has been much appreciated by
Members of the Expedition. I regard it as
a most desirable addition to necessary
food articles of a Polar Expedition.'**

'Home Sweet Home'
From the painting by G.E. Collins R.B.A., 1905

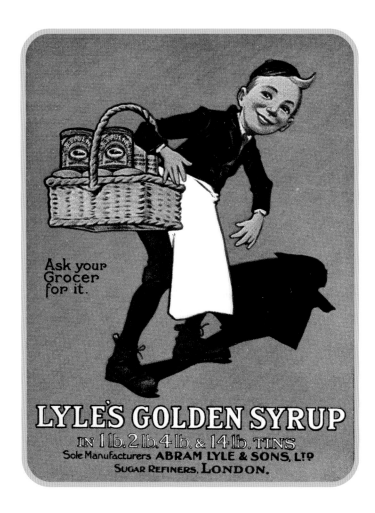

Ask your grocer for it!
An advertisement from the 1900s

Bengal Mango & Ginger Chutney

MAKES 2 X 500ML JARS

6 medium fresh mangoes
   (about 2kg)
200g light muscovado sugar
200g Lyle's Golden Syrup
$1/_2$ teaspoon cumin seeds
1 teaspoon coriander seeds
$1/_2$ teaspoon mustard seeds
8 cardamom pods
2 teaspoons paprika
$1/_2$ teaspoon cayenne pepper
$1/_2$ teaspoon turmeric
$1/_2$ teaspoon ground cloves
50g root ginger, peeled and finely
   chopped
6 cloves garlic, peeled and finely
   chopped
1 level teaspoon salt
500ml white vinegar (distilled malt)
2 medium onions, peeled and
   finely chopped

Peel and stone the mangoes over a large bowl to catch any juices and chop the flesh into cubes, scraping off any flesh clinging to the stone and skin. Add to this the sugar and syrup, mix well and leave to one side while you prepare the spices.

In a dry frying pan over a medium heat roast the cumin, coriander, mustard seeds and cardamom pods for a couple of minutes until they begin to crackle then tip them into a pestle and mortar and lightly crush to release the flavours.

Tip the roasted spices into a large heavy based pan and add the sweet mango mixture followed by all the remaining ingredients. Bring the mixture up to a simmer and then leave it very gently bubbling away for 3 hours. (Leave the lid on for the first hour and then uncovered for the rest.) Keep an eye after 2 hours as the liquid will almost evaporate and you will be left with a syrupy consistency which may tend to stick, so it will need to be stirred from time to time.

Remove the pan from the heat and leave to stand for at least 20 minutes before bottling in sterilised jars. Seal while still warm then leave to cool. Label and date your delicious chutney, which you will need to leave in a cool, dark place for 6 weeks to get the full and fantastic Indian flavour.

Lemon Syrup Pancake Stack

SERVES 4

For the pancakes
275g plain flour
$2^1/_2$ teaspoons baking powder
1 level teaspoon salt
3 tablespoons caster sugar
220ml milk
3 medium free-range eggs
50g unsalted butter, melted
250g Mascarpone
small punnet of blueberries

For the syrup
4 tablespoons Lyle's Golden Syrup
juice and zest of a large lemon

Sieve the flour, baking powder and salt into a bowl and add the caster sugar.

In another bowl whisk together the milk, eggs and melted butter. Add this to the flour mixture and gently whisk together to make a thick batter – it may not be totally smooth so don't worry as its best not to overwork the batter.

Lightly coat a large heavy based frying pan with a little oil and then drop in dessertspoons of the batter mixture in batches to fit the pan. Cook the pancakes over a low to medium heat until a few bubbles appear on the surface and the underside is golden, then flip them over. Keep going until you have used up all the batter, keeping the pancakes warm under foil.

In the meantime put the syrup and lemon in a pan and gently warm. On a warm serving plate arrange the pancakes in a stack spreading Mascarpone with whole blueberries between each pancake and finish by drizzling generously with the lemon syrup. Devour while still warm. Heavenly!

Coconut & Cranberry Flapjacks

MAKES ABOUT 16 FLAPJACKS

200g unsalted butter
50g Demerara sugar
8 tablespoons Lyle's Golden Syrup
350g rolled oats
100g dessicated coconut
150g semi-dried cranberries

Preheat the oven to 150C/300F/ Gas 2.

Heat the butter, sugar and syrup very gently in a saucepan until the butter has melted and all the sugar has dissolved. Remove from the heat and stir in the oats, coconut and cranberries.

Transfer the mixture to a suitable greased baking tray (20cm x 30cm /8"x12") and very gently press it in to fit the tin.

Bake in the centre of the oven for 40 minutes or until just golden. Allow to cool a little and cut into squares.

The flapjacks can be stored in an airtight container for up to a week.

PERFECTION!

TRIPLE-MICHELIN-STARRED CHEF HESTON BLUMENTHAL, SEARCHING FOR THE ULTIMATE INGREDIENTS WITH WHICH TO MAKE TREACLE TART, DECLARED THERE TO BE NO SUPERIOR ALTERNATIVE TO LYLE'S GOLDEN SYRUP!

Mulled Winter Wine

SERVES 6–8

1 medium orange
15 wholes cloves
300ml orange juice
75cl bottle red wine (Chilean Merlot is ideal)
4 tablespoons brandy (60ml)
3 tablespoons Lyle's Golden Syrup
1 cinnamon stick, about 8cm long
$\frac{1}{4}$ teaspoon ground ginger
good grate of nutmeg
2 fresh peeled and segmented satsumas
500ml lemonade

Stud the orange with the cloves, wrap in foil and roast in a medium oven (180C/350F/Gas 4) for 20 minutes. Meanwhile, put all the other ingredients into a large saucepan finally adding the roasted orange. Bring almost to the boil and then reduce the heat down to a very gentle simmer for about 20 minutes. Check for taste, temperature (you want it warm not too hot) and add more golden syrup if needed.

When ready to serve remove the pan from the heat and ladle the warming aromatic wine into suitable glasses (with a teaspoon in each to avoid cracking the glass).

LYLE'S LEGEND & LORE

GOLDEN OLDIE

IN 2007, GUINNESS WORLD RECORDS recognised Lyle's Golden Syrup as having the world's oldest branding (packaging). The famous green and gold tin has remained virtually unchanged since 1885! The Lyle's arch and lion-and-bees logo have dressed the tin for all of that time and have been familiar to generation after generation of families in Britain and throughout the world. Lyle's can boast to being older than Coca Cola (1886), Marmite (1902), and Cadbury's Dairy Milk (1905)! In 2008, at 125 years of age, and to celebrate this milestone, the tin undergoes a special birthday makeover with limited-edition gold tins hitting the shelves.

Rhubarb & Syrup Cream Flan

SERVES 6–8

300g rhubarb, cut into 4cm
  lengths
2 tablespoons Lyle's Golden Syrup
butter for greasing
100ml milk
150ml double cream
100g caster sugar
3 medium free-range eggs
25g plain flour
pinch salt
1 tablespoon Amaretto
icing sugar to dust

Preheat the oven to 190C/375F/ Gas 5.

Cook the rhubarb and golden syrup in a pan very gently until the rhubarb gets to the al dente stage. (This means only just tender.) Using a slotted spoon place the rhubarb in a buttered 25cm flan dish, spreading it out evenly over the base.

Whisk together all the remaining ingredients, except the icing sugar,

until thick and creamy. Pour the mixture over the rhubarb and bake in the centre of the oven for 25–30 minutes. When ready the surface of the flan will have risen with a more golden border around the edge of the dish. When removed from the oven the flan will sink in the centre – don't worry this is meant to happen as the egg custard sets.

Dust with icing sugar and serve as spoonfuls of warm flan or allow to cool and cut into slices.

LYLE'S LOVES...
PANCAKES

LYLE'S GOLDEN SYRUP is the perfect topping for all kinds of sweet and savoury pancakes, but did you know...

Ralf Laue of Germany is the fastest pancake tosser in the world, flipping one pancake 416 times inside two minutes!

Since 1455, every Shrove Tuesday, the town of Olney, in England holds an annual pancake race. Legend has it that the tradition began when a woman of the town became so engrossed in making pancakes that she lost track of time until she heard the bells of the church ringing for the shriving service. Wearing her apron and still carrying her skillet with pancake, she set off for the church at a sprint. And so began the custom of the pancake race!

It comes in big tins too!
A Show card from the 1900s

Malaysian King Prawns with Sticky Wild Rice

SERVES 4

For the chilli paste
3 birds eye chillies, roughly
   chopped
1 small shallot, sliced
1 small stalk of lemongrass, finely
   sliced
1 clove garlic, finely chopped
2 teaspoons lime juice
1 teaspoon fresh chopped
   coriander stems (reserving
   leaves for garnish later)
1 teaspoon coarse sea salt
1 tablespoon Lyle's Golden Syrup

400g raw peeled king prawns
400ml coconut milk mixed with
   400ml water
150g wild rice
100g basmati rice
1 tablespoons Lyle's Golden Syrup

Pound all the chilli paste
ingredients with a pestle and
mortar or whizz using a hand
blender to make a thick paste.

Put the coconut milk and water
into a pan and bring to the boil.
Add the wild rice and simmer for
30 minutes. Next add the basmati
rice (you may need to add a little
boiling water to ensure there is
enough liquid) and simmer for
10 minutes. When the rice is
cooked drain it without rinsing,
return it to the pan and stir in the
golden syrup then leave covered
to keep warm.

Put the chilli paste into a frying
pan and heat gently. Add the raw
prawns and cook for 3–4 minutes
until they turn pretty pink and are
well coated with the chilli paste.

Arrange the sticky rice in warmed
serving bowls, lay the prawns on
top, scatter with coriander leaves
and serve.

Purveyors of only the finest goods
A 19th-century emporium selling lyle's golden syrup

Roast Chicken with Garlic & Lemon

SERVES 4–6

1 medium to large free-range chicken
4 unwaxed lemons (if you can't get unwaxed use regular ones but scrub the skin well under hot water)
8 cloves garlic, unpeeled
6 shallots, peeled
4 good sprigs fresh thyme
2 tablespoons olive oil
175ml white wine
2 tablespoons Lyle's Golden Syrup
sea salt and black pepper

Preheat the oven to 150C/300F/Gas 2.

Cut the chicken up into small joints and large chunks and put into a roasting pan. Cut each lemon (still with the skin on) into 8 chunks and add to the chicken together with the garlic cloves and shallots. Break up the thyme sprigs, discarding any woody stems and scatter over the chicken then spoon in the olive oil and massage everything well together with your hands so that all the ingredients are mixed.

Pour the wine over everything and then drizzle with the syrup. Season with sea salt and lots of freshly ground black pepper. Cover the roasting pan very tightly with foil and then put in the oven for $1^1/_2$ hours.

Remove the foil and turn the oven up to 220C/425F/Gas 7. Make sure all the chicken pieces are skin side up and then return to the oven for another 20 minutes or until all the edges of the lemons, shallots and garlic are dark golden brown.

Serve straight from the oven to the centre of the table for your guests to tuck into.

ROYAL APPROVAL

LYLE'S GOLDEN SYRUP WAS AWARDED THE ROYAL WARRANT IN 1911. IT'S BEEN PROUDLY DISPLAYED ON THE TIN EVER SINCE.

Endive, Mango & date Salad

For the salad
1 endive (French, curly, slightly
  bitter lettuce; note that chicory
  is also called endive but for this
  use the full-blown lettuce)
1 fresh mango
1 red pepper, de-seeded,
  quartered and finely sliced
4 ready to eat dates
handful of parsley, chopped

For the dressing
(these ingredients should be at
  room temperature)
1 heaped teaspoon Dijon mustard
$1/_2$ teaspoon celery salt
good grind of black pepper
1 tablespoon Lyle's Golden Syrup
2 tablespoons red wine vinegar
2 tablespoons olive oil
3 tablespoons walnut oil

Separate the leaves of the endive, putting aside any that are not fresh, wash the remainder in cold water and shake dry. Now place the leaves around the edge of the salad bowl working your way inwards in a way I can only describe as rebuilding the lettuce. Depending on the size you will probably only need to use about half of the lettuce.

Using a small sharp knife take the mango and slide the knife into the flesh working round the stone, first from one side and then the other. Pull the two sides apart and discard the stone. Now criss-cross the flesh inside the mango halves with the knife and turn inside out and voilá you have great little cubes of mango. Carefully cut them from the outer skin and pile them into the centre of the endive 'flower' followed by the colourful slithers of red pepper and topped with sliced dates.

In a blender put the mustard, salt and pepper, golden syrup, vinegar and olive oil and blitz until the mixture thickens. Finally stir in the walnut oil but do not blitz again. Drizzle the vinaigrette with a small ladle around the lettuce and then moving in over the mango and peppers, adding a flourish of parsley to complete the dish.

Caribbean Banana Bread

MAKES A 450G LOAF

250g plain white flour
$1/_2$ teaspoon salt
1 teaspoon baking powder
100g unsalted butter or margarine
2 medium free-range eggs
2 tablespoons Lyle's Golden Syrup
100g caster sugar
1 large, ripe banana
1 tablespoon shelled pecan nuts,
   roughly chopped

Preheat the oven to 180C/350F/ Gas 4.

Prepare a 1lb loaf tin by buttering and flouring it and cutting a piece of baking parchment to fit the base.

Sieve the flour, salt and baking powder into a large bowl and then gradually add the butter or margarine in small cubes, rubbing the mixture with your fingertips until you have the look of fairly coarse breadcrumbs.

Whisk the eggs in a separate bowl, then add in the golden syrup and sugar and carry on whisking until the mixture is really creamy. Roughly mash the banana and add it to the egg mixture together with the pecan nuts.

Fold the flour into the egg, syrup and banana and combine until the ingredients are well mixed. Transfer the mixture into the loaf tin and spread evenly with the back of a spoon.

Bake in the centre of the hot oven for 30 minutes, or until golden and cooked through. Remove from the oven, allow to cool a little so that the bread comes away easily from the side of the tin and then turn out onto a cooling rack, carefully removing the paper from the base. This banana bread is delicious eaten warm – especially with an extra drizzle of golden syrup.

Syrup Sponge Pudding

SERVES 4

75g softened unsalted butter, plus
   a little for greasing
75g soft light brown sugar
2 large eggs, beaten
100g self-raising flour
1 level teaspoon baking powder
1 tablespoon milk

For the sauce
3 tablespoons Lyle's Golden Syrup
   plus extra to serve
4 tablespoons freshly squeezed
   orange juice

Butter the inside of a 1 pint pudding basin.

Take a large mixing bowl and beat together the butter and sugar until it is really soft and light. An electric whisk is ideal for this. Gradually add the beaten eggs, sieve in the flour and baking powder and finally add the milk. Beat the mixture well until it is thoroughly blended and you have a dropping consistency. Pour the mixture into the basin, making a nice level surface with the back of a spoon.

Line a sheet of foil with a sheet of greaseproof paper and fold to make a pleat in the centre – this will allow for expansion as the pudding rises. Cover the basin with the lined foil and wrap around the rim firmly. Then tie round with a piece of string to secure the foil in place. Stand the basin in a steamer or in a pan of simmering water, put the lid on the pan and steam for $1^1/_2$ hours, keeping an eye on the water level and topping up with boiling water as necessary.

Combine the sauce ingredients in a small pan and heat gently. When the pudding is cooked, remove from the pan, unwrap and ease the edges of the pudding away from the basin with a palette knife. Turn out onto a warmed plate and spoon over loads of golden syrup, which will soak into the sponge. Finally pour the warm orange syrup over the pudding and serve.

Delivering the goods
a selection of vintage vehicles

Red Cabbage Braised with Orange & Cranberries

MAKES ABOUT 8 PORTIONS

50g unsalted butter
2 red onions, peeled and sliced
1 medium red cabbage,
   (700–800g) finely sliced with
   outer leaves removed
200g fresh cranberries
$1/2$ teaspoon ground cinnamon
$1/2$ teaspoon ground ginger
5 tablespoons Lyle's Golden Syrup
4 tablespoons red wine vinegar
juice and zest of a large orange
salt and pepper

This is worth making as a whole and freezing in batches for future use.

In a large heavy based saucepan melt the butter, add the onions and let them sweat gently for 10 minutes with the lid on. Turn up the heat, add the red cabbage, mix well with the onions, cover the pan again and reduce to a simmer for a further 10 minutes.

Combine all the remaining ingredients in a bowl and add to the pan, stirring to mix everything together. Cover the pan; turn the heat down to the lowest setting and cook for 1 hour. Check and stir occasionally – there should be sufficient liquid for the cabbage to poach but you can always add a splash more orange juice if required.

Remove the saucepan lid, season with a little salt and pepper and continue cooking for a further 15 minutes, or until there is very little liquid left in the pan which means it is ready to serve.

Red cabbage goes especially well with any roast meats or casseroles and makes a rich and colourful display on the plate.

Herrings with Sweet Dill Mustard

SERVES 4

4 herrings, filleted
400ml white wine vinegar
200ml water
1 cinnamon stick, about 5cm
1 teaspoon allspice berries
1 teaspoon black peppercorns
4 whole cloves
1 large onion, finely sliced
2 tablespoons Lyle's Golden Syrup

For the sweet dill mustard
2 tablespoons Dijon mustard
1 tablespoon white wine vinegar
90ml whipping cream
1 tablespoon Lyle's Golden Syrup
2 tablespoons chopped fresh dill
   plus a few fronds for garnish

Slice each herring fillet into
3 diagonal strips.

Put the vinegar, water, spices, onion and syrup into a pan and bring to the boil. Simmer for 15 minutes and then add the herring strips, skin side up, simmering gently for a further 15 minutes.

Allow to cool then tip the herring mixture into a shallow dish, remove the cinnamon stick, then cover and refrigerate overnight.

About an hour before serving whisk together all the sweet dill mustard ingredients, except the dill, in a small bowl until it is thick and creamy. Stir in the chopped dill and leave in the fridge to infuse all the lovely flavours.

Now lift the herring fillets and onions out of the dish with a slotted spoon (leaving the spices behind) onto serving plates and spoon over the mustard dressing. Scatter the remaining dill sprigs over the top. A crispy salad and chunks of warm crusty bread, or better still pumpernickel, are all you need to enjoy this perfect lunch.

ABRAM LYLE & SONS Limited
SUGAR REFINERS.
OUT OF THE STRONG CAME FORTH SWEETNESS.

LYLE'S LEGEND & LORE

THE LION & THE BEES

The illustration of a dead lion with bees swarming round its head has adorned the tin for almost all of the syrup's 125 years. The illustration has been modified slightly over time, and refers to a passage from The Book of Judges in which Samson kills a lion. Samson later notices that bees have formed a honeycomb in the carcass of the dead animal, and muses, 'Out of the eater came forth meat and out of the strong came forth sweetness'. Lyle was a deeply religious man, and the second half of the passage obviously appealed and must have struck Lyle as a fitting proverb for his syrup – within his strong metal gold-and-green tin lay the most wonderful sweetness of all.

Sunshine Fruits in Orange, Mint & Yoghurt

SERVES 4

2 peaches – obviously in season is best but in any event select them from a good fruiterer
16 fresh strawberries
4 dessertspoons blackcurrants (you can use tinned and drained)
zest and juice of $\frac{1}{2}$ orange
1 tablespoon Lyle's Golden Syrup
4 tablespoons thick natural yoghurt, plus extra for garnish
4 mint leaves, chopped and 4 mint sprigs for garnish
1 teaspoon crushed pink peppercorns

Halve the peaches, remove the stone and cut each half into thin segments.

Hull the strawberries and slice in half, top and tail the currants if using fresh.

Place the zest and orange juice into a bowl with the juice of the orange; add the golden syrup, the 4 tablespoons of yoghurt and the chopped mint leaves. Mix this dressing thoroughly. Now drizzle the yoghurt mixture over the fruit, sprinkle with the crushed pink peppercorns and place one final teaspoon of yoghurt on the side, onto which you can place a sprig of mint and then serve.

Brown Bread Golden Syrup Ice Cream

MAKES ABOUT 1 LITRE

100g brown breadcrumbs
50g soft brown sugar
400ml double cream
1 tablespoon dark rum
2 tablespoons Lyle's Golden Syrup
50g icing sugar

Preheat the oven to 180C/350F/ Gas 4.

Mix together the breadcrumbs and the sugar and bake in the oven for 10 minutes, stirring a couple of times then remove and leave aside to cool.

Whisk the double cream until fairly firm and then add the rum, fold in the golden syrup and sieved icing sugar. Pour into a suitable plastic container and freeze for 2 hours.

Remove from the freezer and beat the ice cream well for a couple of minutes. Finally fold in the baked breadcrumbs and sugar. Return to the freezer for a further 2–3 hours or overnight.

Roast Lamb with Crushed Rosemary Glaze

SERVES 3–4

1 whole bulb of garlic with the top
   cut off
olive oil
coarse sea salt
1 whole orange cut into 8 chunks
3 good stems of rosemary
$1/2$ leg of lamb (around 1kg)
2 tablespoons Lyle's Golden Syrup
black pepper

Heat the oven to 200C/400F/Gas 6.

Put the garlic bulb into a roasting dish, drizzle with olive oil and sprinkle with sea salt. Place the dish in the oven and roast for 20 minutes. Remove and cool the garlic until cool enough to handle and then squeeze out the soft cloves into the roasting dish. Add to this the orange chunks and the leaves plucked from the rosemary sprigs crushed with the back of a spoon to release their pungent flavour.

Using a sharp knife cut insertions in the raw lamb like a criss-cross. Place the lamb in an open plastic bag and add all the ingredients from the roasting dish. Seal up the bag and shake the lot. Place in the fridge for at least one hour shaking as before every 10 minutes. You can do this the night before you want your roast, if preferred.

Keep the oven ready at 180C/350F/ Gas 4. Place the leg of lamb in a roasting dish and coat with golden syrup spreading it into the slits. Tuck the orange segments in under the joint and massage the rosemary and garlic into the lamb emptying any juicy bits from the marinade bag into the dish. Season with plenty of black pepper.

You will need to cook the joint for 20 minutes per 1lb (450g) plus 20 minutes. This will leave the outside crispy and the inside still slightly pink. Baste the joint a few times to keep the full flavour of the juices infusing into the lamb.

When cooked remove and leave to rest for 10 minutes covered loosely with kitchen foil. Strain the remaining juices to add to your gravy and your rosemary roast lamb is ready to enjoy.

Cinnamon Gingerbread Hearts

MAKES 15–20 HEARTS

300g plain flour, plus extra for
    kneading
$1/2$ teaspoon salt
1 teaspoon baking powder
1 teaspoon ground ginger
$1^1/2$ teaspoons ground cinnamon
$1/4$ teaspoon freshly grated nutmeg
60g softened butter
100g caster sugar
6 tablespoons Lyle's Golden Syrup
1 egg yolk

Preheat the oven to 180C/350F/ Gas 4.

Sieve the flour, salt, baking powder and spices into a bowl.

In a larger bowl beat together the butter, sugar and syrup until you have a stiff but creamy mixture. Add the egg yolk and beat really well. Now gently blend in the flour mixture until you have a firm dough.

On a well floured board, roll out the dough to about 1cm thick. If it feels too sticky add extra flour so that you can knead the mixture into a fairly firm dough. Chill for 30 minutes.

Using a heart shaped biscuit cutter cut out as many as the dough will allow. Re-roll the dough to use up the remainder for more hearts. Place them on a greased baking tray, allowing 2–3cm between each biscuit, as they will expand, and cook in the centre of the oven for 8–10 minutes until just golden.

Cool on a wire rack and then store in an airtight container. These biscuits are delicious served with Baked Apples with Prunes in Cinnamon Syrup (page 196).

At Christmas time it's great fun to hang these on the tree. As the hearts are just beginning to cool carefully pierce a hole through with a skewer near the top of the biscuit, wide enough to squeeze a thin ribbon through. When cool you can hang them on the Christmas tree.

Good Boys!
A retro-style advertisement from 2005

Strawberry & Blueberry Smoothie

SERVES 2

250g natural yoghurt
225g strawberries, hulled
75g blueberries
1–2 tablespoons Lyle's Golden
  Syrup (according to your
  morning taste buds)
4 ice cubes
2 sprigs fresh mint

(Seasonal fruit will vary in sweetness so when blitzing the ingredients start with the lesser amount of syrup and increase it as necessary.)

This couldn't be simpler. Simply blitz together the yoghurt, fruit, syrup and ice for about 30 seconds.

Pour into a tall glass and garnish with a sprig of mint. For an extra wholesome start to the day you can sprinkle a spoonful of your favourite muesli on top and serve with a long spoon as well.

Courgettes in White Wine & Golden Syrup

SERVES 4

500g courgettes
1 medium onion
1 clove garlic
1 tablespoon olive oil
200ml dry white wine
salt and black pepper
1 tablespoon Lyle's Golden Syrup
12 seedless grapes, halved

Top, tail and peel the courgettes and cut slices on the diagonal about 1cm thick.

Peel the onion and cut it in half. Lay each half face down and slice into thin slithers. Peel the clove of garlic and finely dice.

In a deep frying pan gently heat the olive oil and fry the onion and garlic for 2–3 minutes until soft and transparent – you don't want them crispy. Now lay the slices of courgette on top, Turn up the heat to medium high and pour over the white wine. Season with salt and plenty of freshly milled black pepper and let the courgettes gently poach for 8–10 minutes turning several times until the liquid has almost gone. Drizzle the golden syrup over the courgettes, turn once or twice to glaze. Finally toss in the grapes, just enough to warm them, and serve as an easy lunch or to accompany fresh grilled fish or white meat.

This recipe works equally well with sliced, cooked beetroot.

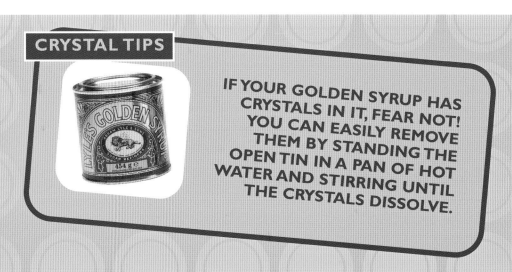

CRYSTAL TIPS

IF YOUR GOLDEN SYRUP HAS CRYSTALS IN IT, FEAR NOT! YOU CAN EASILY REMOVE THEM BY STANDING THE OPEN TIN IN A PAN OF HOT WATER AND STIRRING UNTIL THE CRYSTALS DISSOLVE.

Thai Fried Bananas

SERVES 4

For the batter
150g rice flour
160ml water
50g dessicated coconut
1 tablespoon plain flour
1 tablespoon Lyle's Golden Syrup
1 level tablespoon sesame seeds
1 teaspoon baking powder
pinch salt

corn oil for deep-frying
4 slightly green bananas

For the sauce
400ml tin of coconut milk
1 tablespoon Lyle's Golden Syrup

In a large bowl whisk together all the batter ingredients and leave to stand.

Pour the tin of coconut milk into a saucepan over a fairly high heat and reduce the milk by half (keep the tin as an easy measure). Reduce the heat, add the golden syrup and stir well and then keep the sauce warm until you are ready for it.

Heat the oil in a wok or deep fat fryer. A good hint here is to toss a small cube of bread into the oil and if it sizzles immediately then the oil is hot enough. Peel the bananas and cut each one in half lengthways and then in half widthways. Dip the banana pieces into the coconut batter and then deep fry them until just golden – about 2 minutes on each side. Remove with a slotted spoon, drain on kitchen paper and keep warm. In 4 warmed bowls stack the fried banana pieces and drizzle with the thick creamy coconut milk. Serve immediately.

LYLE'S LOVES...
ICE CREAM

ICE CREAM AND SYRUP are a marriage made in heaven. For precision drizzles, why not try squirting from a Lyle's Squeezy Syrup bottle? Ice cream pre-dates our beloved syrup by many, many years. Indeed, legend has it that...

● **In Roman times, Emperor Nero might have come up with the precursor to ice-cream. He used to send slaves up into the mountains to collect snow and ice with which to make flavoured ices!**

● **The ice cream cone was invented by a New York City ice cream vendor in 1896, to prevent customers from stealing his serving glasses!**

Pork Medallions with Sweet Mustard Crust

SERVES 4

600g pork fillet
2 teaspoons ready made English
  mustard
2 tablespoons Lyle's Golden Syrup
2 tablespoons ready-made apple
  sauce
good grind of black pepper
100g fresh breadcrumbs
sunflower oil for frying
parsley, chopped for scattering
wedges of lemon

Cut the pork fillet into 1cm wide slices and then placing the slices – now called medallions – between two sheets of clingfilm pummel them with a steak hammer or rolling pin until they are about half the thickness and twice as wide. This also tenderises the meat. In a small mixing bowl place the mustard, golden syrup, apple sauce and black pepper and mix well together. Put the breadcrumbs in a shallow dish.

Pick up each medallion and spread one side with the sauce mixture then press into the breadcrumbs. Repeat with the other side so that the medallions are completely coated – this can get quite messy – then set aside on a plate covered with greaseproof paper. Chill these in a refrigerator for 1 hour to set the crust.

Heat the oil in a frying pan, and sauté the medallions in batches for 3–4 minutes on each side until they are a glorious golden colour. Drain on kitchen paper and keep warm while you cook the remainder.

Serve with a scattering of parsley and wedges of lemon.

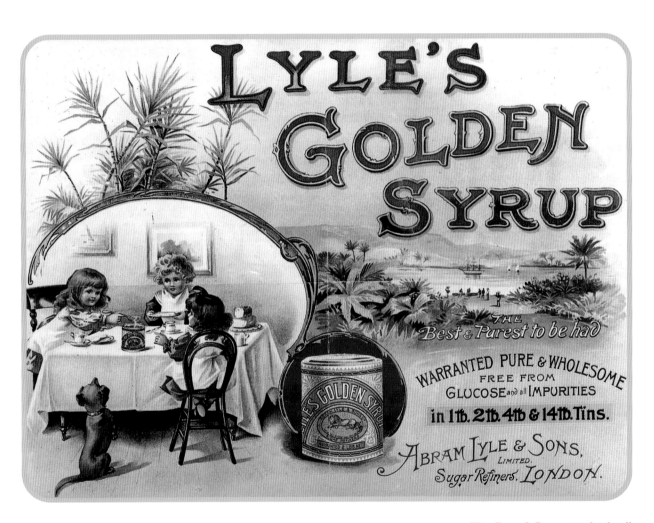

The Best & Purest to be had!
An advertisement from the 1900s

Golden Syrup Beignets

MAKES 10–12 'LITTLE DOUGHNUTS'

120ml water
60g unsalted butter
1 tablespoon Lyle's Golden Syrup
$^{1}/_{2}$ teaspoon salt
75g plain flour
3 medium free-range eggs
2 teaspoons vanilla extract
caster sugar to dust

Combine the water, butter, syrup and salt in a saucepan and bring to the boil. Remove the pan from the heat; add the flour and stir like mad until it all comes together and looks a little shiny. Continue to cook and stir for 2–3 minutes and you will find that the mixture comes away from the side of the pan. Transfer the mixture to a bowl, allow to cool a little and then add the eggs, one at a time, beating each one in by hand for a couple of minutes, finally adding the vanilla.

Heat a deep fat fryer to 190C/375F and dip a ladle into the oil to coat. Drop a good tablespoon of the batter into the ladle and carefully lower the ladle into the oil. Turn the ladle to release the beignet and repeat with more of the batter, frying 4–5 beignets at a time until puffy and golden all over. Drain on kitchen paper and dust with caster sugar. Your beignets should be crispy on the outside and soft and yielding in the middle.

Serve these delicious beignets with good hot coffee in the morning for a perfectly indulgent start to the day.

Rum & Golden Syrup Hot Fruit Salad

SERVES 6

4 tablespoons Lyle's Golden Syrup
2 tablespoons Malibu
2 good sprigs fresh mint
1 medium pineapple
3 greengages or red plums
2 peaches
2 bananas

Preheat the oven to 180C/350F/ Gas 4.

In a small pan gently heat the syrup and Malibu until well mixed and runny. Remove from the heat and add finely sliced leaves from the mint sprigs, reserving a few for later. Leave aside to infuse.

Next prepare the fruit using a large shallow dish. Peel the pineapple leaving the leaves still attached and cut into 6 segments lengthways. Wrap the leaves in foil to avoid them burning. Cut the plums in half and remove the stones. Stone the peaches and cut into quarters. Peel the bananas and cut each into 3 large diagonal slices. Put all the fruit into the dish and pour the rum syrup over everything.

Preheat the grill to high. (If you have a ridged griddle pan you can use this on top of the cooker instead of grilling and you will get gorgeously scorched lines on your fruit as you would on the barbecue). Start with the pineapple, then plums, and then peaches and lay the fruit pieces, flesh side down, on the grill rack or griddle turning once or twice until browned. Transfer the fruits to a baking dish and put into the oven as you go. Cook in the oven for 10 minutes and then lastly grill or griddle the banana, (the softest fruit) and add it to the oven dish to cook for a further 5 minutes.

Unwrap the foil from the pineapple leaves and serve the golden fruits drizzled with the remaining juices and garnished with the reserved mint leaves.

Fruit & Nut Muffins with Drambuie Cream

MAKES 9–12 CAKES

200g self-raising flour
2 teaspoons baking powder
$1/_2$ teaspoon salt
$1/_2$ teaspoon ground cinnamon
$1/_4$ teaspoon ground nutmeg
100g caster sugar
60g chopped mixed fruit
50g walnuts, finely chopped
2 tablespoons Lyle's Golden Syrup
50g melted butter
200ml milk
1 egg

For the Drambuie Cream
400ml double cream
1 tablespoon Lyle's Golden Syrup
2 tablespoons Drambuie

You will need a non-stick muffin tin
  for this recipe.

Preheat the oven to 220C/425F/
Gas 7.

Into a large bowl sieve the flour,
baking powder, salt, cinnamon and
nutmeg and then add the sugar
and stir in the dried fruit and nuts.

In a separate bowl add the golden
syrup to the melted butter and mix
well with a fork. Add the milk and
egg and whisk again.

Gradually pour the milk and egg
mix into the flour and stir until all
the ingredients are combined into a
lumpy mixture – do not overwork it.
Spoon the mixture into the muffin
cups to about two thirds full and
bake in the centre of the hot oven
for 15 minutes or until the muffins
are well risen and golden.

Whisk the cream until really thick
and then stir in the syrup and
Drambuie. Serve with the muffins
for a perfect pud.

Greek Beef Stifado with Baby Onions

SERVES 4

50ml olive oil
500g braising steak, cut into
    largish cubes
250g small cooking onions, peeled
    (plunge them into boiling water
    for a few minutes prior to make
    peeling easier)
100ml red wine
2 tablespoons Lyle's Golden Syrup
1 tablespoon red wine vinegar
3 cloves garlic, roughly chopped
400g tin peeled, chopped
    tomatoes
2 teaspoons dried oregano
2 bay leaves
1 cinnamon stick (about 6cm)
pinch grated nutmeg
pinch ground allspice
salt and freshly ground black
    pepper
500ml good beef stock

Heat about half of the olive oil in a heavy based saucepan and seal the beef in batches, lifting it out with a slotted spoon and keeping aside.

Add the remaining oil into the pan. Sauté the onions gently keeping them whole, until they are lightly golden and just softening. Remove them from the pan with a slotted spoon and keep aside. Add the red wine to the pan followed by the golden syrup and the vinegar, scraping all the good bits from the bottom of the pan and cook for a few more minutes.

Return the meat to the pan and add the garlic, tomatoes, herbs and spices then season with the salt and pepper. Finally add enough beef stock to make a rich gravy. Cook over a very low heat for 1 hour.

Next add the onions and continue cooking for a further $1^1/_2$ hours, with an occasional stir, until the meat is meltingly tender. When the stifado is cooked remove it from the heat and leave covered for about half an hour.

It should be served warm not piping hot and traditionally with fresh crusty bread and salad. I once had stifado served with crumbled feta cheese on top, which gave a delicious salty contrast to the sweetness of the dish.

Granny Smith Toffee Apples

MAKES 6 TOFFEE APPLES

6 Granny Smith apples
250g Demerara sugar
100ml water
$\frac{1}{2}$ teaspoon vinegar
2 tablespoons Lyle's Golden Syrup
25g butter
6 tablespoons unsalted peanuts,
  crushed

You will need 6 strong wooden skewers and ideally an extra pair of hands (or the kids) as the last stage of making these toffee apples happens very quickly.

Push a wooden skewer into each apple and set aside.

In a heavy based pan warm the sugar and water over a medium heat until all the grains have dissolved, swirling the pan rather than stirring the liquid. Do not use a high heat, as this will crystallise the liquid. Next add the vinegar, syrup and butter.

Bring the mixture up to the boil watching all the time (very important) without stirring until it reaches what is called the 'hard crack' stage. This is when half a teaspoon of the sugary mixture hardens into a ball when dropped in a bowl of cold water or sets hard on a very cold plate. The timing will vary according to your pan size and the temperature so just keep checking until it happens. Now you have toffee!

Prepare a tray with the crushed peanuts in and then holding the skewer dip each apple into the hot toffee, swirling it around to completely coat. Then immediately roll the toffee apple in the crushed peanuts for the outer coating and stand on a buttered baking tray. Repeat with the remaining apples.

If they are not to be eaten that day its best to wrap them in cellophane and they will keep in the fridge for several days.

Filo-Topped Bougatsa Pudding

MAKES 12 PORTIONS

900ml milk
100g caster sugar
1 vanilla bean, split in half
  lengthways (or 2 teaspoons
  vanilla extract)
75g semolina
100g unsalted butter, melted
4 large eggs, lightly beaten
500g ready made filo pastry (12
  sheets)
2 tablespoons Lyle's Golden
  Syrup, warmed
1 tablespoon icing sugar
1 teaspoon ground cinnamon

Preheat the oven to 180C/350F/Gas 4

Place the milk, caster sugar and vanilla pod (or extract) into a saucepan and bring to the boil. Gradually add the semolina stirring all the time and then turn down he heat to medium. Cook for 10–12 minutes until the semolina begins to thicken, stirring continuously and then remove the pan from the heat. (If your semolina has gone lumpy, don't worry simply strain it through a sieve into another pan.) Allow to cool a little and then remove the vanilla pod (if using), scraping any seeds into the mixture. Add a tablespoon of the melted butter and the beaten eggs and stir into the semolina mixture, which will now be like a very thick custard. Use a deep rectangular baking dish 25cm x 30cm or similar (about 10" x 12") and brush the bottom with melted butter. Lay 6 sheets of filo pastry in the dish, brushing each sheet with melted butter as you add it and allowing the pastry to overhang the sides of the dish. Pour the semolina custard into the dish. Cover with all but 1 of the remaining sheets of filo, brushing each with butter and this time drizzling each sheet with the warmed syrup as well. Fold in the overhanging pastry to encase the custard and fold the final sheet of filo in half and cut to fit the dish snugly on top. Using a pair of scissors (and this is a bit tricky) score the pastry into portions by just cutting through the last double layer of filo. Too much pressure, or cutting too deep will make the pastry move about and the custard leak out.

Bake in the middle of the oven for 10 minutes and then reduce the heat to 150C/300F/Gas 2 for a further 40 minutes. Remove from the oven, dust with the icing sugar and cinnamon (do not mix them together first as the colour contrast looks better) and pop it back in for 10 minutes. Remove and cool a little before serving warm with poached pears.

Sicilian Aubergine & Pine Nut Polpettes

MAKES 18 POLPETTES

1 medium aubergine
75g raisins, roughly chopped
50g toasted pine nuts
75g Pecorino cheese, finely grated
   (you could use Parmesan)
2 tablespoons Lyle's Golden Syrup
pinch grated nutmeg
little salt and a good grind of black
   pepper
2 free range eggs, beaten
200g fresh white breadcrumbs
flour for dusting
sunflower oil for frying

Peel and chunk the aubergine and put in a saucepan. Cover with water, bring to the boil and cook for 10 minutes. Drain through a sieve and then using a potato masher gently press out the remaining water and leave to cool.

Into a large bowl put the raisins, pine nuts, Pecorino, syrup and nutmeg and mix well together. Add the aubergine and mash into the fruity mixture with a wooden spoon. Then season with salt and pepper, add in $1/2$ of the beaten egg and about $2/3$ of the breadcrumbs until you have a consistency when mixed that will hold together when pressed – but not too sticky.

Pick up about a tablespoon of the mixture at a time and roll into balls about the size of a golf ball (weighing about 35g). Roll the balls in flour, dip into the remaining egg and then the breadcrumbs. Chill in the fridge for at least half an hour to set the coating.

Heat the oil in a frying pan or deep fat fryer to 190C/375F. Add the polpettes, turning them over as they cook for about 5 minutes or until golden brown and crispy. Drain on kitchen paper and serve just warm as a starter with a watercress and rocket salad.

Quail Roasted in Madeira with Bacon-Wrapped Figs

SERVES 2

20g unsalted butter
4 oven ready quail
2 tablespoons Lyle's Golden Syrup
1 teaspoon mixed dried herbs
freshly ground black pepper
4 bay leaves
12 rashers streaky bacon
vegetable oil
2 fresh figs
200ml Madeira wine
1 teaspoon plain flour
handful black grapes, halved

Preheat the oven to 200C/400F/ Gas 6.

Divide the butter into 4, put a knob inside each quail and tie up the legs with string. Drizzle each bird with a teaspoon of golden syrup, scatter with the mixed herbs, season with pepper and lay a bay leaf on top of each.

Take 8 of the bacon rashers, stretch them out with a knife and wrap each way around the quail in the shape of a cross. Place the birds in an oiled roasting tin and roast in the oven for 15 minutes.

Carefully, using a sharp knife, peel and quarter the figs. Stretch out the remaining bacon rashers, cut each into 2 and wrap around each piece of fig. Remove the quail from the oven and turn it up to 220C/425F/ Gas 7. Remove the bacon from the birds, leaving it in the tin for flavour, and add the wrapped figs. Drizzle the quail with the remaining golden syrup and add $^3/_4$ of the Madeira to the roasting tin. Return the quail to the oven for a further 15 minutes.

When the birds are cooked remove them from the roasting tin using 2 forks upending each as you do so to drain out any buttery juices from inside the quail. Put them onto a warm dish to rest for at least 5 minutes, together with the wrapped figs.

When the juices in the roasting tin have cooled a little sprinkle in the flour and add the rest of the Madeira. Put the tin on top of the stove over a gentle heat; stir all the juices to thicken into syrupy gravy and throw in the grapes to warm. Arrange the quail and figs on warm serving plates and spoon over the gravy and grapes to serve.

THE WARTIME MAKESHIFT

THE ANNIVERSARY FACELIFT

THE CARDBOARD TIN
THE TIN HAS CHANGED LITTLE IN 125 YEARS, THOUGH THE CARDBOARD EDITION
ABOVE WAS PUT INTO PRODUCTION DURING THE YEARS OF THE FIRST WORLD
WAR WHEN METAL WAS IN SHORT SUPPLY.

THE ANNIVERSARY TIN
TO CELEBRATE 125 YEARS, LIMITED-EDITION GOLD ANNIVERSARY TINS (LEFT) ARE
PRODUCED TO MARK THE INCREDIBLE MILESTONE IN UNDERSTATED ELEGANCE.

Sweet Marinated Lamb, Bacon and Apricot Brochettes

SERVES 4

2 tablespoons light soy sauce
1 teaspoon Dijon mustard
2 tablespoons Lyle's Golden Syrup
1 tablespoon lemon juice
2 shallots, finely diced
1 teaspoon dried mixed herbs
8 rashers smoked streaky bacon
600g lamb (neck fillet is ideal) cut
   into 24 slices
16 dried apricots (half-cooked or
   ready to eat)

In a bowl whisk together the soy, mustard, golden syrup and lemon juice and then add the shallots and herbs to make a marinade.

Cut each rasher of bacon in half and roll up into a sausage. Now alternately thread the lamb, bacon and apricots onto 8 bamboo skewers (3 lamb, 2 bacon and 2 apricots per skewer) and lay the brochettes out in a large, shallow dish. Pour the marinade over them, cover with clingfilm and leave for at least 2 hours, turning the brochettes in the juices once or twice.

Preheat the grill to medium hot, line the grill tray with foil, lay the brochettes on the rack and brush with loads of marinade. Cook for about 5 minutes on each side for pinkish lamb, or longer to your liking, basting with more marinade as they cook.

Serve with fluffy rice and a crunchy white cabbage and caper salad dressed only with olive oil, lemon juice, salt and pepper.

Carrot & Coriander Salad with Sweet Vinaigrette

SERVES 4–6

For the salad
2 large carrots, washed, peeled and grated

2 shallots, finely diced

25g fresh coriander, roughly chopped (must be fresh, not dried)

1 cos style lettuce (Little Gem or romaine are great)

100g pimento-stuffed olives, each one cut into 3 rings

1 teaspoon sesame seeds

coarse sea salt

For the dressing
1 heaped teaspoon wholegrain mustard

freshly milled black pepper

5 tablespoons olive oil

1 tablespoon Lyle's Golden Syrup

1 tablespoon cider vinegar or white wine vinegar

2 tablespoons orange juice

In a salad bowl place the grated carrots, diced shallots and coriander and mix together gently. In a blender put the mustard, black pepper, olive oil, golden syrup, vinegar and orange juice and whiz until it thickens. This can also be done by hand with a bowl and whisk, the only difference is that you will need to add the olive oil last and a little at a time as you whisk it so that it emulsifies nicely. Drizzle the dressing over the salad and fold it together to coat everything.

Remove the leaves from the lettuce, wash in fresh water and dry. You will need 1 large leaf or 2–3 small ones per person. Arrange the leaves on serving plates and then fill with the dressed carrot and coriander salad. Scatter with the olive rings, arranging a few around the plate, sprinkle with the sesame seeds, a little coarse sea salt and serve.

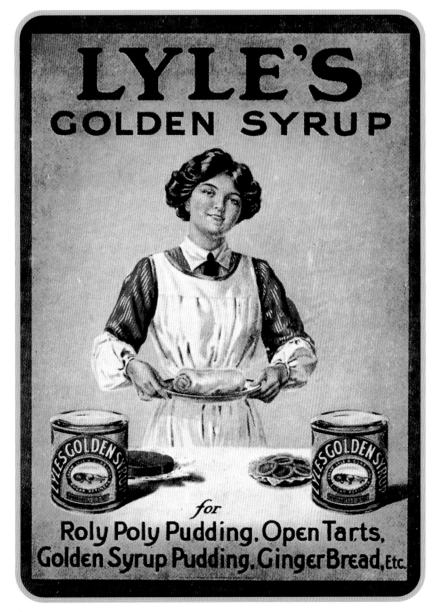

A must for the home baker!
An advertisement from the 1900s

Fillet Steak Strips with Sweet Ginger Stir-Fry

SERVES 2

Stir-fry sauce
5cm piece root ginger finely chopped
3 tablespoons dry sherry
1 tablespoon dark soy sauce
1 tablespoon Lyle's Golden Syrup
$\frac{1}{2}$ teaspoon Chinese five spice powder

2 fillet steaks (about 150g each)
1 tablespoon sesame oil
4 baby corn
100g sugar snap peas
1 small red pepper, deseeded and thinly sliced
handful of Chinese leaves or cabbage, shredded
1 teaspoon of toasted sesame seeds

Put all the stir-fry sauce ingredients into a shallow dish, mix well and add the steaks, turning them to coat thoroughly. Cover and leave to marinate for at least 1 hour.

Heat a lightly oiled griddle or heavy based frying pan until just beginning to smoke slightly. Remove the steaks from the marinade (keeping the juice for the stir-fry) and sear on both sides to seal in the juices. Cook for a further 3–4 minutes on each side. (If you prefer your steaks medium or more – cook on!) Remove from the pan and rest the steaks for 5 minutes, keeping them warm.

Meanwhile heat the sesame oil in a wok and add first the baby corn, then the sugar snaps, then the peppers and finally the Chinese leaves allowing each to cook for 2–3 minutes before adding the next. Cook everything quickly over a high heat. Add the remaining marinade to the wok, stir a few more times to heat through and your vegetables are ready to slide onto hot serving plates. Slice the steaks very thinly and arrange in a pile on top of the vegetables finishing with a final flourish of toasted sesame seeds.

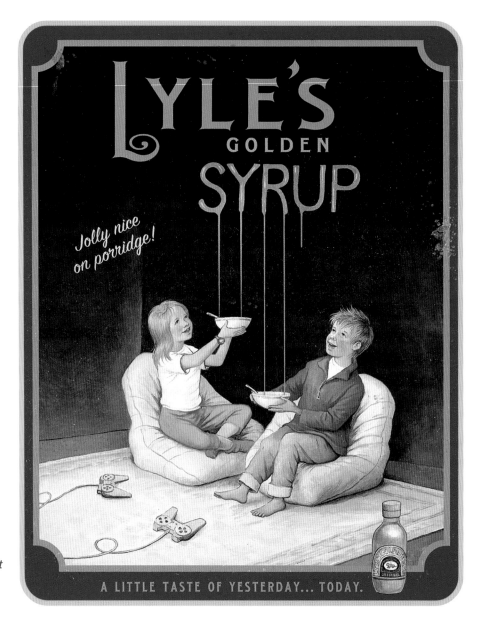

Catch it whilst you can!
A retro-style advertisement from 2005

Rich Parkin

150g self-raising flour
1 level teaspoon bicarbonate of
 soda
$1/2$ teaspoon ground cinnamon
1 teaspoon ground ginger
100g medium oatmeal
75g butter
150g Lyle's Golden Syrup
1 egg, beaten
2 tablespoons milk
75g candied peel, finely chopped
50g soft brown sugar

Preheat the oven to 150C/300F/
Gas 2.

Butter and flour a 1lb loaf tin and
cut a piece of baking parchment to
fit the base.

Sift the flour, soda, cinnamon and
ginger into a large bowl and then
stir in the oatmeal.

In a small pan gently heat the
butter and syrup until melted. Beat
the egg with the milk. Gradually
add the buttery syrup to the dry
ingredients, stirring as you go to
make a thick mixture. Then add the
egg and milk, stirring until smooth
and finally the candied peel and
sugar. Pour the mixture into your
prepared tin and bake in the centre
of the oven for 1 hour.

The Parkin, which will keep moist
for a considerable time in an
airtight tin, should not be eaten
until 24 hours after baking. This
makes the perfect accompaniment
to a brew of Yorkshire Tea.

Golden Sunset Cocktail

MAKES 4 TALL GLASSES

4 tablespoons Lyle's Golden Syrup
800ml freshly squeezed orange
    juice (about 8 oranges)
200ml freshly squeezed pink
    grapefruit juice
    (about 1 grapefruit)
juice of a lime
4 shots of Tequila (optional)
4 slices of orange for garnish
4 mint sprigs and ice to serve

In a small pan gently warm the golden syrup together with about a quarter of the orange juice, until it is dissolved. Pour into a large glass jug, add in the other fresh juices and stir until thoroughly mixed. Chill for 1 hour in the fridge.

Put some ice into each glass, pour in the Tequila (if using) and pour the juice mixture over it. Make one cut from the outside to the centre of each orange slice and wedge onto the rim of the glass. Finish with a sprig of mint, serve and then close your eyes and imagine you're in the Caribbean.

A little tip here is to pour the lime juice into an ice tray and freeze it adding it to the drinks giving extra colour, flavour and zing (1 lime makes 2 ice cubes).

Lyle's Orange Buttercream Gâteau

4 medium free-range eggs
75g caster sugar
100g unsalted butter, softened
1 rounded tablespoon Lyle's
    Golden Syrup
zest of an orange (1 tablespoon)
1 tablespoon orange juice
40g self-raising flour
50g fine fresh breadcrumbs
75g ground almonds

For the decoration
100g candied orange peel
50g dark chocolate
150g unsalted butter
300g icing sugar
1 dessertspoon Cointreau

Preheat the oven to 150C/300F/ Gas 2. It is important with this recipe to have all your ingredients ready and a 23cm/9" cake tin lined with baking parchment.

Separate the eggs, with the yolks in one bowl and the whites in another. Add the caster sugar to the egg yolks and whisk really well until you have a thick, creamy consistency. Lift your whisk from the mixture; draw a figure of 8 with the drizzling cream and if the '8' stays until you have completed the figure it is whisked enough. Now beat in the softened butter, the golden syrup and the orange zest and juice. Make sure that your whisk is completely clean and free of any grease (otherwise this won't work) and whisk the egg whites until you have really stiff peaks.

Mix the flour, breadcrumbs and almonds together and add them to the egg yolk mixture then fold in the egg whites in a few big airy sweeps. Your mixture will look rather like scrambled eggs. Pour the mixture into the lined cake tin and bake in the centre of the oven for 1 hour until risen and golden. This is a rich gateâu not a sponge so do not expect it to rise as much. Remove from the oven and leave for 5 minutes before transferring to a wire rack.

While the cake cools prepare the icing and decoration. Chop the butter up into small pieces, place in a mixing bowl and beat until it is smooth and creamy. Gradually add the icing sugar while mixing slowly until it is well combined. Mix in the Cointreau then whisk the icing vigorously until it is smooth and creamy. Chill in the fridge.

Melt the chocolate in a double boiler or in a bowl over a pan of simmering water. Cut the candied peel into little leaf shapes about 5cm long and dip half of each leaf into the melted chocolate. Lay each leaf on some greaseproof paper for the chocolate to set and when all are done chill in the fridge. When the cake has cooled split it through the middle and spread a third of the icing mixture on the base. Sandwich the cake together again and spread the remainder on the top and round the sides of the cake. You can make a smooth finish with a palette knife otherwise use the back of a spoon or a fork for a more fun effect. Dip a spoon into the remainder of the chocolate and then drizzle very fine strands of chocolate over the butter icing. Finish by adding the chocolate dipped candied orange in a circle on top of the cake.

THE HP SAUCE
RECIPE COLLECTION

Scallop, Chorizo & Warm Potato Salad

SERVES 2

300g potatoes, peeled and cooked
4 tablespoons mayonnaise
2 teaspoons olive oil
1 teaspoon malt vinegar
1 heaped teaspoon chopped
   chives
pinch of salt
25g unsalted butter
2 tablespoons HP Sauce
2 tablespoons fresh lemon juice
freshly ground black pepper
8 king scallops
50g chorizo, diced into 1cm bits
smoked paprika

Slice the potatoes while still warm in half and then cut them into $\frac{1}{2}$cm slices.

In a bowl mix the mayonnaise with the olive oil, vinegar, chives and salt then add the potatoes and carefully mix them together. Set aside and keep warm.

In a frying pan melt the butter and then add the HP Sauce, lemon juice and black pepper. Now add the scallops over a medium heat and roll them in the juices. They will need about 2–3 minutes on each

side basting as they cook. Add the chorizo and cook until warmed through. It will go hard if cooked too long.

Spoon a helping of warm potato salad onto a plate and make a nest in the centre. Place the scallop and chorizo mixture in the middle, dust with smoked paprika and serve.

A HUMBLE PLACE OF ORIGIN

It was in 1875 that an ambitious young man arrived in the manor of Aston to establish the Midland Vinegar Company. Edwin Samson Moore knew that labour, in this part of the Midlands, was cheap and that the water in the area was hard – essential for the brewing of

Tuscan Three Meat Stew

SERVES 8

2 tablespoons olive oil
300g shallots, peeled and roughly
  chopped
5 cloves garlic, finely diced
6 stems celery, diced
1 teaspoon dried thyme
1 teaspoon freshly chopped
  rosemary
6 bay leaves
500g diced pork
500g diced lamb
500g diced braising steak
$^1/_4$ teaspoon salt
lots of freshly ground black pepper
400g tin chopped tomatoes
2 tablespoons tomato purée
3 tablespoons HP Sauce
150g pitted green olives
1 bottle Italian red wine

Heat the olive oil in a large flameproof casserole and add the shallots, garlic, celery and herbs. Sauté gently for 5–6 minutes and then add in the meats.

Brown the meat all over for a further 5 minutes letting the juices run and then season with the salt and pepper. Add all the remaining ingredients to the casserole, stir well to combine and put the

casserole in the oven at 70C/150F/Gas $^1/_4$ for 3 hours.

After 3 hours remove the lid of the casserole, stir the stew gently and return to the oven uncovered for a further 2 hours so that the liquid reduces and you have a deliciously rich stew with thick gravy.

Serve traditionally with papardelle pasta and a crunchy green salad.

vinegar. Moore's cousin invested in the business, which helped to provide a stable platform from which the company could grow and rival the other vinegar brewers in the area. Potato chips from France had just taken the country by storm and it became all the rage to partner them with fried fish. Moore probably didn't know that a national culinary institution was in the making, but he did know that a liberal shake of vinegar improved the dish beyond doubt. Vinegar was a blossoming industry. The business prospered. Moore's eldest son, Edwin, joined the firm in 1890, and as the century drew to a close, a man of less ambition might have been forgiven for being very satisfied with his lot in life. But not so Moore the Elder, for he had a much bigger dream. **Continued on page 266....**

Couscous-Stuffed Peppers

SERVES 2

2 red peppers
salt and pepper
150g of mixed antipasti in olive oil
100g couscous
125ml vegetable stock
1 onion, peeled and chopped
1 clove garlic, peeled and crushed
4 cherry tomatoes, roughly
    chopped
2 tablespoons HP Sauce
200g Feta cheese, crumbled
fresh torn basil leaves

Preheat the oven to 180C/350F/ Gas 4.

Cut the peppers in half lengthways and remove the seeds. Brush them all over with a little oil from the antipasto, lay them in a baking dish and season with salt and pepper. Roast in the oven for 15 minutes.

Put the couscous into a bowl and add hot vegetable stock. Leave to stand for 5 minutes and then fluff it up with a fork. Using a little more oil from the antipasti fry the onion and garlic until softened and then add the cherry tomatoes and HP Sauce and cook for a couple of minutes.

Tip the onion mixture into the couscous, add the diced mixed antipasto and the crumbled Feta and stir the whole lot together. Remove the peppers from the oven and pack in the couscous mixture so that it is mounded. Return them to the oven for a further 15 minutes until the topping is golden.

Serve with a scattering of basil, a mixed leafy salad and a good dollop of minted yoghurt.

Right
A 1920s advert...
This little piggy ran
all the way home!

The Great British Sausage Sandwich

MAKES 4 SANDWICHES

4 large sausages
8 slices granary or sourdough
  bread
butter
wholegrain mustard
HP Sauce
piccalilli
2–3 sliced tomatoes

Cook the sausages for
12–15 minutes and keep warm.

Spread each slice of bread with
butter, then spread 4 of the slices
with mustard and 4 with HP
Sauce.

Cut each sausage into 3 slices
lengthways and place on top of
the mustard coated bread. Add a
generous dollop of piccalilli and
cover with tomato slices.

Top with the HP bread slices,
cut in half and serve to a delighted
audience.

Grilled Tuna with HP Lime Marinade

SERVES 4

4 fresh tuna steaks
5 tablespoons lime juice
3 tablespoons HP Sauce
4 spring onions
25g sesame seeds, toasted

Lay the tuna steaks in a shallow dish, mix together the lime juice and HP Sauce and pour it over them. Leave in the fridge to marinate for 2 hours.

Trim off any tired ends of the spring onion leaves and cut off the root. Working up from the root 'end' slice the leaves off at about 8cm and set aside the spare green tops, finely sliced into matchstick lengths.

Take the white part of the spring onion and starting 2cm in from the root end using a small sharp knife make a cut through up to the other end. Rotate the spring onion and repeat until you have made half a dozen cuts and the feathery slithers of the spring onion have opened up. Put them into ice-cold water and leave in the fridge for hour when they will have formed pretty curls.

Set the grill to medium high and cook the tuna steaks for 2–3 minutes on each side, all the time basting with the marinade. Serve sprinkled with toasted sesame seeds and the reserved sliced green onion tops. Remove the spring onions from the water, drain on kitchen paper and arrange on top of the tuna.

Finish with a drizzle of the marinade juice around the plate and a few handmade chips.

Left
A 1930s advert...
Making scraps a
thing of the past!

Hot Tamarind Chicken

SERVES 2

2 free range chicken breasts
1 tablespoon HP Sauce
1 teaspoon tamarind paste
$\frac{1}{2}$ teaspoon sea salt
1 tablespoon vegetable oil
1 onion, chopped
2 cloves garlic, finely diced
1 stalk lemongrass, finely sliced
1 green pepper, deseeded and
  sliced
4 green chillies, deseeded and
  finely diced
1 tomato, roughly chopped
4 kaffir lime leaves, crumbled

Cut 3 shallow slits in each chicken breast. Mix together the HP, tamarind and salt and spread this over the meat and into the slits. Cover and leave to marinate for 1 hour.

Heat the vegetable oil in a frying pan and add the onion and garlic. Fry for 3–4 minutes. Reduce to a low heat and add in the lemongrass, pepper, chillies and tomatoes and cook for a further 5 minutes, moving the mixture gently around the pan.

Now nestle the marinated chicken breasts cut side down, together with any remaining marinade, into the mixture, add the lime leaves and 150ml of water, cover and simmer very gently for 30 minutes turning the chicken once. Add a little more water if needed and spoon the mixture over the chicken from time to time. Remove the lid for the last 5 minutes to reduce the liquid.

A CANCELLED DEBT AND A HANDSOME PROCUREMENT

Whilst driven to expanding the Midland Vinegar Company inventory in new and exciting ways, Moore also had to busy himself with some of the more everyday demands of running a business. Amongst

Bacon & Sweetcorn Fritters

FOR 4 PEOPLE

100g self-raising flour
4 tablespoons milk
$1/2$ teaspoon baking powder
1 free range egg, beaten
2 tablespoons HP Sauce
325g tin of sweetcorn kernels
6 rashers back bacon, grilled and
    diced
vegetable oil for frying
maple syrup to serve

Make a stiff batter by putting the sieved flour and baking powder into a bowl, make a well in the centre for the egg and gradually add the milk. Beat well and then add the HP Sauce and beat for a further minute. Fold in the drained sweetcorn and diced bacon so that they are well mixed with the batter and refrigerate for 20 minutes.

Oil a griddle or heavy frying pan over a medium-high heat and spoon on tablespoons of the mixture. Cook for 2–3 minutes, turning once, until golden brown. Continue until all the mixture is used and then serve in stacks drizzled with maple syrup.

these more mundane requirements was the chasing up of accounts that had fallen into arrears. One such account was with a grocer by the name of Mr F. G. Garton. Moore and son visited the grocer personally to see if they might succeed in settling the debt. They introduced themselves to Mr Garton and removed themselves to an area behind the shop that would allow for discretion. There they were greeted by the most heavenly smell emanating from a copper which contained a rich, exotic-looking sauce. It tasted no less wonderful than it smelled and Moore realised immediately that he had stumbled upon something quite special; the very thing which would fulfil his most ardent business dream. There was then just one other small matter that was to delay by mere seconds the cancellation of Mr Garton's bad debt and the offering of £150 for the purchase of the grocer's piquant sauce recipe. That small matter was the detail of a name. **Continued on page 278....**

HP King Duck

SERVES 4

For the pancakes
125g self-raising flour
$1/_2$ tsp salt
1 medium free range egg, beaten
25g butter, melted
150ml milk
vegetable oil for frying

$1/_2$ small cucumber
4 spring onions, white and green
   parts
4 tablespoons HP Sauce
1 tablespoon runny honey, plus
   extra for brushing
$1/_4$ teaspoon Chinese five-spice
   powder
1 teaspoon redcurrant jelly
1 tablespoon dark soy sauce
2 duck breasts
salt
sesame oil for frying

First prepare the pancake batter. Mix the sieved flour with the salt. Gradually whisk in the egg, butter and milk to form a smooth thick batter. Chill for 30 minutes.

Slice the cucumber into 4cm chunks. Take each chunk and cut into thin matchstick strips. Top and tail the spring onions, cut into 4cm pieces and slice each piece into fine shreds. Set aside. Mix together the HP, honey, spice powder, redcurrant jelly and soy in a small bowl, making sure the jelly is well dispersed and leave until ready to serve.

Heat a little oil in a frying pan and add 1 tablespoon of the batter. Spread it out with the back of a spoon until you have about an 8cm round. Gently cook for 1–2 minutes until bubbles surface. Flip over and cook for another minute. You want to achieve thin crispy pancakes. Repeat to make 8 small pancakes. (You will probably have some batter left over for seconds!)

Put the duck breasts into a shallow dish and pour boiling water over the skin. This will help it crisp when cooking. Drain and pat dry with kitchen paper. Season the skin with a little salt. Heat a heavy based pan with a small amount of sesame oil. Put the duck breasts in over a medium to high heat skin side down to crisp and cook for 5 minutes. Reduce the heat, turn the duck over and cook for 5–6 minutes for pink or longer for well done. While the flesh side is cooking brush honey over the skin side. Remove the duck breasts and leave to rest for 5 minutes, then cut into thin diagonal slices.

For each person take 1 pancake, lay on some duck slices, drizzle with the sauce then lay on some cucumber, then some spring onion. Repeat the process with a second pancake.

Slow-Cooked Barbecue Pork Belly

SERVES 6–8
FOR A BARBECUE PARTY

2kg pork belly, prepared in 1 piece
1 litre Coca-Cola
$\frac{1}{2}$ teaspoon freshly chopped
   ginger
3 whole cloves
1 cinnamon stick (about 10cm
   long)
3 star anise

For the marinade
200g soft dark brown sugar
300ml malt vinegar
$\frac{1}{2}$ teaspoon ground cinnamon
$\frac{1}{2}$ teaspoon ground allspice
4 tablespoons HP Sauce
2 heaped teaspoons horseradish
   sauce
200ml dark rum
fresh coriander to garnish

Preheat the oven to 150C/300F/ Gas 2.

Put the pork belly into a suitable size deep ovenproof dish to lay it out flat. In a saucepan put the Coca-Cola, ginger, cloves, cinnamon and star anise and bring to the boil. Simmer for 10 minutes and then pour over the pork. Cook in the oven for $2\frac{1}{2}$ hours by which time the meat should be very tender.

Lift out the pork, drain and discard the liquid, and leave aside to cool in the dish.

Now make the marinade. Put the sugar, vinegar, cinnamon and allspice into a pan and bring to the boil. Turn down the heat and keep cooking until the liquid has reduced by half. Remove from the heat and stir in the HP Sauce, horseradish and rum. Let the marinade cool before pouring it over the pork belly. Put in the fridge covered with clingfilm to infuse for 3–4 hours.

Time to fire up the barbie or, if the clouds roll in, heat the grill to medium high. Arrange the pork over the hot coals, preferably with the lid down for it to take on the delicious smokiness, and cook for 10 minutes or until it is heated totally through. To serve, slice up the tender pork and scatter with freshly chopped coriander.

Left
From the 1930s...
In celebrated tabletop company!

Everything goes with

HP

SAUCE

Right
From the 1940s...
HP: helping young men
to clear their plates!

Welsh Rarebit... the HP Way

FOR 4 PEOPLE

50ml traditional ale
1 tablespoon HP Sauce
1 teaspoon prepared English
 mustard
1 teaspoon dry English mustard
$1/_4$ teaspoon cayenne pepper
300g mature Cheddar cheese,
 grated
1 ciabatta loaf
pinch of paprika
mixed leaves to serve

Put the beer, HP Sauce, mustards and cayenne in a pan and bring to a simmer. Remove from the stove and add the grated cheese, a little at a time, until you have the consistency of porridge.

Cut the ciabatta in half and then split each half and toast lightly. Spoon the cheesy mixture over the 4 ciabatta pieces and sprinkle the tops with paprika.

Place under a hot grill until bubbling with golden flecks. Serve each rarebit topped with a handful of mixed leaves.

Gujerati Mango & Lentil Curry

SERVES 4

$\frac{1}{2}$ teaspoon cumin seeds
$\frac{1}{2}$ teaspoon black mustard seeds
2 cloves of garlic, crushed
1 onion, peeled and chopped
$\frac{1}{2}$ teaspoon salt
1 tablespoon vegetable oil
1 tablespoon brown sugar
250g red lentils, soaked overnight
  in water, rinsed and drained
4 tablespoons HP Sauce
2 chillies, finely chopped
$\frac{1}{2}$ teaspoon turmeric
400ml vegetable stock
2 large ripe mangoes, peeled and
  cubed

Dry fry the cumin and mustard seeds in a small pan until they begin to pop and lightly colour, releasing their wonderful aroma, then tip them into a pestle and mortar and grind them to fully unleash their flavour.

Put the ground spices together with the garlic, onion and salt into a blender and process to a paste. Heat the oil in a heavy based pan and add the paste, cooking over a gentle heat and stirring all the time until it just begins to brown.

Add the sugar, lentils, HP, chillies and turmeric together with the stock, bring up to the boil and then simmer for 20 minutes. Toss in the mango chunks and cook for a further 10 minutes until you have a thick rich sauce.

Serve with chapatti or naan breads.

King Prawn Patia with Muscovado & Yoghurt

SERVES 4

4 tablespoons natural yoghurt
1 medium onion, chopped
2 cloves garlic
3cm piece of fresh ginger, peeled
  and diced
1 teaspoon coriander seeds
1 teaspoon cumin seeds
1 teaspoon black mustard seeds
2 tablespoons vegetable oil
2 teaspoons paprika
$\frac{1}{2}$ teaspoon cayenne
$\frac{1}{2}$ teaspoon turmeric
2 tablespoons light muscovado
  sugar
1 tablespoon white wine vinegar
2 tablespoons tomato purée
2 tablespoons HP Sauce
500g peeled king prawns

Put the yoghurt, onion, garlic and ginger into a blender and blitz with 3 tablespoons of water to make a paste.

In a hot frying pan or wok dry roast the coriander, cumin and black mustard seeds until they start to pop – about 20–30 seconds – and then crush them lightly in a pestle and mortar to release the flavours. Return the pan to the heat add the oil, the crushed spices, paprika, cayenne and turmeric and cook very gently for 2 minutes, being careful not to burn the spices.

Add the yoghurt paste to the pan of spices and fry gently for 8–10 minutes, stirring from time to time until the mixture turns a golden colour. While this is cooking mix together the sugar, vinegar, tomato purée and HP Sauce and pour it into the pan to make a fairly thick mixture. Add a splash of water if it is too thick and simmer gently for 5 minutes.

Toss in the prawns, season with a little salt if required, and cook just long enough to heat the prawns through without overcooking them. You should have a thick, 'grainy' sauce that will coat the prawns perfectly. Serve on a bed of jasmine rice.

Right
A c.1930s advert....
A sauce for celebration!

Peach-Glazed Pork Fillet

SERVES 2

300g pork tenderloin, sliced into
   1cm-thick medallions
salt and pepper
3 tablespoons peach conserve
2 tablespoons HP Sauce
1 tablespoon balsamic vinegar
$\frac{1}{4}$ teaspoon ground cumin
chopped parsley

Season the pork medallions with salt and pepper.

Melt the peach conserve in a pan by mashing any fruit pieces and add the HP sauce, balsamic vinegar, cumin and a good grind of black pepper and stir them all together. Allow to cool and then pour over the pork medallions. Leave to marinate for 1 hour.

Line a grill rack with foil and heat the grill to medium. Using some tongs remove the pork from the marinade and lay out the medallions on the grill pan. Baste with plenty of the marinade and grill for 8–10 minutes, turning and basting as it cooks.

Serve scattered with chopped parsley or coriander.

HOUSES OF PARLIAMENT SAUCE

Deluxe Steak Burgers

MAKES 6 BURGERS

650g best lean minced rump steak
2 rashers unsmoked back bacon, diced
1 medium onion, finely diced
1 clove garlic, finely diced
1 medium free range egg
1 teaspoon anchovy essence
2 tablespoons HP Sauce
$\frac{1}{2}$ teaspoon dried thyme
$\frac{1}{2}$ teaspoon dried sage
pinch of salt
freshly ground black pepper
1 tablespoon plain flour
olive oil

Place all the ingredients, except the flour and oil, into a large mixing bowl and combine together. You can use a wooden spoon but your hands will do the job much better. Add the flour and work it in evenly to help bind the mixture.

Divide the mixture into 6 equal patties making sure you squeeze each one quite firmly to make a good solid burger.

Place the burgers onto greaseproof paper and pop into the fridge for about an hour. You can leave them longer but the idea is to get the mixture to set so that they stay in good shape while cooking.

Heat about 1 tablespoon of olive oil in a frying pan or griddle (or brushed onto a barbecue) and when the oil is hot pop in (or on) the burgers. Cook them for 5–8 minutes and turn over for another 5–8 minutes.

years to come. Serendipity had led Moore and son to within smelling distance of Mr Garton's brew, but perhaps he believed it was fate when Moore was gifted with the most apt of names for the grocer's concoction. Through an open door his gaze landed upon the cart which Garton used to transport his goods to customers. Propped there, against the spokes of one wheel, was a board with thick painted words exclaiming GARTON'S HP SAUCE! A fittingly snappy appellation, he didn't doubt, but, 'Why the letters HP?', Moore asked of the grocer. Rumour had it, revealed Garton, that a bottle of his sauce had been spotted at one of the restaurants of the Houses of Parliament! Goodness gracious – could there be a more apt symbol to win over the British nation? Moore was intoxicated with joy. He had found his sauce, he had found its name; he didn't doubt it would find the people, it was now all just a question of timing. Continued on page 288.

Deep Vegetable and HP Pie

SERVES 4–6

1/2 tablespoon olive oil
1 large potato, peeled and very
  thinly sliced
1 medium aubergine, skin on and
  cut into 1/2cm slices
1 leek, washed and very thinly
  sliced
2 medium courgettes, skin on and
  cut into 1/2cm rings
salt and black pepper
1 clove garlic finely diced
mixed dried herbs
350ml double cream
3 tablespoons HP Sauce
1 1/2 leaves gelatine

You will need an ovenproof dish about 25cm x 20cm.

Preheat the over to 180C/350F/ Gas 4.

Drizzle a little oil into the base of the dish. Start by forming a layer of potato slices then a layer of aubergine, then leeks and courgettes. Season well, add the garlic and herbs and then repeat the layers again.

In a saucepan heat the cream and HP Sauce and when warm add the gelatine according to the instructions on the packet. Ladle the HP cream mixture over the vegetables and finally sprinkle the mixed herbs on the top.

Loosely cover with foil, place the dish in the centre of the oven and cook for 20 minutes. Remove the foil and return to the oven for a further 15 minutes until the top coating is golden brown.

Serve hot as it is or press the top down gently with a spatula and leave the dish to cool – it will then easily cut into thick slices when thoroughly cold. Perfect for lunches, picnics and parties.

Right
From the 1950s...
Famous double-acts
endorse our beloved HP.

Lenny the Lion : If I was a real lion I would insist on having my lion-tamers dished up with H.P. Sauce. *Everything* goes with H.P. Sauce.

Cynthia doesn't say.

Terry Hall : If you were a real lion you wouldn't get the chance – *I'd* bag the lion's share of the H.P. Sauce. You wouldn't dip a whisker in this H.P. Tomato Ketchup either. I love it – it's so rich in tomato ! Like you and me, Lenny, H.P. Sauce and Tomato Ketchup are a really . . .

Happy Pair!

Hylda Baker says:
That's our Cynthia up there with the bottle of H.P. Sauce. She doesn't say much, but she knows, you know ! She knows that everything goes with H.P. Sauce. She knows that H.P. Tomato Ketchup is *so* rich in tomato. And she knows I know she knows there's nothing like H.P. on the table to make us a really . . .

Happy Pair!

She knows, you know !

Brunch Wrap

MAKES 4 WRAPS

500g puff pastry (defrosted if
   frozen)
4 tablespoons HP Sauce
4 rashers streaky bacon, lightly
   grilled
100g tin of baked beans
4 small tomatoes, sliced
2 eggs, hardboiled and sliced
2 pork sausages, cooked
freshly milled black pepper
milk for brushing

Pre-heat the oven to 190C/375F/ Gas 5.

On a lightly floured surface roll out the pastry to about $\frac{1}{2}$ cm thick and cut out 4 x 16cm squares. Take each piece with the 4 points like a compass facing north, south, east and west. Roll out the east and west sides so that you have an elongated diamond – these will be wrapping over the filling. Spread each piece of pastry with a tablespoon of HP Sauce.

Now for the filling. Lay first a rasher of bacon in each top to bottom, then a spoon of beans spread out, then slices of tomatoes, then the egg and finally half a sausage cut lengthways. Season with pepper.

Take each one and fold the larger flaps into the centre over the filling. Seal with a little water. Brush with a little milk and place on a baking tray lined with parchment. Bake in the centre of the oven for 15 minutes until the wraps are puffy and golden. Leave to rest a few minutes before serving.

THE ASTON FACTORY THAT WAS HOME TO HP SAUCE FOR SO MANY YEARS WAS UNIQUE IN THAT THE SITE WAS DIVIDED BY THE A38(M) MOTORWAY. A PIPELINE WAS USED TO CARRY VINEGAR FROM ONE SIDE OF THE FACTORY ABOVE SEVEN LANES OF THE ASTON EXPRESSWAY AND OVER TO THE OTHER! IN THE 1970S, THE PIPELINE LEAKED, DAMAGING THE PAINTWORK OF THE PASSING TRAFFIC BELOW!

What a blessing that eggs are such good value at this time of year. There are so many satisfying meals to make with them – that are really easy too! And eggs are so much more exciting, when you add a drop of HP to the recipe. The pure flavour of finest tomatoes in HP Tomato Ketchup. The rich flavour of blended fruits and spices in HP Sauce. Who else but HP gives you so much goodness!

6 beat-the-clock ways with
eggs & HP*

Buttered Eggs

4 rashers streaky bacon
1 oz butter or margarine
1 tablespoon HP Tomato Ketchup
2 eggs

Cut streaky rashers in half and put 4 halves each into 2 individual ovenproof dishes. Cream the butter or margarine with the HP Tomato Ketchup. Break an egg over bacon in each dish. Top with the butter and ketchup mixture. Bake in a fairly hot oven for 10 minutes, or until egg is set. Add a dash of HP Sauce on it—makes a marvellous quick snack.

Blushing Rarebit

4 oz grated cheese
1 tablespoon HP Tomato Ketchup
½ oz butter or margarine
2 slices bread
2 eggs

Put grated cheese, HP Tomato Ketchup and butter or margarine into small thick saucepan. Melt mixture gradually, stirring over low heat. Toast bread slices, and spread thickly with hot cheese mixture. Put under grill until golden brown. Poach eggs until set. Top each hot rarebit with a poached egg. Serve with HP Sauce on it—delicious!

Stuffed Eggs

4 eggs
HP Tomato Ketchup

Hard boil eggs, allowing 2 for each person. Cut eggs in half, putting yolks into bowl. Mash yolks with 1 tablespoon HP Tomato Ketchup until soft. Refill egg halves, and serve with salad, and to top it all, HP Sauce—marvellous!

Egg Pasties

¼ lb. short pastry
Filling:
2 hard-boiled eggs
2 skinned pork sausages
or ¼ lb. sausage meat
1 tablespoon HP Tomato Ketchup
1 teaspoon chopped parsley
salt and pepper

Filling: chop hard-boiled eggs, put in a bowl with sausage meat, HP Tomato Ketchup, parsley and seasoning. Blend thoroughly.
Roll pastry thinly into a square. Cut in four. Divide filling in four and put a portion on each pastry square. Damp edges and fold into a triangle, sealing edges firmly. Put on a greased baking sheet, brush with a little milk and bake at 400°F. – Gas 6 for 10 minutes. Reduce heat to 350°F. – Gas 3-4 and cook for a further 15 minutes. Serve hot or cold with HP Sauce on it.

Zippy Popovers

2 oz flour
pinch of salt
pinch of cayenne pepper
1 egg
1 tablespoon HP Sauce
5 tablespoons milk
1 tablespoon finely chopped onion
2 tablespoons grated cheese
HP Tomato Ketchup

Sift flour with seasonings into bowl, hollow out the centre and drop in egg and 3 tablespoons of the milk. Beat with wooden spoon, gradually drawing in flour from basin sides and adding rest of milk to make smooth batter. Stir in HP Sauce, chopped onion and grated cheese.
Divide cooking fat between 12 patty tins and put in hot oven (450°F. – Gas 8) until fat is very hot, remove from oven. Give batter a stir, then divide between tins. Put back in oven and cook for about 15 minutes or until well risen and golden brown. Serve hot with HP Tomato Ketchup on it!

Portuguese Omelet

1 onion
1 tomato
almonds
few sultanas
seasoning, herbs
a little oil
HP Tomato Ketchup

Chop an onion finely, and cook until transparent in oil. Add a chopped tomato, a few chopped almonds, a few sultanas, seasoning and herbs. Blend when cooked with a tablespoon HP Tomato Ketchup.
Make a 3-egg omelet, fold and pour hot onion and tomato mixture over, topping with a very little finely grated cheese, and a final touch of HP Sauce. Fabulous!

*HP—in it and on it! HP Sauce, HP Tomato Ketchup

Lamb & Mint Pasties

MAKES 6 PASTIES

450g lamb, cut into 1cm cubes
150g potatoes
75g carrots
100g of turnip and swede mixed
1 large onion, roughly chopped
$1/_2$ teaspoon dried thyme
1 teaspoon good ready-made mint
    sauce
$1^1/_2$ tablespoons HP Sauce
salt and pepper
1kg pack of readymade short
    crust pastry
1 dessertspoon sunflower oil
1 free-range egg
1 tablespoon fresh milk

Pour the sunflower oil into a large saucepan adding the onion. Cook over a medium heat until the onion is transparent but not coloured.

Add the lamb to the onion. Continue to cook until all the lamb is sealed, this should take about 10 minutes. Keeping the same heat add the thyme, HP Sauce, a pinch of salt and a very generous grind of black pepper – pasties need pepper!

When the lamb is approaching tender, after about 30–40 minutes, add the remaining vegetables and the mint sauce and mix all together well in the pan.

Continue to cook until the vegetable pieces are just softening. Test the mixture and adjust the seasoning to your taste, set aside to cool.

Roll out the short crust pastry to a little under $1/_2$cm thick on a clean cool, well floured surface. Lay a small plate, ideally 20cm diameter,

over the pastry and cut round it. Remove the excess pastry. Brush around the edge of the pastry circle with cold water. Place 140g of the lamb mix into the centre and bring the top and the bottom of the circle together over the mixture pinching it together to make a 2cm joint from side to side. Fold 1cm of pastry over the end. Now here is the clever bit, using your thumb and fore finger squeeze the pastry joint together and crimp it all along the edge until it looks like a traditional pasty. Brush the outside with a half-and-half beaten-egg-and-milk mixture. This will give the cooked pasty a lovely golden sheen.

Place the made pasties on baking parchment on a flat tray and cook at 180C/350F/Gas 4 for the first 15 minutes reducing to 150C/300F/Gas 2 for another 12 minutes. Remove from the oven and place on a cooling tray for the pastry to set.

Left
From c.1930...
Egg-cellent ideas
abound in the sixties!

HP SA

-always with Fish

No 319/2

Left
*From c.1930...
It's fine for fish!*

Calf's Liver & Pancetta with Caramelised Red Onions

FOR 4 FRIENDS

40g butter
1 large red onion, thinly sliced
½ tablespoon Demerara sugar
1 tablespoon red wine vinegar
salt and black pepper
12 rashers pancetta (or streaky bacon)
600g calf's liver, thinly sliced
2 tablespoons HP Sauce
freshly chopped parsley

First, caramelise the onions. In a pan melt half the butter and cook the onions until softened. Now add the sugar, red wine vinegar and season with salt and pepper. Cover and cook for 10 minutes over a low heat until caramelised.

Pop the pancetta under a medium grill until its just getting crispy around the edges, remove and roughly dice.

Season the liver with salt and pepper. Using a frying pan, heat the remaining butter until it begins to bubble and then slide in the liver. The object here is to brown the outside and still leave the liver pink inside, which should take no more than 2 minutes on each side. Stack the liver to one side of the pan, add the HP Sauce, the pancetta and the caramelised onions and quickly mix together. You don't want to cook the liver any longer than is necessary.

Serve as a stack with the caramelised onions on top and a flourish of freshly chopped parsley.

DR HILL PROCLAIMS

Doctor Alfred Hill was the first head of Birmingham's Health Department, and served as a public analyst, passing fit for public consumption all manner of foodstuffs. He had tested each and every one of the products manufactured by the Midland Vinegar Company. His were the crucial first words of approval and, in a manner that seemed fitting as the furore of a

Middle Eastern Hot Pepper Dip

SERVES 6

1 large red pepper
3 cloves garlic, peeled
½ teaspoon salt
1 onion, finely diced
70g fresh white breadcrumbs
50g walnuts, toasted under a grill
   for 3–4 minutes and finely
   chopped
1 tablespoon fresh lemon juice
2 tablespoons HP Sauce
1 teaspoon ground cumin
1 teaspoon chilli powder
150ml olive oil
warmed pitta bread, to serve
mint leaves, to garnish

Char the pepper under a hot grill or over a flame using a pair of tongs. Pop it into a paper bag and close. Leave for 5 minutes and then you will find the skin easy to remove from the soft flesh. Discard any seeds and pith and roughly chop the pepper, then pop it into a food processor.

Chop the garlic roughly on a board and mash with the salt to make a paste. Add this to the processor together with the onion, breadcrumbs, walnuts, lemon juice, HP Sauce, cumin and chilli. Blend all these ingredients together until you have a smooth paste. Now gradually add the olive oil, with the blender still going.

Transfer the pepper dip to a bowl and serve at room temperature with warm pitta bread and mint leaves. This dip is also great with kebabs, grilled meat and fish.

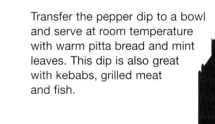

new century still hung thick in the air, his endorsement for the company's newest product sounded like a bell-ring of joy, proudly announcing the arrival of a very special sauce: 'I beg to report that I have analysed the sample of Garton's H.P. Sauce and find it to be made from the best materials. The well-known Midland

there is no better, is used in its preparation. It is of a pleasant and piquant flavour and is in every respect a THOROUGHLY GOOD SAUCE.' It was 1903. Thousands of green glass bottles of the sauce adorned the windows of food stores across the nation. Hill had had his say, now the public would have theirs. **Continued on page**

Cheesy Tortillas with Ratatouille

SERVES 4

½ tablespoon olive oil
1 onion, roughly chopped
1 clove garlic, finely chopped
1 small red pepper, deseeded and
  roughly chopped
1 small aubergine, skin on and
  diced into 2cm cubes
1 courgette, skin on and diced into
  2cm cubes
1 teaspoon fresh chopped
  oregano (or ½ teaspoon dried
  oregano)
salt and freshly ground black
  pepper
2 large tomatoes, skinned and
  roughly chopped
3 tablespoons HP Sauce
4 flour tortillas
200g grated Cheddar

Start by making the ratatouille. First heat the olive oil in a large frying pan and cook the onions and garlic until just softened, add the diced peppers, aubergine and courgettes and mix well together. Add the oregano, season well with salt and pepper and cook fairly quickly to retain the crunch of vegetables for about 8 minutes. Now add the tomatoes and HP Sauce, stir and cook for a further 2–3 minutes.

Brush a separate frying pan with oil over a medium heat and lay in one tortilla at a time. After a couple of minutes sprinkle with a quarter of the cheese, allow it to melt and then fold the fritatta in half and in half again and remove from the pan to a warm serving plate. Repeat with the other tortillas.

Now spoon oodles of the ratatouille half over the tortilla and half onto the plate and serve.

Oxtail Soup

SERVES 6

1kg oxtail, trimmed and cut into
  pieces
25g unsalted butter
1/2 tablespoon olive oil
2 stalks celery, chopped
1 onion, diced, skin on
1 small turnip, diced
1 carrot, diced
500ml beef stock
3 tablespoons HP Sauce
6 peppercorns
2 cloves
small piece of mace
small bunch herbs
salt and black pepper
1 tablespoon sherry

Brown the oxtail in the butter and oil in a large casserole pan. Add the vegetables, the stock, HP Sauce and 1 litre of water. Bring to the boil adding the peppercorns, cloves, mace and herbs. Season with salt and freshly ground black pepper.

Cover the casserole, turn the heat down to a simmer and cook for 2 1/2 hours until the meat is really tender and falling away from the bones.

Allow to cool a little and then strain the whole lot through a colander or sieve into a suitable bowl. Cover the liquid and chill in the fridge for 1 hour. Discard the vegetables and bones together with any fat or skin from the oxtail, leaving you with just the meat. Break this up into small pieces and set aside.

When the liquid has chilled you will be able to easily skim off any fat on the surface. Put the remaining jellied juices into a saucepan and if it needs to be thicker bring to the boil and reduce until you have the desired consistency. Add in the meat and cook for 5 minutes then check the seasoning. Remove from the heat, stir in the sherry and serve.

A SAUCE OF
HAUTE QUALITÉS...
...A KIND OF FRENCH PRIMER

Singapore Peanut Noodles

SERVES 2–4

100g Chinese dried medium egg
    noodles (or 200g fresh noodles)
2 tablespoons sesame oil
1 bunch spring onions, sliced
1 teaspoon freshly grated ginger
3 tablespoons peanut butter
2 tablespoons HP Sauce
1 teaspoon sugar
1 teaspoon chilli flakes
100ml vegetable stock
100g fresh beansprouts
50g roasted, unsalted peanuts,
    crushed

Put the egg noodles into a pan of boiling water, cover and remove from the heat for about 5 minutes while the noodles rehydrate.

In a wok or large frying pan heat the sesame oil, add the onions and ginger and cook over a gentle heat until tender. Stir in the peanut butter, HP Sauce, sugar, chilli flakes and stock and combine over the heat for 2–3 minutes.

Swizzle the noodles with a fork to loosen them and then drain. Tip the beansprouts into the wok, turning them in the sauce for a couple of minutes and then add in the noodles and toss the whole lot

together. Tip out onto a warm serving dish and scatter with the crushed peanuts.

As well as being a great vegetarian option you can also add prawns, cooked chicken or pork and it's a great way of using up leftovers. Simply add them at the same time as you stir in the peanut butter.

In September 1914, the Great War had begun and an uncertainty and gloom hung over the country. For the first time in the company's history, women took up positions in the factory, as the male workforce left to go and fight for their country. The wives and girlfriends helped maintain production and ensured that supplies of HP could be sent out to the troops. Indeed, it was said that a smattering of HP was all that made the soldiers' rations of bully beef bearable! And it was towards the end of the war that Moore introduced to

the HP label what would become for many British children their first education in foreign language: the famous paragraph exclaiming the wonders of HP Sauce, written in French. Some thought it a tribute to our allies in the war; others assumed it a nod to the vast quantity of sauce devoured by the troops in France. It was, in fact, a clever attempt to 'upmarket' the sauce and align it with the splendours of French cuisine.
Continued on page 304....

SAUCE
SAUCE
SAUCE
SAUCE

Cette sauce de premier choix possède les plus hautes qualités digestives.

C'est un assortiment de fruits d'Orient, d'épices et de Vinaigre de "Malt" pur.

Elle est absolument pure, appétissante et délicieuse avec les viandes chaudes ou froides.

POISSON.

JAMBON.

FROMAGE.

SALADE, &c.,

et pour relever le goût des

SOUPES.

HACHIS.

RAGOÛTS, &c.

SEULS FABRICANTS:

THE MIDLAND VINEGAR Cº LIMITED
LONDRES ET BIRMINGHAM.

Certificate of Purity

This sauce is free from artificial colouring and preservatives and conforms with pure food laws throughout the world.

It is made from fruits and spices of the highest quality, blended with pure malt vinegar of our own brewing.

All ingredients are regularly tested and examined for quality and purity in our own laboratories and the whole manufacture is under strict analytical control.

As an independent assurance of purity, samples of H.P. SAUCE are regularly taken for analysis by Messrs. Bostock Hill & Rigby, Public Analysts and Consulting Chemists.

THE MIDLAND VINEGAR Cº LIMITED
LONDON AND BIRMINGHAM.

HOUSES OF PARLIAMENT

IS A COMBINATION OF THE CHOICEST

ORIENTAL FRUITS SPICES AND PURE MALT VINEGAR

BLENDED WITH THE UTMOST CARE TO ENSURE A

DIGESTIVE RELISH

EVEN FOR THE MOST FICKLE APPETITE. THIS OBJECT HAVING BEEN ATTAINED BY YEARS OF PRACTICAL EXPERIENCE IN THE SAUCE TRADE.

MANUFACTURED BY SOLE PROPRIETORS-

THE MIDLAND VINEGAR Cº LIMITED
LONDON AND BIRMINGHAM.

Cette sauce de premier choix possède les plus hautes qualités digestives.

C'est un assortiment de fruits d'Orient, d'épices et de Vinaigre de "Malt" pur.

Elle est absolument pure, appétissante et délicieuse avec les viandes chaudes ou froides.

POISSON.

JAMBON.

FROMAGE.

SALADE, &c.,

et pour relever le goût des

SOUPES.

HACHIS.

RAGOÛTS, &c.

SEULS FABRICANTS:

THE MIDLAND VINEGAR Cº LIMITED
LONDRES ET BIRMINGHAM.

This Label is also protected under the Trade Marks Acts in Great Britain and many other countries.

MARQUE DÉPOSÉE

GARTON'S
HP
SAUCE

MARQUE DÉPOSÉE

GARTON'S
HP
SAUCE

REGD U.S. PAT. OFF.

GARTON'S
HP
SAUCE

REGD TRADE MARK.

GARTON'S
HP
SAUCE

MARQUE DÉPOSÉE

Cette sauce de premier choix possède les plus hautes qualités digestives.

C'est un assortiment de fruits d'Orient, d'épices et de Vinaigre de "Malt" pur.

Elle est absolument pure, appétissante et délicieuse avec les viandes chaudes ou froides.

POISSON

Certificate of Purity

This sauce is free from artificial colouring and preservatives and conforms with pure food laws throughout the world.

It is made from fruits and spices of the highest quality, blended with pure malt vinegar of our own brewing.

HOUSES OF PARLIAMENT

IS A COMBINATION OF THE CHOICEST

Cette sauce de premier choix possède les plus hautes qualités digestives.

C'est un assortiment de fruits d'Orient, d'épices et de Vinaigre de "Malt" pur.

Elle est absolument pure, appétissante et délicieuse avec les viandes chaudes ou froides.

SAUCE

REGᵈ TRADE MARK.

SAUCE

This Label is also protected under the Trade Marks Acts in Great Britain and many other countries.

MARQUE DÉPOSÉE

SAUCE

HOUSES OF PARLIAMENT

IS A COMBINATION OF
THE CHOICEST
ORIENTAL FRUITS
SPICES AND
PURE MALT VINEGAR
BLENDED WITH THE UTMOST
CARE TO ENSURE A
DIGESTIVE RELISH
EVEN FOR THE MOST FICKLE APPETITE.
THIS OBJECT HAVING BEEN ATTAINED
BY YEARS OF PRACTICAL EXPERIENCE
IN THE SAUCE TRADE.

MANUFACTURED BY
SOLE PROPRIETORS-

THE MIDLAND VINEGAR Cᵒ
LIMITED
LONDON
AND
BIRMINGHAM.

REGᵈ U.S. PAT. OFF.

Certificate of Purity

This sauce is free from artificial colouring and preservatives
and conforms with pure food
laws throughout the world.

It is made from fruits and
spices of the highest quality,
blended with pure malt vinegar
of our own brewing.

All ingredients are regularly
tested and examined for quality
and purity in our own laboratories and the whole manufacture is under strict analytical
control.

As an independent assurance
of purity, samples of H.P. SAUCE
are regularly taken for analysis by
Messrs. Bostock Hill & Rigby,
Public Analysts and Consulting
Chemists.

Cette sauce de premier
choix possède les plus
hautes qualités digestives.

C'est un assortiment de
fruits d'Orient, d'épices et
de Vinaigre de "Malt" pur.

Elle est absolument pure,
appétissante et délicieuse
avec les viandes chaudes
ou froides.

POISSON,
JAMBON,
FROMAGE,
SALADE, &c.,
et pour relever le goût des
SOUPES,
HACHIS,
RAGOÛTS, &c.

SEULS FABRICANTS :

THE MIDLAND VINEGAR Cᵒ
LIMITED
LONDRES
ET
BIRMINGHAM.

E 42

GARTON'S

HP

REGᵈ TRADE MARK.

SAUCE

GARTON'S

HP

MARQUE DÉPOSÉE

SAUCE

GARTON'S

HP

REGᵈ U.S. PAT. OFF.

SAUCE

Certificate of Purity

This sauce is free from artificial colouring and preservatives
and conforms with pure food
laws throughout the world.

It is made from fruits and
spices of the highest quality,

HOUSES OF PARLIAMENT

IS A COMBINATION

Cette sauce de premier
choix possède les plus
hautes qualités digestives.

C'est un assortiment de
fruits d'Orient, d'épices et
de Vinaigre de "Malt" pur.

Elle est absolument pure,
appétissante et délicieuse

Roast Poussin with Garlic & Herbs

SERVES 2

2 small heads of garlic, complete
  and unpeeled
olive oil
salt and fresh black pepper
2 poussin (oven ready)
4 sprigs fresh thyme
4 sprigs fresh rosemary
2 medium potatoes, peeled and
  sliced
50g unsalted butter, melted
2 tablespoons HP Sauce

Pre-heat the oven to 200C/400F/ Gas 6.

Take the 2 heads of garlic and trim across the top taking off about 1cm. Drizzle with a little olive oil, season with plenty of salt and pepper, place in a roasting tin and roast for 15 minutes.

Remove the garlic from the oven and allow them to cool enough to handle. Put one head of garlic into each poussin together with 2 sprigs of each of the herbs. Season the poussin with salt and pepper and put them into the roasting tin. Now tuck the sliced potatoes under and round the poussin in the tin.

Whisk the butter and HP Sauce together and brush it all over the poussins pouring the remainder over the sliced potatoes. Roast in the centre of the hot oven for 40 minutes.

When cooked, remove the poussin, allow to rest for a few minutes and then serve with the golden potatoes and your favourite vegetables.

Give your chips yum, mum.

And your fish.
And shepherd's pie. And sausages.
Not to mention cold meat salad.
And stew. The lot, in fact.

The fabulous HP Sauce adds
taste to it all. Good, rich, spicy taste
that makes food a little bit special.

For dad. And the children.
And you, dear mum.

The fabulous HP Sauce.

HP Steak & Mushroom Jackets

SERVES 4

olive oil
4 baking potatoes
sea salt
1 red onion, sliced
200g sliced closed cup
    mushrooms
2 tablespoons HP Sauce
100ml beef stock
100ml white wine
1 tablespoon Dijon mustard
good dash Tabasco sauce
400g fillet steak
salt and pepper
100g blue cheese
chopped fresh chives

Heat the oven to 180C/350F/Gas 4.

Drizzle a little olive oil over the potatoes and then turn the potatoes in your hands to cover them completely in the oil. Place them on a baking tray, sprinkle with sea salt and bake in the oven for 1 hour. The salt and oil will give the potatoes a good crispy skin.

Heat the oil in a pan, add the onions and mushrooms and sauté for 5–6 minutes until softened. Mix together the HP Sauce, stock, wine, mustard and Tabasco and add this to the pan. Cook gently for about 8 minutes until the sauce is thickened.

Meanwhile heat the grill to medium-high, season the steak and cook for approximately 10 minutes depending on how thick it is and how rare you like your steak (for a fillet that is 2.5cm thick, 10 minutes should give you a medium-rare steak). Turn once during cooking. Remove the steak and rest it for 5 minutes, keeping it warm. Cut the steak into slices and add it to the onion and mushroom mixture and stir.

Cut the potatoes with a cross halfway through and then squeeze with fingers and thumbs to open them up. Pack in the steak and mushroom mixture and then sprinkle with crumbled blue cheese and scatter with chopped chives.

Left
Sound advice for
60s mums.

Brisket with Figs & Rum

SERVES 6

1.5 kg brisket
1 litre good beef stock
1 large onion, peeled and roughly
  chopped
2 stalks of celery, roughly chopped
2 carrots, peeled and chopped
2–3 sprigs thyme
2 bay leaves
12 black peppercorns
1 tablespoon brown sugar
250g dried figs
100ml rum
2 tablespoons HP Sauce

Put the brisket into a suitable size pan and pour over the stock. Add the vegetables, herbs, peppercorns and sugar and bring up to the boil. Turn down the heat to just simmering and cook covered for 4 hours.

While this is cooking soak the figs in the rum.

Preheat the oven to 180C/350F/ Gas 4. Remove the brisket from the liquid and cover and keep warm. Strain the juices from the pan, discarding half the liquid and retaining the vegetables.

Place the brisket in a roasting tin with the vegetables tucked in around it and cook in the oven for 30 minutes after which time the outside will become golden and crispy.

Put the reserved liquid back into a saucepan over a high heat and reduce it down to half again. Add the figs, rum and HP Sauce and simmer for 20 minutes while the meat is finishing in the oven. If the gravy needs further thickening, add a teaspoon of cornflour mixed with an equal amount of water.

Serve thick succulent slices of brisket and vegetables doused with fig and rum gravy.

IT WAS IN 1940, AS A RESULT OF WARTIME RATIONING WHICH CUT THE PRINTED MATTER ON LABELS TO A BARE MINIMUM, THAT THE LINK TO THE RECIPE'S ORIGINAL OWNER, 'GARTON'S', WAS DROPPED FROM THE LABEL, NEVER TO RETURN.

Hunters' Chicken

SERVES 4–6

1 free-range chicken
salt and black pepper
2 tablespoons olive oil
2 onions, sliced
200g button mushrooms
200ml vermouth or white wine
200ml chicken stock
2 tablespoon tomato purée
3 tablespoons HP Sauce
1 tablespoon chopped fresh
 tarragon
400g fresh chopped tomatoes
1 tablespoon chopped fresh
 parsley
crème fraîche, to serve

Preheat the oven to 180C/350F/ Gas 4.

Cut the chicken into 10 pieces, including each breast into 2 and the legs in half. Season well with salt and freshly ground black pepper

Heat the oil in a frying pan and brown the chicken pieces for a few minutes. You may need to do this in a couple of batches. Lift the chicken from the pan with a slotted spoon and place in an ovenproof casserole.

Now cook the onions and mushrooms in the same frying pan for 5 minutes, stirring occasionally, until they begin to soften. Add the vermouth, stock, tomato purée and HP Sauce, together with the tarragon and cook for a further 5 minutes, then tip into the casserole with the chicken. Place the casserole in the oven and cook for 1 hour.

Remove from the oven, and skim off any excess oil from the juice. Stir in the tomatoes, return it to the oven and cook uncovered for a further 20 minutes while the sauce reduces. (You can thicken it with a little cornflour mixed with a splash of water, if desired.)

Scatter with the parsley and leave to rest for 5 minutes before serving with a swirl of crème fraîche and some good chunky roast potatoes.

Honey-grilled Salmon with Kiwi & Cucumber Salsa

SERVES 4

2 tablespoons HP Sauce
1 teaspoon Dijon mustard
2 tablespoons runny honey
1 tablespoon sesame oil
4 salmon fillets (approximately 200g each)
salt and pepper

For the salsa
2 tablespoons lime juice
1 tablespoon runny honey
2 firm kiwi fruits, peeled and diced
$\frac{1}{4}$ cucumber, unpeeled and finely diced
$\frac{1}{2}$ green pepper, deseeded and finely diced
1 small onion, finely chopped
1 small green chilli, deseeded and finely diced
2 heaped tablespoons fresh coriander, chopped

In a small bowl mix together the HP Sauce, mustard, honey and sesame oil. Brush the salmon fillets with this mixture, season with salt and pepper and leave in the fridge for 30 minutes.

Combine the lime juice and honey in a bowl and toss in the kiwi, cucumber, green pepper, onion, chilli and coriander turning them all in the juices. Leave this covered at room temperature while the salmon marinates.

Heat the grill to medium high and cook the fillets for 8–10 minutes, depending on the thickness, basting more mixture over them as they cook.

Serve the salmon with the salsa piled on top.

Maple HP Rib Chops

SERVES 4

1kg pork rib chops
1 litre chicken stock
6 tablespoons maple syrup
2 tablespoons brown sugar
2 tablespoons cider vinegar
2 tablespoons HP Sauce
1 heaped teaspoon mustard
    powder

Put the rib chops into a large saucepan with the stock, adding extra water to cover, and bring to the boil. Turn down the heat to a very gentle simmer, cover and cook for 45–60 minutes until tender.

Drain the ribs, discarding the stock, and put them into a large shallow dish. Warm the syrup, sugar, vinegar, HP Sauce and mustard powder in a pan for 5 minutes. Remove from the heat and pour the syrupy mixture over the ribs, turning them and making sure they are well coated. Allow to cool and then pop in the fridge for 2–3 hours to marinate.

When the barbecue is in full swing and the coals at perfect cooking temperature lay on the ribs and cook for 10 minutes, basting with any remaining marinade, or until the ribs are golden brown and ready to devour.

If you haven't got a barbecue these will cook perfectly on a griddle on the stove.

HAROLD'S PREFERENCE

In 1964, a casual remark did more to pique interest in HP Sauce than the marketing-campaign or selling-strategy dreams of any company executive of the era could have wished for. A new government had been elected to power, led by Harold Wilson. He was

Stuffed Butternut Squash

SERVES 4

2 small butternut squash
2 tablespoons olive oil
celery salt and freshly milled black
    pepper
1 small red chilli, finely diced
2 cloves garlic, finely chopped
200g chestnut mushrooms, sliced
100ml dry cider
3 tablespoons HP Sauce
400g tin cannellini beans, drained
2 tablespoons chopped flat leaf
    parsley, to garnish

Heat the oven to 180C/350F/Gas 4. Cut the butternut squash in half lengthways without removing the skin and scoop out the seeds. Brush the flesh with a little of the olive oil and season with salt and pepper. Put the squash in a baking tin, cover with foil and roast for 45–60 minutes, depending on the size, until they are soft all the way through.

Heat the remaining oil in a pan and gently fry the chilli, garlic and mushrooms for 3–4 minutes. Add the cider, HP Sauce and beans, season with celery salt and black pepper and simmer for a further 5 minutes, or until the juices have reduced down, and then stir in a good tablespoon of chopped parsley.

When the squash is cooked place one half on each plate and fill with the beany mixture spooning any remaining on the side. Scatter with the remaining parsley.

to the question of whether her husband had any bad habits, she quipped that if he did have a fault it was that he drowned everything she cooked in HP Sauce! This was publicity on an unprecedented scale; the media leapt on the comment, and her words were widely satirised by columnists and commentators of the day. The Prime Minister decided neither to confirm nor refute the statement. After all, a preference for the sauce suggested that he was a man of the people, a man of popular tastes! HP Sauce's connections with

the Houses of Parliament now seemed irrefutable. It wasn't until 1975, on the occasion of the centenary celebration of the Midland Vinegar Company, with the renowned fan of the sauce as the Company's guest of honour, that the former Prime Minister revealed that his wife's innocent remark from over a decade ago was inaccurate only so much as it wasn't HP Sauce for which he had a particular penchant, but Worcestershire Sauce! He left the company assembled there dumbfounded, but the myth prevailed. Continued on page 312

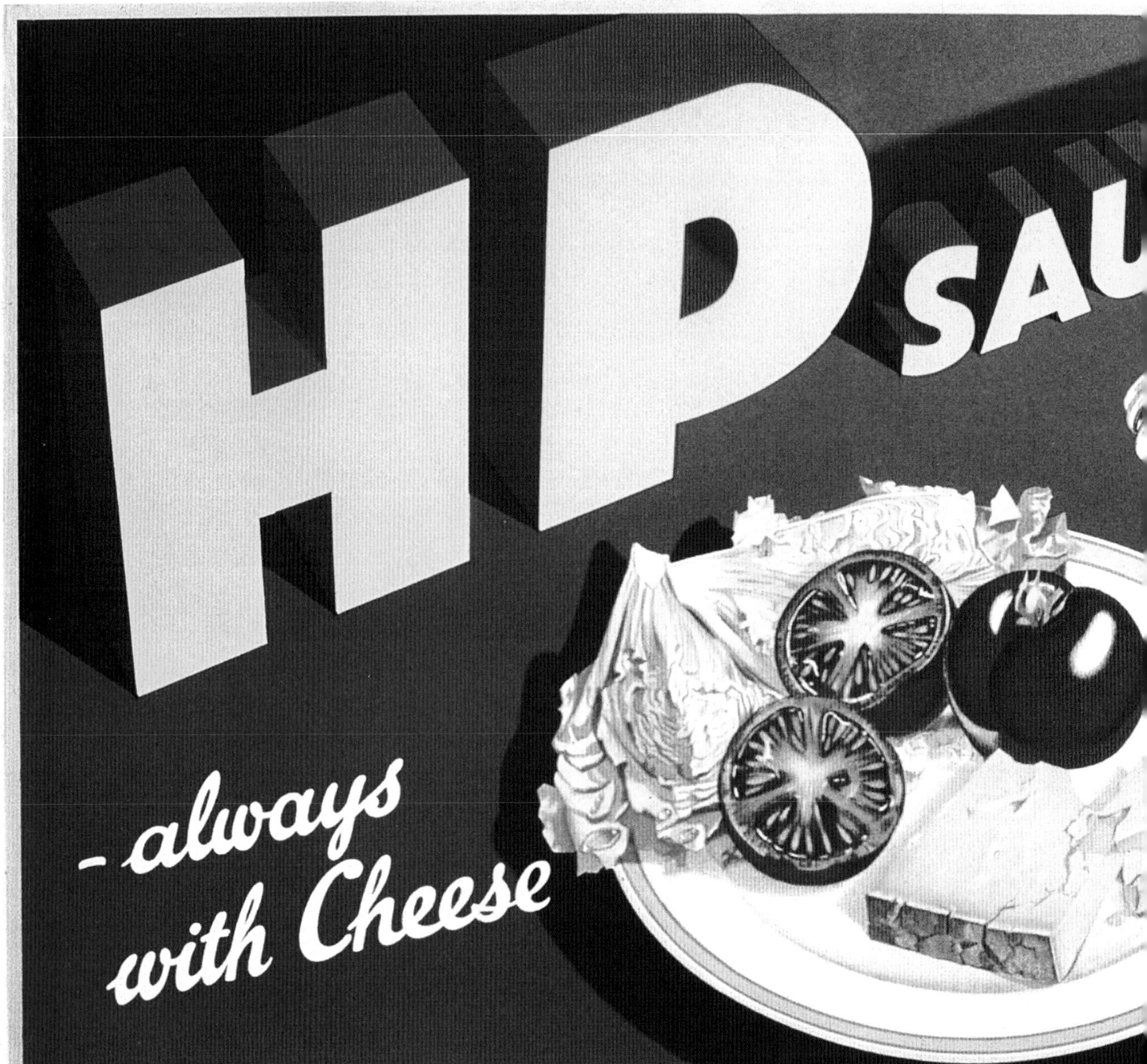
HP
- always
with Cheese

Left
From c.1930...
It's champion with cheese!

Devilled Lamb & Apricot Kebabs

MAKES 4 LARGE KEBABS

2 tablespoons HP Sauce
2 teaspoons wholegrain mustard
1 teaspoon medium curry paste
1 tablespoon runny honey
2 tablespoons lemon juice
1 teaspoon fresh thyme leaves
500g lamb neck fillet
freshly milled black pepper
24 ready-to-eat dried apricots

4 bamboo skewers soaked in
   water to stop them burning
   during cooking.

In a bowl mix together the HP Sauce, mustard, curry paste, honey, lemon juice and thyme.

Cut the lamb into 1cm thick discs. Season them with plenty of black pepper and toss them into the bowl of marinade. Leave for 1 hour.

Thread the lamb and apricot alternately on the skewers and then pop them under a hot grill or on the barbecue, brushing with any remaining sauce for 8–10 minutes until cooked to your liking. Serve with crispy baked potatoes and a leafy salad.

Lamb Tagine with Prunes, Olives & Almonds

For the tagine spice mix
1 tablespoon ground ginger
1 tablespoon ground black pepper
1 tablespoon turmeric
2 teaspoons ground cinnamon
1 teaspoon grated nutmeg

For the tagine
1kg lamb, diced into large chunks
2 tablespoons tagine spice mix
1 tablespoons olive oil
400ml lamb or beef stock
3 tablespoons HP Sauce
1 tablespoon honey
1 tablespoon dark brown sugar
150g ready to eat prunes, stoned
10 green olives, stoned and halved
50g slivered almonds, toasted in a
    dry frying pan
freshly chopped parsley, to serve

Mix together the tagine spices into an airtight jar. You will have enough to make this recipe at least twice and the spices will keep for a few months.

Put the lamb into a dish and sprinkle the 2 tablespoons of spice mix over the meat, coating it thoroughly, then cover and leave in the fridge for at least 2 hours.

Preheat the oven to 150C/300F/ Gas 2. Heat the olive oil in a frying pan, sear the lamb chunks all over in batches and transfer them with a slotted spoon to an ovenproof casserole. Pour in the stock, HP Sauce and honey, cover and cook in the oven for 2 hours.

Remove the casserole from the oven, stir in the sugar, prunes and olives and cook for a further half hour. Remove and rest for 0 minutes before serving scattered with almonds and parsley.

Florentine Pasta

SERVES 2

1 tablespoons olive oil
1 clove garlic, minced
2 shallots, finely diced
1 tablespoon Marsala wine
2 tablespoons HP Sauce
200ml double cream
100g Parmesan cheese, 3/4
  grated and $\frac{1}{4}$ left for shavings
100g washed baby leaf spinach,
  stalks removed
1 tablespoon pine nuts, toasted
  for 3 minutes in a dry pan
salt and pepper
200g linguine, or your favourite
  pasta

Heat the oil and butter in a large frying pan and add the garlic and shallots. Cook for 3 minutes until just softened and add the Marsala and HP Sauce. Add the cream and the grated Parmesan, bring up to the boil and then add the spinach. Cover and cook over a low heat until the spinach is just wilted and tender. Season with plenty of freshly ground black pepper.

Cook and drain the pasta and then toss with the creamy spinach mixture. Serve with shavings of Parmesan and the toasted pine nuts.

IN 1940 CAME THE FIRST EVER INSTANCE OF THE CLOSELY GUARDED SECRETS OF THE HP RECIPE LEAVING THE COUNTRY. WITH TRANSATLANTIC JOURNEYS FAR TOO PERILOUS TO SHIP SAUCE TO CANADA, THE RECIPE WAS INSTEAD TRANSLATED INTO CODE AND SENT IN TWO HALVES ACROSS THE OCEAN, WITH THE METHOD FOLLOWING ON IN A THIRD ENVELOPE!

Beef on the Bone with Chop House Butter

For the chop house butter
2 red onions, peeled, halved and finely chopped
2 teaspoons coarsely ground black pepper
2 tablespoon extra virgin rapeseed oil
splash red wine
1 tablespoon chopped thyme leaves
1 tablespoon freshly grated horseradish
500g butter, at room temperature
1 tablespoon Henderson's relish

2 tablespoons HP Sauce
1 tablespoon Tewksbury Mustard
2 teaspoons Gentleman's Relish
(You can freeze the leftover butter for use another time)

2 x T-Bone steaks, around 350g each

To prepare the butter, gently cook the red onions and black pepper in the rapeseed oil for 1–2 minutes then remove from the heat and mix well with all of the other ingredients.

Roll the butter mixture in clingfilm or greaseproof into a 3cm cylinder and store in the fridge for at least 20 minutes to firm up.

Season the steaks with a little salt and pepper and brush with vegetable oil.

Heat a griddle pan until smoking, and cook the beef cuts for 3–4 minutes on each side (for medium rare), or until cooked to your liking.

Serve the grilled steaks with two 1cm-thick rounds of the Chop House Butter, melting over each steak.

HAPPY DAYS... A SAUCE WITH SOME PUNCH

Venison Tartare

SERVES 4–6

4 shallots, finely diced
2 juniper berries, crushed
1 teaspoon capers, rinsed and
    finely chopped
1 fresh lime, half for juice and half
    for garnish
1 tablespoon olive oil
2 cloves garlic, minced
sprig of dill, finely chopped
dash Tabasco sauce
1 teaspoon paprika
salt and freshly ground black pepper
500g fresh venison, loin or fillet
    preferably
1 large egg yolk
2 level tablespoons HP Sauce
$\frac{1}{2}$ teaspoon made English
    mustard

First make the tartare seasoning by mixing together in a bowl the shallots, juniper, capers, lime juice, olive oil, garlic and dill. Then add the Tabasco, paprika, salt and pepper and mix altogether. Cover and leave in the refrigerator for 6 hours or overnight.

Roughly chop the venison and put in a food processor with the tartare seasoning. Blitz as long as it takes to create a mince, not a paste. Transfer the venison to a bowl and add the egg yolks, HP Sauce and mustard. Mix together well.

Divide the mixture into equal patties, forking the surface to enhance their look and serve with toast triangles and a rocket and watercress salad.

In the 1980s, it fell to a man of the people to sell the sauce of the people. Frank Bruno was establishing himself as one of the world's best boxers and was much loved by the people of Britain. HP had signed Bruno and the commentator with whom he had such a cuddly rapport, Harry Carpenter, to film a commercial for television. The voiceover began: 'How to get on the *wrong* side of Frank Bruno:', and Frank was promptly served with a plate of food to which he responded by scowled. The voiceover then interjected once more: 'How to get on the *right* side of Frank Bruno:', and Frank was duly passed the HP Sauce, after which he broke into a merrily whistled tune of 'Happy Days Are Here Again'. The voiceover concluded, 'Only one sauce can give Frank's favourite foods the necessary punch!' A nation almost certainly nodded in agreement! More than two decades later, you would be hard pressed to find a sauce that delivers a more knockout flavour!

Shepherd's Pie

SERVES 4

1 tablespoon vegetable oil
1 onion diced
500g lean minced lamb
1 large carrot
2 sticks celery
400g tin chopped tomatoes
2 sprigs thyme and 1 bay leaf tied
   together
HP Sauce
1 lamb or beef stock cube
salt and pepper
150g mushrooms, roughly
   chopped
1 tablespoon plain flour
800g potatoes, peeled
knob of butter
milk
2 teaspoons readymade
   horseradish sauce

Heat the oil in a pan and cook the onions until softened. Add in the mince and brown the meat – about 8 minutes – then follow with the carrots and celery. Pour in the tomatoes then add the herbs, HP Sauce, crumble in the stock cube, season well with salt and pepper and cook for 20 minutes over a medium heat.

Add in the mushrooms, sprinkle in the flour and taste the sauce, adjust the seasoning if necessary. Cook for a further 20 minutes by which time you should have a thick, rich, meaty mixture.

Remove from the cooker and leave to cool for 10 minutes. Discard the herb sprig and pour the meat and vegetables, with all the delicious juices, into an ovenproof serving dish with sides at least 5cm high.

Cut the potatoes into roughly even chunks about 5cm square and boil in salted water until cooked, then drain. Mash them until creamy by adding the butter, milk, horseradish and season with pepper. Leave aside to cool a little.

Preheat the oven to 180C/350F/ Gas 4. Now gently spread the mashed potato over the lamb and fork it level leaving symmetrical fork lines on top. Bake for 20–30 minutes until your forked mash is golden brown and crispy.

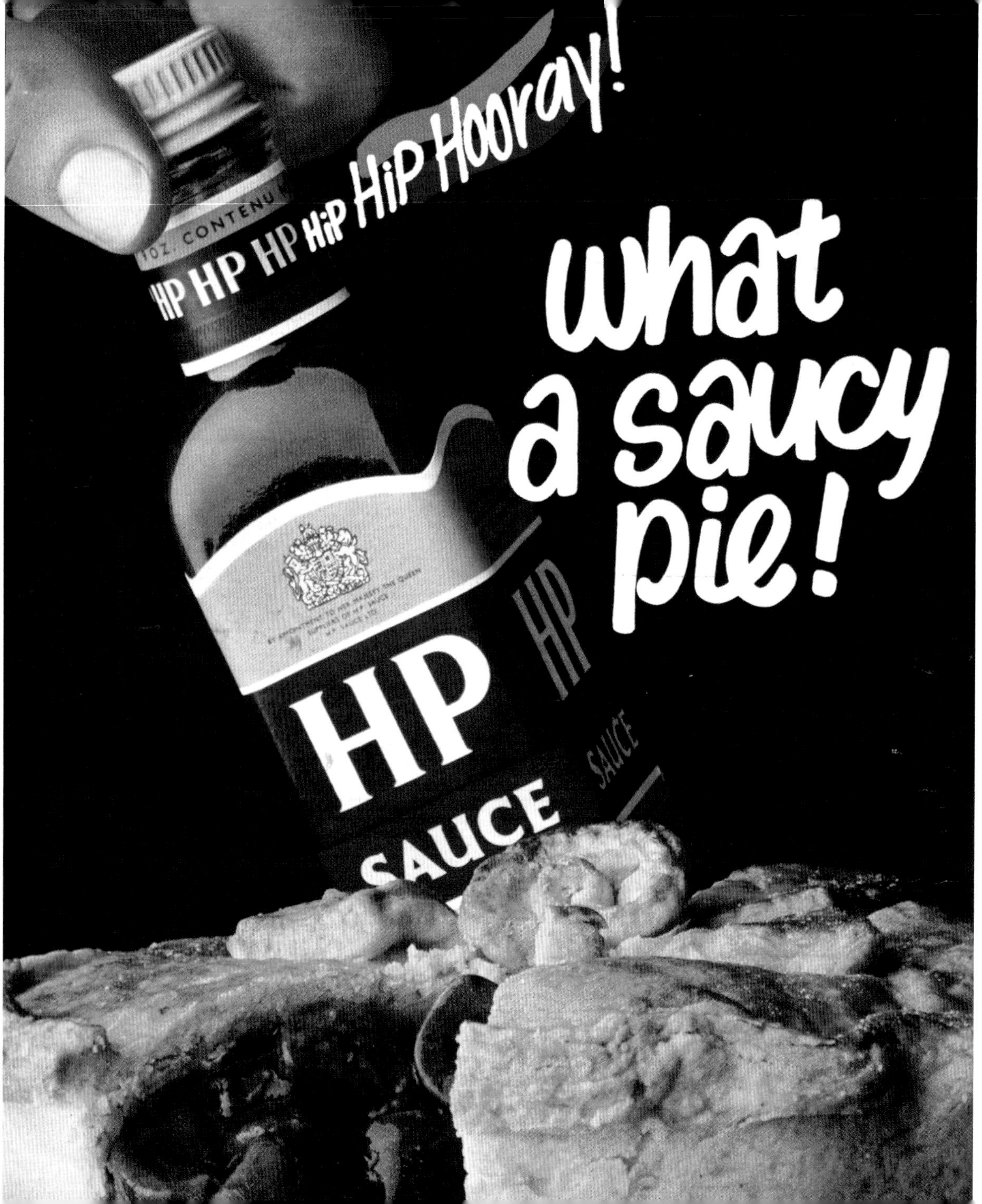
HP HP HP HiP HiP Hooray!
what a saucy pie!
HP
SAUCE
HP
SAUCE

Mulligatawny Soup

SERVES 6

1 tablespoon vegetable oil
1 onion, chopped
2 cloves garlic, finely chopped
$^1/_2$ teaspoon grated fresh ginger
$^1/_2$ teaspoon chilli powder
pinch ground cinnamon
2 teaspoons curry paste
1 carrot, peeled and chopped
1 apple, peeled, cored and
  chopped
1 large potato, peeled and diced
200g red lentils, rinsed and
  drained
1 litre chicken stock
1 tablespoon soft dark brown
  sugar
2 tablespoons HP Sauce
$^1/_2$ tablespoon lemon juice
1 tin coconut milk

Heat the oil in a large pan and gently cook the onions, garlic and ginger until just turning golden. Add the chilli, cinnamon and curry paste and cook for a further minute.

Next add the carrot, apple, potato, lentils, stock and sugar. Bring to the boil and then simmer gently for 20 minutes so that the vegetables are tender. Remove from the heat and allow to cool a little. Blend in a processor until you have a smooth purée.

Return the purée to the pan and add the HP Sauce, lemon juice and coconut milk and reheat for 5 minutes. Great served with warm naan bread and chopped boiled eggs on the side.

Left
A cheeky caption
for this late '60s
magazine advert.

Spicy Oriental Lettuce Shells

MAKES 8 STARTER PORTIONS

50g dried cellophane noodles or fine egg noodles
2 tablespoons HP Sauce
1 teaspoon chilli paste
1 teaspoon garlic purée
1 teaspoon five spice powder
1 tablespoon toasted sesame oil
2 tablespoons chopped fresh coriander
150g shredded roast chicken (reclaimed from your Sunday lunch!)
8 nest shaped crispy lettuce leaves (iceberg or similar)

Cover the noodles with boiling water and leave aside for 5 minutes for them to rehydrate. Drain, cool and roughly chop the noodles.

Whisk together the HP Sauce, chilli, garlic, spice and sesame oil until well combined and then add in the coriander.

Into the sauce tip the chicken and noodles and toss well to coat. Divide the chicken mixture between the lettuce leaves so that you can pick them up, roll them up and munch!

Right
HP Vinegar, from which our HP Sauce story begins!

HP
MALT
VINEGAR

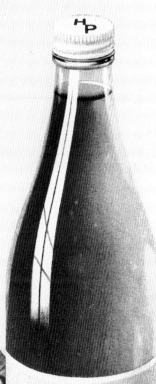

HP MALT VINEGAR

HOUSES OF PARLIAMENT

HP
MALT VINEGAR
GENUINE VINEGAR
BREWED & BOTTLED BY H.P. SAUCE LTD. ASTON CROSS, BIRMINGHAM

BRITAIN'S BEST BREW

Mexican Beef & Bean Wraps

MAKES 4 WRAPS

1 tablespoon vegetable oil
1 Spanish onion, diced
1 green chilli, finely diced
250g minced lean beef
1 tomato, roughly chopped
1 tablespoon tomato purée
1 tablespoon HP Sauce
salt and pepper
$1/2$ tin refried beans, or red kidney
   beans, drained and rinsed
1 tablespoon chopped oregano
4 flour tortillas
shredded lettuce
1 avocado, peeled, stoned and
   sliced at the last minute
50g strong Cheddar, grated
sour cream, to serve

Heat the oil in a pan and fry the onions and chilli until soft. Add in the minced beef and cook until browned. Next add the tomato, tomato purée and HP Sauce, season with salt and pepper and cook gently for 20 minutes, adding a splash of water if the mixture is too dry.

Stir the beans and oregano into the beef mixture and cook for a further 10–15 minutes, stirring occasionally, as it will be fairly dry.

Warm the tortillas in the oven according to the packet instructions. Onto each tortilla lay some shredded lettuce, a few slices of avocado, a good dollop of beef and beans, a sprinkling of cheese and a spoonful of sour cream. Fold the tortilla first up from the bottom, then wrap over the sides to form an envelope and serve.

OVER THE DECADES, THE SAUCE MIGHT HAVE CHANGED ITS LOOK, BUT IT REMAINS AS PIQUANT AND PLEASANT AS THE BATCH WHICH FIRST APPEARED ON SHOP SHELVES IN 1903.

WITCH SAUCE?

HP SAUCE...
...OF COURSE!

Pheasant with Date & Red Wine Sauce

SERVES 2

1 oven ready pheasant
1 tablespoon olive oil
500ml chicken stock
200ml red wine
2 tablespoons port
2 tablespoons HP Sauce
250g dates, halved and stoned
salt and freshly ground black
  pepper

Preheat the oven to 200C/400F/ Gas 6.

Using a sharp knife or a pair of poultry shears cut the pheasant in half down the centre and then cut each half into 2 equal portions.

Place the pheasant pieces in a large bowl. Drizzle the olive oil over them and with your hands make sure the meat is all lightly coated. Season with salt and freshly ground black pepper.

Heat a dry heavy-based frying pan. Add the pheasant pieces and sauté to colour. Turn them over and when the pieces are browned, place them in a deep roasting pan skin side down.

Put the stock, wine, port and HP Sauce into a saucepan and bring to the boil. Pour the liquid over the pheasant. Put the roasting pan in the oven and cook uncovered for 30 minutes, turning the pheasant to skin side up half way through to crisp it. Add the dates at this stage.

Remove from the oven and lift out the pheasant portions and dates, keep warm and rest for 5 minutes. Put the roasting tin on the top of the stove, turn up the heat to high and reduce the gravy to a thick sauce, this will take about 5 minutes.

Arrange the pheasant portions and dates on warmed serving plates and pour over the rich sauce.

Crab Claws with Ginger & Coriander

SERVES 4 AS A STARTER

1 tablespoon sesame oil
100g thinly sliced shallots
2 cloves garlic, finely chopped
1 tablespoon fresh ginger, peeled
  and finely diced
1 heaped teaspoon hot chilli flakes
2 tablespoons HP Sauce
2 tablespoons runny honey
1 tablespoon fish sauce
16 crab claws
chopped fresh coriander, to serve
wedges of lime, to serve
sourdough bread, to serve

Sprinkle a little oil into a wok over a medium heat and when it's hot add the shallots, garlic and ginger and stir-fry for 3–4 minutes with a pinch of salt.

Remove the wok from the heat and add the chilli flakes, stir in the HP Sauce, honey and fish sauce and then return to the heat. When the mixture is bubbling toss in the crab claws and turn them to coat heating the claws through for 2–3 minutes.

Tip out onto serving plates, scatter with coriander, add wedges of lime and warm chunks of sourdough bread.

THE BOVRIL RECIPE COLLECTION

BOVRIL

THE GUARANTEED F
OF PRIME OX I

DESIGNED & PRINTED BY NATHANIEL LLOYD & C.º QUEEN VICTORIA S.T LONDON.

RIL BO

RODUCT
EEF

THE GUA
OF

Venison, Beetroot & Red Wine Casserole

SERVES 6

1kg diced venison
2 tablespoons seasoned flour
2–3 tablespoons vegetable oil
12 shallots
12 juniper berries
1 heaped tablespoon redcurrant
   jelly
350ml red wine
1 tablespoon Bovril
12 uncooked baby beetroots,
   peeled
300ml beef stock
2 tablespoons chopped mixed
   fresh thyme and parsley

Preheat the oven to
160C/325F/Gas 3.

Put the venison into a large bowl,
sprinkle over the seasoned flour
and toss it all to coat. Heat a little
of the oil in a large frying pan and
brown off the venison in batches
without overcrowding the
pan, adding more oil as required.

Transfer the meat with a slotted
spoon to a casserole dish.

Heat the remaining oil in the frying
pan and cook the shallots for
5 minutes. Then add the juniper
berries, lightly crushed, the
redcurrant jelly, red wine, Bovril,
beetroot, stock and half the
herbs and bring up to the boil.
Pour this into the casserole
dish over the venison, stir
everything together and
cover and cook for
2 hours.

Remove the casserole from the
oven, check the seasoning, scatter
with the remaining fresh herbs
and serve with some delicious
celeriac mash.

Staggering Stories of STRENGTH

Cheesy Chicken Tagliatelle

SERVES 2–3

3 teaspoons Bovril
300ml hot milk
50g unsalted butter
3 tablespoons olive oil
1 red onion, roughly chopped
2 cloves garlic, finely diced
1 tablespoon tomato purée
1 teaspoon mixed herbs
350g chicken breasts, cut roughly
  into 1.5cm chunks
100ml white wine
300g tagliatelle

salt and freshly ground black
  pepper
100g Parmesan, grated
fresh parsley, chopped

First, dissolve 2 teaspoons of the Bovril in the hot milk. Heat the butter and oil over a medium heat in a frying pan and add the onion, garlic, tomato purée and mixed herbs. Mix well together. When the onion begins to colour, add the chicken and cook for 10 minutes. Turn up the heat and pour in the wine and the milk with Bovril.

Season well and simmer for 15 minutes or until the sauce has thickened and the chicken is well coated and tender. You may need to add a drop of water to get the right consistency for the tagliatelle sauce. Meanwhile, bring some water to the boil in a separate pan and add the last teaspoon of Bovril. Slide in the tagliatelle and cook for 5–6 minutes or until it's *al dente*. Drain the pasta and serve in warm pasta bowls. Spoon over the chicken sauce adding grated Parmesan and a flourish of parsley.

Hard of Hearing

In 2007, so-called Ironman of Leicester, Manjit Singh, pulled off the astonishing feat of towing a seven-and-a-half-tonne aircraft nearly four metres using just clamps and rope... attached to his ears! The stunt, at East Midlands Airport in Derby, resulted in 57-year-old Singh setting a world record – he has 25 stacked against his name. It took Singh a long time to psych up for the attempt, and then ten worrying seconds of stubborn resistance before the 'Jetstream 41' passenger plane slowly started to inch forward down the runway. When he's not piling a load onto his lobes, he's busy setting or breaking other world records which involve pulling double-decker buses with his hair, doing push-ups on his fingertips and inflating weather balloons using raw lung power.

Bovril & Rice Bread

For the rice
60g rice, uncooked

For the rest of the loaf
30g unsalted butter
1 medium onion, finely chopped
500g strong plain white flour
7g active yeast (or one sachet)
1 teaspoon sea salt
1 tablespoon fresh thyme leaves
1 tablespoon Bovril dissolved in
   150ml boiling water
150ml cold water

Boil the rice for 7 minutes until cooked through but not too soft. Tip into a sieve, rinse with water from a freshly boiled kettle and set aside.

While the rice is cooking, heat the butter in a small frying pan and sauté the onion until soft, but not browned. In a large bowl, combine the flour, yeast and salt, then mix in the rice, onion and thyme.

Add the cold water to the Bovril and stir into the other ingredients. It will be a little stickier than normal. Knead for 4–5 minutes (either by hand or using a freestanding mixer) adding a little extra flour if necessary. Leave to rise in a warm place until doubled in size.

Knock back the dough by gently pushing your fist into the centre and knead again for a couple of minutes. Form into a loaf and transfer to an oiled tin. Leave to prove again for about an hour until well risen.

While the loaf is on its second proving pre-heat your oven to 220C/425F/Gas 7. Put in the loaf and bake for 10 minutes then reduce the heat to 200C/400F/Gas 6 for a further 20 minutes.

The loaf is cooked if it sounds hollow when rapped on the bottom.

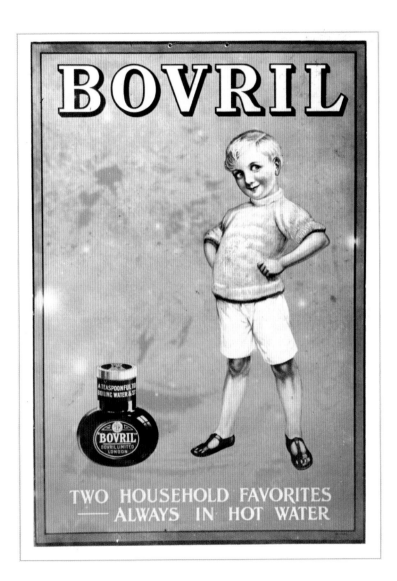

Left
In need of hot water!
c. end of 19th Century

Almond Brittle

**TO BE EATEN ON ITS
OWN OR TO DECORATE
8 DESSERTS**

175g golden caster sugar
2 tablespoons golden syrup
4 tablespoons warm water
1 teaspoon Bovril
50g butter
$\frac{1}{4}$ teaspoon smoked paprika
150g toasted flaked almonds

In a heavy-based pan over a medium heat mix together the sugar, golden syrup, warm water and the Bovril. Cook until the mixture is a light golden brown, which should take between 10 and 15 minutes. Remove from the heat and add the butter, paprika and almonds and mix them all together.

Pour the mixture out onto a prepared baking sheet and spread out about $\frac{1}{2}$ cm thick. Leave it to cool completely and then break up into pieces.

ATCHOO!

The power of a good sneeze can exceed 100 miles per hour. The potency of a sneeze can be attributed to the number of organs involved in the process; not just the nose and mouth, but the muscles of the face, throat and chest.

Consommé

SERVES 6

750g shin of beef, diced
2 tablespoons Bovril dissolved in
    300ml boiling water
1.5 litres water
1 medium onion, roughly chopped
1 medium carrot, roughly chopped
1 bay leaf
sea salt and freshly ground black
    pepper
small wine glass of dry sherry
1 or 2 egg whites with their shells,
    to clarify (optional)

Put all the ingredients except the seasoning, sherry and the egg whites into a large saucepan. Bring to the boil, removing any scum that forms during cooking. Lower the heat so that the liquid is just at simmering point and cover. Leave to cook for at least an hour.

Strain through a sieve lined with muslin. If not sufficiently clear return to the pan with the unwhisked egg whites and the shells and simmer for a further 10–15 minutes.

Sieve again and return to a clean pan. Add the sherry and season to taste.

This is excellent served with a garnish of freshly cooked vegetables cut into julienne strips and some warm crusty bread.

Bovine cuteness 1915

Hummus, Rocket & Red Onion Wrap

MAKES A BATCH OF HUMMUS FOR 8–10

225g chickpeas, soaked overnight
in cold water
2 bay leaves
sprig of thyme
1 onion, quartered
2 teaspoons Bovril
6 black peppercorns
3 cloves fresh garlic, peeled and
diced
3 tablespoons light tahini (sesame
paste)
4 tablespoons olive oil
3 tablespoons freshly squeezed
lemon juice
4–5 tablespoons chickpea water
$\frac{1}{2}$ teaspoon ground cumin

For each wrap
1 soft flour tortilla
2 tablespoons hummus
$\frac{1}{4}$ small red onion, finely sliced
small handful fresh rocket or
watercress
1 heaped teaspoon natural
yoghurt

Drain and rinse the chickpeas, tip into a large saucepan and cover with fresh water. Add the bay leaves, thyme, onion quarters, Bovril and peppercorns and bring to the boil. Boil rapidly for 10 minutes then turn down the heat and simmer for 1 hour until the chickpeas are soft. Drain, reserving at least 5 tablespoons of the chickpea water and allow to cool. Remove the bay leaves and any stems of thyme and put the chickpeas, onion and peppercorns into a food processor adding the garlic, tahini, half the olive oil, the lemon juice, half the chickpea water and the cumin. Blitz to a coarse purée. Now, with the motor running, add the remaining olive oil and remaining chickpea water until you have the right consistency.

You may need to add more chickpea water – you want to end up with a firm, textured consistency. Check and adjust the seasoning to your taste. For the wraps, simply warm the tortillas and spread with the hummus. Top with the red onion and the rocket and finish with a dollop of yoghurt. Roll up the wrap and devour.

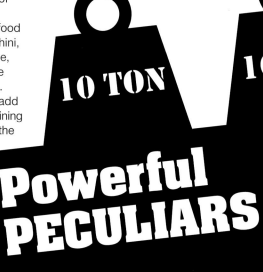

10 TON   10

Powerful
PECULIARS

Beef and Mushroom Stroganoff

SERVES 4–6

500g rump steak, trimmed of any
  fat
90g unsalted butter
500g button mushrooms, thinly
  sliced
2 large onions, finely sliced
1 dessertspoon Bovril dissolved in
  300ml boiling water
300ml soured cream
nutmeg
sea salt and freshly ground black
  pepper

Cut the steak into thin strips about $\frac{1}{2}$cm wide and no more than 6cm long.

Melt the butter in a large sauté pan and cook the onions gently until they are very soft but not browned, then remove from the pan and keep to one side. Turn up the heat and add the meat a few pieces at a time and brown. Set aside with the onions.

When all the meat has been browned, reduce the heat, add the mushrooms and cook until starting to soften. You may need to add some extra butter at this point. Return the onion and meat to the pan and pour in the Bovril stock. Bring to the boil and simmer everything together for 10 minutes.

Season and then add the soured cream and a grating of nutmeg. Bring just up to simmering point and then serve with boiled or steamed rice and a green salad.

Strong horny type

The strongest creature on earth? Hmmm... The elephant? Nope, not even close. Whilst our trunked friends can carry loads of up to several tonnes, a proportional evaluation of a very tiny compatriot of Dumbo's reveals strength of an extraordinary kind. Whilst an African elephant can carry about 25 per cent of its own body weight, the rhinoceros beetle can carry an eye-bulging 850 times its own weight (that's the equivalent of Dumbo simultaneously piggy-backing 850 of his brothers and sisters). Such is the rhinoceros beetle's strength that he can forage through the leaves and foliage on jungle floors and burrow underground to safety. Despite their immense power, they live on a modest diet of rotting fruit and sap – not a protein shake in sight!

Sausage Jambalaya

SERVES 4

2 tablespoons olive oil
2 onions, chopped
2 spring onions, chopped
1 green pepper, deseeded and
  diced
1 tablespoon chopped fresh
  parsley
400g tin chopped tomatoes
1 tablespoon tomato ketchup
2 cloves garlic, finely diced
$1/_2$ teaspoon dried mint
1 tablespoon Bovril, dissolved in
  300ml warm water
300g long grain rice
salt
400g smoked sausage, cut into
  chunks
$1/_4$ teaspoon cayenne pepper

Heat the oil in a deep frying pan
and sauté the onions, spring
onions, pepper and parsley for
5 minutes.

Add the tomatoes, tomato ketchup,
garlic, mint and Bovril stock and
bring up to a simmer. Add the rice,
a pinch of salt, the sausage and
cayenne and then enough water to
cover the ingredients by about 3cm.

Cook until at least half of the liquid
has been absorbed and then cover
and simmer over a very low heat for
45 minutes, resisting the temptation
to lift the lid until the end when
you will have a delicious red
jambalaya.

The spider is one of the world's finest unsung engineers. Their webs are powerful prey-catching tools. The strongest web belongs to the Golden Orb Web Spider, which can be 6 metres tall and 2 metres wide and last for several years.

Bovril Lamb Kebabs

MAKES 10 BIG KEBABS

1kg lamb neck fillet, cut into
  2.5cm chunks
2 teaspoons Bovril
20 small dried apricots
2 red peppers, deseeded and cut
  into 3cm square pieces
20 cherry tomatoes
salt and pepper
chopped fresh mint, to garnish

You will need 10 wooden or metal skewers

Place the diced lamb into a dish and spoon over the Bovril, turning the pieces over until they are all coated. Cover and leave for at least one hour.

When you are ready, lift the lamb from the marinade retaining any juices.

Onto each kebab skewer thread a tomato, then a piece of lamb, then a piece of red pepper, then lamb again, an apricot piece and finally lamb. Prepare 10 skewers. Lay them onto a foil covered grill and pour over any remaining marinade. Season well.

Cook under a hot grill until the lamb is browned outside but still pink inside. Serve on a bed of fluffy rice with a shower of mint.

A beef drink bequeathed

John Lawson Johnston was a dietetic expert. In 1874, three years after the French had lost the Franco-Prussian war, Johnston won a contract to supply one million tins of beef – three years' worth of provisions – to the French government. They believed that poor rations for their soldiers had been a chief factor in the defeat of their country. Johnston moved back to Canada, where he felt he would be better able to meet the supply demand for fulfilling the order. Ten years prior to taking on the contract, Johnston had concocted a recipe for a liquid form of beef. A man not prone to pretension, he gave his recipe the name of 'Johnston's Fluid Beef'. Now back in Canada, he began to experiment further with this broth. He used beef

Savoury Bread and Butter Pudding

SERVES 4

2 large slices of slightly stale white
    bread, crusts removed
butter, for spreading
Bovril, for spreading
90g mature Cheddar cheese,
    grated
3 large eggs
600ml full-fat milk

Preheat the oven to
150C/300F/Gas 2.

Spread the bread with softened
butter and then Bovril.

Cut into quarters and arrange half
of the bread in an ovenproof dish
sprinkling over half the cheese.
Repeat.

Beat the eggs with the milk and
strain over the bread and cheese.

Leave to stand for at least
10 minutes before baking for
$1\frac{1}{4}$ hours until just firm. Increase
the heat toward the end of cooking
time to brown the top or place
under a pre-heated grill for a few
minutes to crisp.

parts that were left over from the French government's tinned beef order, and began to reinvent the broth as a concentrate. He hit on a winning formula, and trialled selling a hot beef drink at Montreal's freezing-cold winter carnival. A phenomenon was born. Irony struck a few years later, when fire destroyed the business premises that he used to create the very drink that had brought an unprecedented glow to a city that had been so very, very cold. Johnston returned to London and started again, setting up shop in Shoreditch, and beginning to produce and sell the concentrate once more. It could be purchased in pubs and grocery stores. By 1886, a shorter and somewhat more appealing name had been found: Bovril. He formed the word by combining the rather exotic-sounding *Vril* (picked up from a science fiction novel of the day and referring to an 'electric fluid' with restorative powers) and *bos* (the Latin for cow). He registered the name the following year, and just two years later, more than 3,000 bars and public houses up and down the country could be found to serve Johnston's brilliant beef broth.

Yell for Bovril

Bovril
good and beef

Bovril

Bovril
Warms & Cheers

EUROPEAN CHAMPIONSHIP
HENRI DELAUNAY CUP—QUALIFYING TI

England
V
Northern
Ireland

WEDNESDAY NOVEMBER 22nd 19
KICK-OFF 7.45 p.m.

WEMBLEY

Peanut & Strawberry Ring

SERVES 4–6

You will need a 20cm ring mould

1 packet strawberry jelly
1 banana, sliced
100g peanuts, chopped
1 teaspoon Bovril
250g crushed pineapple, fresh or
   tinned
200ml double cream

Make the jelly according to the packet instructions adding the Bovril and then refrigerate. Allow to part set and then fold in the bananas and peanuts. Spoon into a ring mould and continue chilling until firm – about 4 hours.

Dip the ring mould into a bowl of hot water and then turn out onto a large round plate.

Whip the cream into stiff peaks and fold in the pineapple. Fill the centre with the pineapples and cream – really yummy.

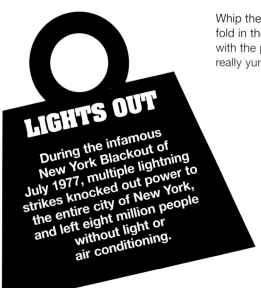

LIGHTS OUT
During the infamous New York Blackout of July 1977, multiple lightning strikes knocked out power to the entire city of New York, and left eight million people without light or air conditioning.

Chilli Beef with Cornbread Topping

SERVES 4

For the chilli
3–4 tablespoons groundnut or
   sunflower oil
1 onion, finely chopped
1 red pepper, cut into strips
1 large clove garlic, chopped
500g minced beef
1 teaspoon ground coriander
1 teaspoon ground cumin
2 or 3 small hot red or green
   chillies, deseeded and finely
   chopped
400g tin chopped tomatoes
2 tablespoons tomato purée
1 dessertspoon Bovril
1 tin red kidney beans, drained
   and rinsed
freshly ground black pepper

For the cornbread
240g cornmeal
$\frac{1}{2}$ teaspoon fine sea salt
1 tablespoon plain flour
2 teaspoons baking powder
1 large egg
275ml buttermilk
handful of grated Cheddar cheese

Heat the oil in a large saucepan and fry the onion, pepper and garlic. Add the minced beef using a wooden spoon to break up any lumps. Cook until just browned.

Add the coriander, cumin and chillies to the meat mixture then tip in the tomatoes and add the tomato purée, the Bovril and kidney beans. Bring to the boil and simmer for 30–40 minutes adding a little hot water if the mixture looks as if it is drying out too much. You need a moist but not sloppy mixture.

Season with freshly ground black pepper and sea salt (if necessary) then turn into a heatproof dish and heat the oven to 200C/400F/Gas 6.

To make the cornbread, mix the dry ingredients in a large bowl then add the egg beaten with the buttermilk.

Pour or drop in spoonfuls over the chilli mixture and sprinkle over some grated Cheddar. Bake for about 30 minutes until golden and bubbling.

Four-Nut Roast

SERVES 4

300g mixed nuts (chestnuts,
   walnuts, almonds and cashews)
4 shallots, finely diced
400g tin chopped tomatoes
1 free-range egg, beaten
150g Emmental cheese
1 teaspoon dried mixed sage and
   mint
1 tablespoon chopped fresh flat
   leaf parsley
2 level teaspoons Bovril mixed
   with 1 tablespoon boiling water

grated zest of half a lemon
salt and pepper

Preheat the oven to 180C/350F/
Gas 4.

Place the mixed nuts on a baking
tray and put in the oven for
8–10 minutes until golden – taking
care not to burn them. Let them
cool and then blitz in a processor
until ground.

Place the ground nuts in a large
bowl add all the other ingredients,
finally seasoning with salt and
pepper. Mix everything together well.

Line a 1lb loaf tin with baking
parchment and spoon in the nutty
mixture and bake for 1 hour until
firm to the touch and golden.

Leave to cool for 10 minutes and
then turn out the nut loaf. Delicious
with cranberry sauce and fresh
peppery watercress.

Bless thy Bovril

Not many storecupboard stocks and spreads come with Papal approval, but an audacious
advert from the end of the nineteenth century depicts the Pope seated on throne and gripping
a steaming mug of hot Bovril in one hand and blessing our beloved beef extract with the
other! The advert was emblazoned with, 'The Two Infallible Powers – The Pope & Bovril'!
And Bovril has remained infallible: worshipping of its meaty goodness has continued
unabated for a hundred years and more! (See illustration over page.)

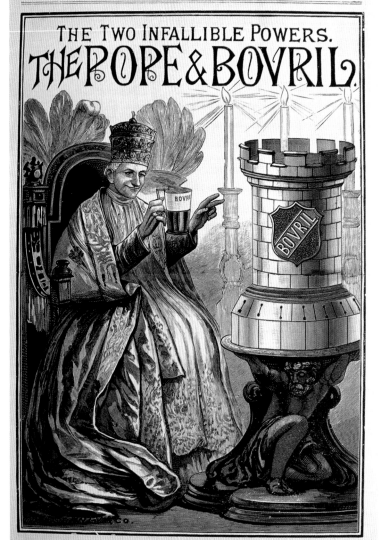

THE ILLUSTRATED SPORTING AND DRAMATIC NEWS. March 1, 1890.—739

The two infallible powers!1890

Pork Chops with Brandied Tomato Gravy

SERVES 2

vegetable oil, for frying
2 pork chops
25g butter
1 tablespoon plain flour
small tin of chopped tomatoes
1 tin consommé
1 tablespoon brandy
1 teaspoon Bovril
chopped parsley, to garnish

Preheat the oven to 180C/350F/ Gas 4. Heat the oil in a frying pan and brown the chops for 2–3 minutes on each side. Transfer the chops to the oven and cook for 8 minutes.

Melt the butter in a pan and then add the flour. Cook for 1 minute, stirring constantly. Add the remaining ingredients, bring up to the boil and then simmer for 5 minutes until the sauce has thickened.

Remove the chops from the oven and onto warm plates. Pour over the rich gravy and serve scattered with parsley.

Chinese-Style Pork with Bovril Sauce

SERVES 4

2 teaspoons light soy sauce
500g pork shoulder, cubed
2 tablespoons groundnut or sunflower oil
2 teaspoons freshly grated ginger
3 cloves garlic, finely grated
1 medium onion, finely sliced
1 red pepper, deseeded and finely sliced
1 rounded teaspoon Bovril dissolved in 300ml boiling water
2 teaspoons cornflour

Sprinkle the soy sauce over the pork pieces in a shallow dish and leave to marinate for half an hour.

Heat the oil in a wok and fry the pork until cooked through, then set aside.

Next, fry the ginger, garlic, onion and pepper. Cook until the vegetables are just tender.

Return the pork to the pan then pour over the Bovril stock. Bring to the boil and simmer for 3–4 minutes so that the meat is thoroughly hot.

Mix the cornflour with three tablespoons of water in a small basin and add to the wok. Stir the contents of the pan until the sauce has thickened. Serve with steamed rice.

Other vegetables can be added like broccoli, spinach, pak choi, bean sprouts and green beans and you can also substitute the pork shoulder for thin slices of rump steak or chicken.

POTENT PONG

The dubious honour of the world's smelliest cheese went to a French effort called Vieux Boulogne, made from cow's milk by cheesemaker Philippe Olivier, and judged by an olfactory panel at Cranfield University in 2004.

PROMOTES THAT SINGING FEELING
–The "accompaniment" of perfect health

Left and Right
Bovril's pyjama-clad advocate of the 1930s

Bovril Noodle Soup

SERVES 2

1 dessertspoon Bovril dissolved in 600ml boiling water
6 slices of fresh ginger the thickness of a pound coin
1 clove garlic, thinly sliced
2 star anise
1 tablespoon nam pla (fish sauce)
freshly ground black pepper
60g egg or rice noodles
120g rump or rib-eye steak, cut into very thin strips
fresh coriander
4 finely sliced spring onions
small handful of beansprouts

Simmer the Bovril stock with the ginger, garlic and star anise for 30 minutes, topping up with extra boiling water as necessary. Strain the liquid, discarding the spices, and garlic and then stir in the nam pla.

Add the noodles to the stock and simmer for a few minutes until just cooked.

Ladle the noodles and stock into warm bowls into which you have placed the strips of meat, which will cook in the heat from the liquid.

Scatter over a little freshly chopped coriander, the spring onions and some beansprouts.

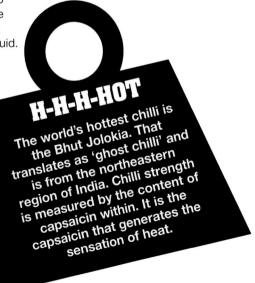

H-H-H-HOT
The world's hottest chilli is the Bhut Jolokia. That translates as 'ghost chilli' and is from the northeastern region of India. Chilli strength is measured by the content of capsaicin within. It is the capsaicin that generates the sensation of heat.

Rabbit Stew

SERVES 4

1 rabbit (approx. 1.5kg)
2 tablespoons seasoned flour
2 tablespoons vegetable oil
200g unsmoked streaky bacon,
    diced
2 onions, roughly chopped
2 sticks of celery, diced
400g chestnut mushrooms, sliced
1 tablespoon Bovril mixed with
    200ml boiling water
300ml dry white wine
few sprigs fresh thyme
2 bay leaves
salt and black pepper
2 slices white bread, crusts
    removed
1 tablespoon Dijon mustard
2 tablespoons brandy
4 tablespoons sour cream

Preheat the oven to 160C/325F/ Gas 3.

Cut the rabbit up into portions and put into a large bowl. Dust with the seasoned flour and turn the pieces to coat all over. Then shake them in a sieve or colander to release the excess flour.

Heat the oil in a large flameproof casserole, add the bacon and onion and cook for a few minutes to release the bacon juices. Add the rabbit pieces and gently brown all over. When this is done add the celery, mushrooms, Bovril stock, wine and herbs and season with salt and pepper.

Spread the bread slices with the mustard and arrange them over the top of the casserole, mustard side down. Put on the lid and pop it into the oven to cook for 1–1$^1/_2$ hours or until the meat is tender.

Remove the casserole from the oven and stir to disperse the bread throughout the juices. Cook, covered, for a further 30 minutes.

Take out the casserole and add the sour cream then leave aside to rest for 10 minutes. When you are ready to serve heat the brandy in a small pan, place the casserole in the centre of the table, flame the brandy and pour it over the rabbit stew – wow!

Spaghetti alla Carrettiera

SERVES 4

2 tablespoons olive oil
50g pancetta, diced
1 clove garlic, finely diced
300g mixed wild mushrooms,
  wiped and roughly sliced
1 level teaspoon Bovril
100ml vermouth (or white wine)
300g dried spaghetti
50g canned tuna, flaked
chopped fresh parsley
freshly grated Parmesan, to serve
salt and black pepper

Heat the olive oil in a large frying pan and gently sauté the pancetta and garlic until the fat on the pancetta has become translucent. Add the mushrooms, Bovril, season with plenty of black pepper, then pour in the vermouth. Cook for 5 minutes.

Heat a large pan of salted water. When boiling, add the pasta and cook for 8–10 minutes until just al dente.

Add the tuna to the mushrooms and bacon, gently mixing it with the other sauce ingredients without breaking it up too much and then scatter the parsley all over. Take off the heat and cover to keep warm while you drain the pasta.

Serve the spaghetti in warm bowls with the sauce spooned over and serve with a bowl of freshly grated Parmesan cheese. The Italians do not traditionally eat Parmesan with fish but it does lend itself rather well to this dish.

The Beautiful Game

Bovril has a long association with football. Traditionally, the winter terraces would be packed with thermos-clutching fanatics, cheering on their team whilst drinking down their warming cup of beef tea. In the 1960s, Chelsea and England striker Jimmy Greaves became the face of Bovril, proclaiming he 'wouldn't be without it'. The first link between football and Bovril was in 1898, when the FA-Cup winning team of that year, Nottingham Forest, put their name (and attributed part of their success!) to the nutritional qualities of the drink. The drink was and still is immensely popular across Scottish football grounds (after all, its inventor was a Scot!).

BOVRIL and a clever Cook.

(One of the prize-winners in the Bovril Competition)

A key component in a cook's craft! c. end of 19th Century.

Steak & Kidney Pudding

SERVES 4

450g diced chuck steak
150g ox kidney, cores removed
   and diced
1 onion, finely chopped
salt and freshly ground black
   pepper
1 teaspoon fresh thyme leaves
$1/4$ teaspoon mustard powder
1 tablespoon plain flour
1 tablespoon Bovril dissolved in
   150ml warm water

For the suet pastry
225g self-raising flour
salt and freshly ground black
   pepper
100g shredded beef suet
6–8 tablespoons cold water

You will need a $1^1/_2$ pint lightly
greased pudding basin

Put the steak and kidney in a bowl together with the onion, thyme and mustard powder then season with salt and plenty of black pepper. Turn the meat to mix well and set aside.

Sift the flour into a large bowl and season with a good pinch of salt and some black pepper. Add the suet and mix well, then gradually add enough of the water to create a soft, elastic dough.

Turn the dough out onto a lightly floured board and cut off about a quarter of it for the lid. Roll out the remaining dough sufficient to line the pudding basin with about a 1cm overhang.

Next, add the flour to the meat mixture and ensure it is coated well. Put it all in a sieve and shake off any excess flour. Add the meat to the pudding basin without pushing it down and then pour in the Bovril stock – enough to fill two-thirds of the way up the meat.

Roll out the remaining suet pastry to create a lid over the meat and then fold the border over and press the pastry together to seal. Cover the bowl with a double layer of foil with a pleat in the middle to allow for expansion and tie this in place with some string. Steam the pudding for 4 hours, topping up with boiling water as required.

To serve, turn out onto a warm plate and cut out wedges of steaming pud.

Bovril and Molasses Pecan Pie

SERVES 6

500g pack short crust pastry
170g light brown sugar
170g molasses
20g melted butter
4 eggs, lightly beaten
1 teaspoon Bovril
1 teaspoon vanilla essence
325g chopped pecans

The pastry must be defrosted completely if you buy frozen.

Pre-heat the oven to 200C/400F/ Gas 6.

Roll out the pastry on a lightly floured surface to about the thickness of a £1 coin and line a 20cm ovenproof flan dish with the pastry, trimming the edges. Put it in the refrigerator for 10 minutes.

In the meantime, in a heavy based pan over a medium heat blend the brown sugar, molasses, butter, eggs, Bovril and vanilla. Cook for a few minutes until all the ingredients are mixed well together then stir in the pecans.

Take the pastry-lined dish from the refrigerator and pour in the pecan mixture. Cook for 10 minutes and then reduce the temperature to 180C/350F/Gas 4 for a further 10 minutes or until the pie has set.

Take it out of the oven and let it cool before serving topped with fresh seasonal fruit.

WED LOCK!

In 2006, the male and female holders of the respective Arm Wrestling Champion of the World titles were Californian husband-and-wife team Allen and Carolyn Fisher. They have been holding hands for over twenty years!

Lemon & Thyme Roast Chicken

SERVES 4–6

1 free-range chicken (about 1.5kg)
2 teaspoons Bovril
1 lemon
freshly ground black pepper
8 rashers smoked streaky bacon
3 cloves garlic, peeled and halved
3 shallots, peeled and halved
2 sprigs fresh thyme

Preheat the oven to 180C/350F/
Gas 4.

Place the chicken in a roasting pan and spread the whole bird with a thin layer of Bovril. Cut the lemon in half and squeeze the juice over the Bovril. Now cover the bird with lashings of freshly milled black pepper and finally lay the rashers of smoked bacon over all of it. Fill the inside of the chicken with the garlic, shallots and thyme and the

remainder of the lemon.

When the oven is up to temperature pop the chicken in and cook for 1½ hours, removing the bacon after 1 hour but keeping it beside the chicken in the pan.

Serve with crispy pan-fried cabbage and baby roast potatoes.

Staggering
Stories of
STRENGTH

Lentil Dhal with Ginger and Coriander

SERVES 4–6

2 tablespoons vegetable oil (or to be totally authentic 60g ghee)
1 medium onion, diced
1 clove garlic, peeled and diced
1 fresh chilli, finely diced
2cm fresh ginger, finely diced
2 tomatoes, skinned and roughly chopped
1 teaspoon turmeric
1 teaspoon cumin seeds
2 teaspoons Bovril
hot water

250g red lentils, washed and drained
2 tablespoons fresh chopped coriander

Heat the oil (or ghee) in a large pan over a medium heat. Add the onion, garlic, chilli and ginger and fry until the onion just begins to colour. Then add the tomatoes, turmeric, cumin, Bovril and a couple of tablespoons of water then add the lentils and turn up the heat to give a rolling boil.

Cook for 5 minutes and then turn the heat to low and let it simmer for 15–20 minutes adding a little more hot water to achieve the right consistency. When it's ready, stir in the fresh coriander and serve.

Thick-necked

Englishman John Evans is a professional 'head balancer'. At more than two metres tall and over twenty-four stone in weight, he's not a man of insignificant size. But the vital statistic is his 24-inch neck. It has enabled him to steady books, bricks and beer barrels using just his anatomical attic for support. He has also balanced people and has branched out into speedboats, quad bikes and automobiles.

His most well-known challenge was balancing a Mini weighing 162kg on his head. A mere sniff of wind can spell disaster for this Derbyshire-born master of stability, since it's only his neck that keeps such huge weights safely propped up. A sway, trip or tumble could cripple him as the loads that he dares to balance are more extreme than any below-neck musculature could possibly cope with. Evans is the holder of 32 World Records and has raised thousands and thousands of pounds for charitable causes.

Cheese and Onion Frittata

SERVES 2-3

4 eggs
50g single cream
freshly ground black pepper
pinch of chilli powder
2 tablespoons Bovril
1 tablespoon butter
1 tablespoon olive oil
2 medium onions, peeled and
  roughly chopped
2 medium potatoes, peeled and
  thinly sliced
50g grated strong mature Cheddar
  cheese
1 heaped teaspoon chopped
  parsley

Pre-heat the grill to medium hot.

In a mixing bowl whisk the eggs, cream, pepper, chilli powder and Bovril. This needs to be light and frothy.

Put the butter and oil into a large frying pan over a medium heat and add the onions and potatoes and fry for 10–12 minutes until they begin to colour.

Pour the egg mixture over the onions and potatoes and cook for 3–4 minutes over a low heat then sprinkle the cheese and parsley over the top. Cook for a further couple of minutes and then put the pan under the grill for another 2 minutes until the cheese melts and just starts to bubble.

Cut into wedges and serve with dressed mixed leaves.

BOVRIL

Bovril soon puts a man on his feet

Right
Bovine invigoration! 1915

Roasted Red Pepper Risotto

Serves 2–3

2 large red peppers
2 tablespoons olive oil
1 teaspoon Bovril
600ml chicken stock
$\frac{1}{2}$ teaspoon ground cumin
$\frac{1}{2}$ teaspoon ground coriander
$\frac{1}{4}$ teaspoon chilli powder
2 leeks, white parts only, finely
   sliced
1 clove garlic
200g Arborio rice
1 tablespoon butter
2 tablespoons grated Parmesan
   cheese

Preheat the oven to 180C/350F/
Gas 4.

Halve and deseed the peppers,
discarding any pith. Heat
1 tablespoon of the olive oil and
stir in the Bovril. Use this to brush
the peppers all over and then put
them in a baking tin in the oven for
15–20 minutes until just beginning
to soften and char. Remove the
peppers, allow to cool a little,
cut into chunks and leave aside.

In a small pan bring the chicken
stock to a simmer then add the
cumin, coriander and chilli.

While this is simmering, heat the
remaining oil and the butter in a
heavy based frying pan and, when
sizzling, add the leeks and sauté for
5 minutes. Then add the garlic and
rice and cook for 1 minute, stirring
all the time. Next add half the stock
and all of the peppers, turn the heat
down to medium, and keep stirring.
Once the liquid is almost absorbed,
still stirring occasionally, gradually
add more stock, a little at a time,
until the rice is tender and creamy
but not dry (you may not need all of
the stock). Remove the pan from
the heat, stir in the cheese and
serve at once.

10 TON 10 TON 10 TON

Powerful
PECULIARS

American Meatloaf

Serves 4–6

30g unsalted butter
1 medium onion, finely chopped
750g minced beef
1 dessertspoon Bovril
1 large free-range egg
120g fresh white breadcrumbs
2 tablespoons chopped parsley
1 tablespoon thyme leaves
 sea salt and freshly ground
        black pepper

Pre heat the oven to 180C/350F/Gas 4.

Melt the butter in a small pan and cook the onion until soft, but not browned.

Combine all the remaining ingredients in a large bowl, add the onion, mixing well, and turn into a greased loaf tin.

Bake for about $1\frac{1}{2}$ hours basting occasionally with stock made from dissolving 1 further teaspoon of Bovril in 150ml boiling water.

Allow to cool a little before turning out to serve.

TON

Strong to the finish

Does spinach make you strong? Well, we have a cartoon character and a data entry error to thank for perpetuating one of the most commonly believed myths in food. Popeye was the heroic, spinach-guzzling Sailorman whose redoubtable physical strength was put down to the gallons of canned green leaves he consumed. But it was some sixty years prior to Popeye's first comic-strip outing, way back in 1870, that one man's mistake was accepted for fact. A German scientist, Dr E. von Wolf, was conducting a study into the iron content of the vegetable. In recording his findings, von Wolf contrived to misplace a decimal point and thus inflated the strength-giving properties of spinach to ten times its actual value! Broccoli and cauliflower actually have a higher iron content.

Moroccan Stuffed Leg of Lamb

SERVES 6–8

60g pine nuts
150g cous cous
250ml boiling water
1 vegetable stock cube
100g frozen petit pois
6 ready to eat dried prunes,
    stoned and roughly chopped
small handful fresh mint, chopped
salt and pepper
boned leg of lamb
2 tablespoons Bovril

Preheat the oven to 180C/350F/ Gas 4.

Spread the pine nuts on a baking sheet and toast them in the oven for 5 minutes until golden. Remove and leave to cool.

Put the cous cous into a bowl. Combine the boiling water and stock cube, stir well then pour it over the cous cous. Leave for 5 minutes and then fluff it up with a fork. Add the peas, prunes, mint and pine nuts, season well and combine all the ingredients.

Spread the lamb out flat on a board and spread half of the Bovril all over the inside of the lamb. Pile the stuffing down the centre of the leg of lamb and then bring up the meat

from the sides. Tie securely into a roll. (Any unused stuffing can be rolled into golf-sized balls and added to the roasting tin for the last half-hour of cooking.)

Put the lamb into a roasting tin and cook for 1–1$\frac{1}{2}$ hours, depending on how you like your lamb cooked. Halfway through the cooking time remove the lamb from the oven, spoon out a couple of tablespoons of the juices and mix with the remaining Bovril. Baste the lamb with these meaty juices and continue cooking.

When the lamb is cooked to your liking, remove it from the oven and leave to stand in a warm dish for 10 minutes to relax the meat before serving in thick, juicy slices.

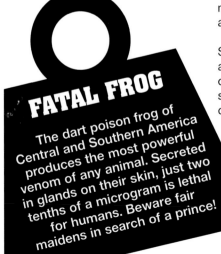

FATAL FROG

The dart poison frog of Central and Southern America produces the most powerful venom of any animal. Secreted in glands on their skin, just two tenths of a microgram is lethal for humans. Beware fair maidens in search of a prince!

Chopper to the rescue!
1958

Oatcakes

MAKES 16 OATCAKES

115g medium oatmeal
1 teaspoon sea salt
115g plain flour
55g lard or butter
1 rounded dessertspoon Bovril

For the egg wash
1 egg beaten with a little milk

Preheat the oven to 180C/350F/ Gas 4.

Mix the oatmeal, salt and flour together in a bowl and rub in the fat as if making pastry. Dissolve the Bovril in three tablespoons of hot water. Add to the other ingredients and mix well. You may need to add a little extra water to give a soft but not sticky dough.

Roll the dough out thinly and cut into rounds using a 7.5cm plain cutter. Arrange the rounds on baking sheets lined with parchment and brush with the egg glaze.

Bake in the centre of the oven for 10 minutes. Remove from the oven and egg wash again. Return to the oven and cook for a further 10 minutes or until firm and nicely browned.

Store in an airtight container when cool.

Sweet and Sour Pot Roast

SERVES 6–8

2kg rolled rib of beef
150g smoked streaky bacon
30g lard
1 tablespoon sunflower oil
1 large onion, finely chopped
2 cloves garlic, diced
4 tablespoons Bovril
250ml red wine vinegar
1 teaspoon mixed dried herbs
1 tablespoon mango chutney
1 tablespoon finely diced stem
  ginger
50g pitted green olives
6 baby shallots

Heat the oven to 220C/425F/Gas 7.

Lay the rib of beef out flat and cover with strips of bacon, roll up and tie and place in a roasting dish with the lard and pop in the oven to brown for 15 minutes.

Meanwhile, in a frying pan heat the cooking oil and sauté the onions and garlic until soft, then add the Bovril, wine vinegar, herbs and mango chutney and mix them well together.

Remove the meat pan from the oven and turn it down to 150C/300F/Gas 2. Tip the contents of the frying pan over the meat, cover with kitchen foil and pop it back in the oven for 1 hour (if you like your beef well done increase this time to $1^1/_2$ hours).

Remove the meat from the oven, add the stem ginger, the olives and the shallots to the roasting pan and cook for a further 20 minutes, still covered.

When the rib of beef is cooked let it stand for 10 minutes, keeping it warm and then serve in thick slices spooning over the thick sauce.

Boldly go with Bovril...

From the earliest advertising, Bovril has been promoted as a healthy hot drink. In those very early years, testimonials rained in from such eminent figures as the Antarctic explorers Robert Falcon Scott and Ernest Shackleton. Abandoned South-Pole supply huts remain where stores of all manner of tinned goods were found, Bovril among them, Indeed, it was Shackleton who would coin the phrase that would become the very lynchpin for a future renowned Bovril advertising campaign: 'It must be Bovril'. The campaign became particularly pertinent during the First World War, when Bovril was being promoted to help ward off 'flu and chills'.

Turkey Bang Bang

SERVES 4–6

For the sauce
2 teaspoons sunflower oil
3 tablespoons peanut butter
2 tablespoons chilli sauce
1 dessertspoon Bovril
1 tablespoon caster sugar
1 tablespoon white wine vinegar
3 tablespoons water

For the meat and salad
1 iceberg lettuce, finely shredded
half a cucumber, in slices or
   batons
small bunch of fresh coriander
small bunch of mint
300g cold turkey
bunch of spring onions, finely
   sliced
half a red pepper, deseeded and
   finely sliced

To make the sauce simply combine all the ingredients in a small bowl.

Next, arrange the shredded lettuce on a large platter, followed by the cucumber, then scatter over the roughly chopped coriander and mint. Drizzle over some of the sauce.

Combine the rest of the sauce with the cold meat cut or torn into even sized pieces and arrange this over the lettuce bed.

To finish, scatter over the finely chopped spring onions and the red pepper which has been very thinly sliced.

Bovril Chips

SERVES 4

750g Maris Piper, King Edwards or
  Sante potatoes
4 tablespoons sunflower oil
2 tablespoons Bovril
$\frac{1}{2}$ teaspoon paprika

Preheat the oven to 180C/350F/
Gas 4.

Peel the potatoes and cut them
into chunky chips. Rinse in cold
water to remove the starch, boil
them in unsalted water for 5
minutes remove and drain. Return
them to the pan and give the pan a
shake to fluff up their edges.

Meanwhile heat the oil with the
paprika and Bovril in a roasting tray
in a hot oven for 5 minutes. Take
the roasting tray out of the oven,
stir the Bovril oil well and carefully
slide in the chips using a slotted
spoon to roll them in the pan juices,
making sure they are all completely
coated. Return the tray to the oven
for 10–12 minutes then take it out
again and pour off the fat. Put it
back in for 5 minutes or until the
Bovril chips are golden and crispy.

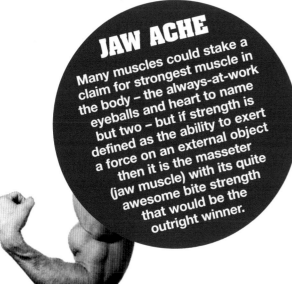

JAW ACHE
Many muscles could stake a
claim for strongest muscle in
the body – the always-at-work
eyeballs and heart to name
but two – but if strength is
defined as the ability to exert
a force on an external object
then it is the masseter
(jaw muscle) with its quite
awesome bite strength
that would be the
outright winner.

Reflective glory
Left *from 1925*
and **this page** *from*
the late 1930s

Puff Pastry Twists

MAKES 20–24 PUFF PASTRY TWISTS

500g readymade puff pastry
Bovril, for spreading
1 egg beaten with 3 tablespoons full-fat milk
1–2 tablespoons poppy seeds

Pre-heat the oven to 220C/425F/ Gas 7. Line two large baking sheets or trays with baking parchment.

Roll out the pastry thinly to something less than the thickness of a pound coin. Spread thinly with Bovril then cut into strips 15cm by 1cm.

Twist the pastry strips into spirals and lay carefully on the baking sheets. Brush with the egg glaze and sprinkle generously with poppy seeds.

Bake for 15–20 minutes until risen, golden and crispy.

Billboard Bovril

Bovril became neon-lit in 1909, when its first electrical advertising sign was erected in London's Piccadilly Circus. The first illuminated signs appeared here in 1893, and Bovril was one of the earliest advertisers, hanging around for many years, as part of what would become the oldest and best-known lights complex in the world. But even when their messages were not illuminated, they were potent. There have been many memorable campaigns over Bovril's long life, with popular characters and advertising slogans that still resonate brightly today. 'Liquid life', 'Bovril, one of the pleasures of life' and 'Yell for Bovril' worked and retain a magic both then and now.

Beef & Onion Flatbreads

SERVES 4

For the bread base
250g strong plain white flour
$\frac{1}{2}$ teaspoon fine sea salt
1 teaspoon active yeast
1 tablespoon olive oil
approx. 125ml warm water

Meat mixture
250g minced beef
1 large clove garlic, finely chopped
1 medium onion, finely chopped
1 teaspoon ground cumin
squeeze of lemon juice or a
    tablespoon pomegranate
    molasses (if available)
2 tablespoons coarsely chopped
    flat leaf parsley
sea salt and black pepper
Bovril for spreading
400g tin chopped tomatoes,
    drained of excess liquid

To make the bread dough mix the flour, salt and yeast together in a large bowl. Dribble in the olive oil and enough warm water to make a soft but not sticky dough. Knead briefly then cover and leave to rise until doubled in size.

While the dough is rising, turn the beef, the garlic and the finely chopped onion into a saucepan and cook gently until the meat loses its pinkness breaking up any lumps with a wooden spoon or fork. Add the ground cumin, the lemon juice or pomegranate molasses and season with salt and black pepper. When the mixture has cooled add the chopped parsley.

Knock back the dough and turn out onto a floured work surface and knead for a couple of minutes until you have springy dough.

Divide into four and roll and stretch each piece into a thin, roughly circular shape. Do this directly onto an oiled baking sheet. You will probably need two sheets.

Spread each of the pieces of dough with Bovril and a quarter of the drained tomato and top with a quarter of the meat mixture.

Leave to prove while you heat the oven to 220C/425F/Gas mark 7. When the oven is hot, slide in the trays and bake for 10–15 minutes until the dough is cooked and just starting to take colour. As soon as the breads come out of the oven cover with a clean tea towel and leave for five minutes. This traps the steam and keeps the bread malleable. You should be able to fold the breads so that they can be eaten with your fingers.

Scatter with more chopped parsley before serving with a crunchy salad.

Hand-Raised Pork Pie

For the filling
675g pork shoulder (because you
 need a bit of fat), coarsely
 chopped
100g unsmoked back bacon,
 coarsely chopped
$1/_2$ teaspoon dried sage
$1/_2$ teaspoon dried thyme
$1/_4$ teaspoon anchovy essence
$1/_4$ teaspoon ground nutmeg
lots of freshly ground black pepper

For the hot water pastry
340g plain flour
$1/_4$ teaspoon ground mace
150ml water
140g lard
2 teaspoons Bovril
1 free-range egg, beaten

For the jellied stock
250ml vegetable stock
$1/_2$ onion, finely diced
1 bay leaf
4 black peppercorns
$1/_2$ teaspoon dried thyme
1 leaf of gelatine – prepare as per
 the packet instructions

You will need a 6"/15cm pork pie
tin or similar cake tin

Preheat the oven to 170C/325F/
Gas 3.

Chop the pork and bacon and put
them into a mixing bowl, add all
the other filling ingredients and
combine them all well. Set aside.

Now, to make the pastry. Sieve the
flour into a dry bowl and add the
lard and Bovril, stir well, and when
all is dissolved pour it into the dry
ingredients immediately. Stir to
form a dough, turn the dough out
onto a working surface and knead
lightly and quickly for 5 minutes,
but no more – it is important to
work with the pastry while it's still
warm. Take $3/_4$ of the dough, make it
into a ball, and place it in the bottom
of your tin. With your fingers work
the dough up the sides of the tin
just leaving enough overlap at the
top to fold over later. The $1/_4$ of
dough left is for the round lid and
decoration.

Pack the the meat mixture firmly
into the pastry case, right up to the
top, and fold over the surplus pastry.
Cut a lid and pop it on the top
pinching the pastry together to
seal. Make a 'steam' hole in the top
and brush the pie with beaten egg.
Cook for about 2 hours. Keep an
eye on it as ovens do vary. It should
come out golden brown. Place on a
cooling tray and leave to cool.

Now for the lush jelly. Pour the
vegetable stock into a pan adding
the onion, bay leaf, peppercorns
and thyme. Bring to the boil and
simmer until reduced to about half.
Strain into another pan and add the
gelatine, stir, allow to cool a little
until syrupy, and then carefully pour
into the cold cooked pork pie via
the steam hole. When the pie is full,
chill in the fridge to set the jelly.

Peanut Bovril Crunchies

MAKES 16–20

butter, for greasing
350g self-raising flour
2 teaspoons baking powder
50g unsalted peanuts, crushed
2 teaspoons Bovril dissolved in
    200ml warm water
150g crunchy peanut butter
milk for brushing

Preheat the oven to 180C/350F/
Gas 4. Grease a baking sheet with
a little butter.

Mix together the sieved flour,
baking powder and half the
peanuts in a bowl. Add the warm
Bovril and the peanut butter and
stir everything together really well
until you have a slightly marbled
mixture.

Spread this out on the baking sheet
with a palette knife to a depth of
1.5 cm, brush with a little milk and
sprinkle over the remaining
peanuts.

Bake in the centre of the oven for
45 minutes then turn out and cool
on a wire rack. Break into chunks
and share them about.

Bovril & Paprika Belly Pork

SERVES 6

1.5kg belly pork in one piece, skin on
1 teaspoon salt
1 tablespoon smoked paprika

For the sauce
3 tablespoons olive oil
2 cloves garlic, chopped
1 teaspoon fresh ginger, grated
1 small red chilli
3 spring onions, chopped
1 teaspoon smoked paprika
1 teaspoon Bovril
1 tablespoon sweet sherry
handful fresh coriander

Preheat the oven to 180C/350F/ Gas 4.

Place the piece of pork on a rack over a baking tin, score it with a sharp knife and pour half a kettle of boiling water over it. Pat it dry with kitchen paper and discard the water. This will help the skin to crisp. Sprinkle the salt and paprika over the skin and rub it in well amongst the slits. Put the pork in the centre of the hot oven, still on its rack over the roasting tin, and cook for 2 hours.

To make the sauce, heat the olive oil and add the garlic, ginger, chilli and spring onions and sauté until just golden. Remove from the heat and tip into a food processor. Add the paprika, Bovril, sherry and coriander and blitz to a smooth sauce.

Mental toughness

In 2008, still basking in the success of its hosting of the Olympic Games, Beijing hosted the first ever World Mind Sports Games. Just shy of 3,000 competitors challenged for 35 gold medals across five different board and card game events – chess, bridge, draughts, Go and Chinese chess: representative of some of the oldest and most sophisticated mental exercises known to man. Delegations from each participating country were asked to bring water from their home country to symbolise the source of human spirit. The waters were mixed together and at the end of the games, each delegation returned home with a sample that represented the combined wisdoms of the world. The Games was the brainchild of Frenchman José Damiani, whose wish it was to stage a mental version of the Games in the same Olympic city that held the physical Games.

Lamb & Leek Casserole

SERVES 4

2 tablespoons sunflower oil
1 onion, roughly chopped
800g diced lamb
450g leeks, diced
1 clove garlic, finely diced
1 teaspoon dried mixed herbs
2 tablespoons Bovril mixed with
   250ml warm water
150ml white wine
500g waxy potatoes, peeled and
   thinly sliced
salt and black pepper
few sprigs of rosemary to garnish

Preheat the oven to 160C/325F/ Gas 3.

Heat the oil in a flameproof casserole on top of the stove and gently fry the onions until translucent. Add the lamb, moving it around the casserole to brown it all over until the juices flow and then add the leeks, garlic and herbs. Cover and cook over a low heat for 10 minutes.

Remove the casserole from the heat and season the lamb with a pinch of salt and plenty of black pepper. Now layer the potatoes all over the top of the lamb mixture and then pour the Bovril stock and wine over the top. Season with a little more salt and pepper. Cover and cook in the oven for 2 hours.

Remove the casserole from the oven, dot a few pieces of butter over the potatoes and return the casserole to the oven for a further 20 minutes to brown and crisp the potato topping. Serve with sprigs of rosemary.

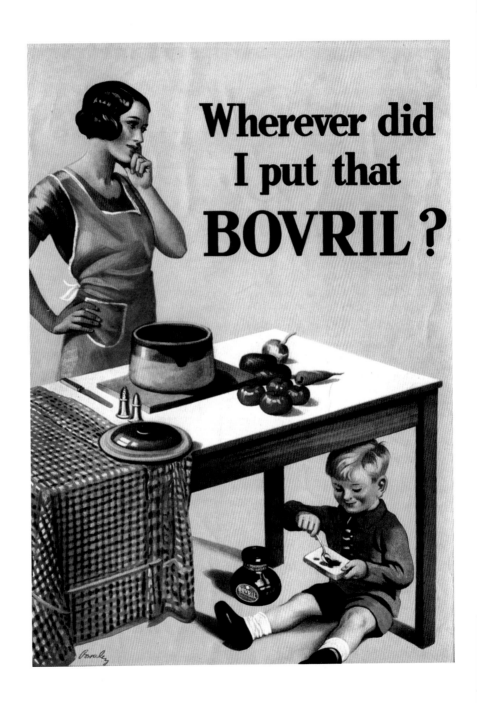

Casserole delayed...
1937

Jewelled Salad with Bovril Vinaigrette

SERVES 4 AS A SIDE DISH

For the Bovril vinaigrette
5 dessertspoons white wine
   vinegar
1 teaspoon whole grain mustard
freshly ground black pepper
2 teaspoons Bovril
9 dessertspoons good olive oil

10 romaine or cos lettuce leaves
4 fresh, firm plum tomatoes
   roughly chopped
1 large red onion, roughly chopped
1 green pepper, deseeded and cut
   into rough chunks
1 yellow pepper, deseeded and
   cut into rough chunks
$\frac{1}{2}$ cucumber cut into 2cm pieces
12 pimento stuffed green olives
finely chopped mint leaves

In a blender put the vinegar, mustard, generous grinds of black pepper and the Bovril and give it a whiz, with the motor still running drizzle in the olive oil and you will have thick vinaigrette. Pour into a jug or bowl and set aside.

Take a salad bowl and line the outside with the lettuce leaves standing them up like soldiers. Mix together the tomatoes, onion, peppers, cucumber and olives and pile them into the centre. Using a dessertspoon or ladle generously drizzle the vinaigrette over the salad and finish with a flourish of mint.

The remaining vinaigrette can be stored in an airtight container in the fridge for up to a week.

A BIG BANG

The most powerful blast ever observed in the universe occurred in March 2008. The gamma ray burst – an explosion of high-energy radiation – occurred 7.5 billion light years away, but could be witnessed with the naked eye.

Mushroom & Oxtail Soup

SERVES 6

1kg oxtail, trimmed and cut into
    pieces
2 large onions, sliced
2 large carrots, sliced
2 sticks celery, sliced
2 bay leaves
20 juniper berries, crushed
1 tablespoon Bovril
30g dried mushrooms
500g button mushrooms
sea salt and freshly ground black
    pepper

Place all the ingredients except the fresh mushrooms in a large casserole or slow cooker.

Cover with boiling water and simmer, covered, on the lowest possible heat preferably in a slow cooker or in a solid fuel stove for 8 hours.

Allow to cool then strain the meat and vegetables from the rich stock. Remove all the bones from the meat, keeping the meat aside, and discard the bones and bay leaves.

In a blender or food processor, strain and reduce the vegetables to a purée with some of the stock and return the purée to a clean saucepan. Add the rest of the oxtail broth, the meat, 600ml of fresh cold water and the button mushrooms, thinly sliced.

Bring to a simmering point and cook for another 15–20 minutes. Check seasoning and adjust if necessary. Serve steaming hot with warm, crusty baguettes.

Bovril-charged!
c.1930

Chopper to the rescue!
1958

Cream Cheese, Bovril & Chive Dip

MAKES ENOUGH FOR 6 TO DIP INTO

200g cream cheese
1 tablespoon smooth peanut
   butter
1 teaspoon Bovril
2 tablespoons double cream
dash Tabasco sauce
1 tablespoon chopped chives

Simply mix all the ingredients together and serve with a plate of crunchy crudités like batons of raw celery, carrots, sweet peppers, cucumber and florets of cauliflower.

Left
Just a little Bovril
c.1950

BOVRIL

Is prepared from **PURE BEEF ONLY**, and is admitted by scientific experts everywhere to be the most perfect form of concentrated nourishment at present known. It contains, besides Peptone, a perceptible powder, which is Albumen and Fibrine, the nutritious constituents of Beef, and by this powder it may be distinguished from clear Beef Tea, which is devoid of staminal properties. **ONE OUNCE** of these constituents contains more real and direct nourishment than **FIFTY OUNCES** of ordinary Meat Extract of Beef Tea. **BOVRIL,** by the simple addition of a spoonful to a cup of boiling water, instantly forms a refreshing, sustaining, and strengthening drink, which has justly been termed a **BOON TO THE AGE.** It is sold everywhere, by the Stores, Chemists, Grocers, and others, in Bottle, Tins, and Lozenges; and is **SERVED HOT** at the leading Hotels, Restaurants, Railway Stations, Temperance Bars, Theatres, and places of Amusement.

SPECIAL NOTICE.

Absolutely purity of everything is guaranteed.

STANLEY RECRUITS HIS STRENGTH WITH BOVRIL

T. KESSANLY & Cᵒ

HEAD OFFICE: 30 FARRINGDON ST

BOVRIL

s the strengthening article of diet
for

THLETES ACTORS, SINGERS, AND PUBLIC SPEAKERS.

ll speak highly of the advantages
erived from such an easily digested
nd strengthening article of diet
s **BOVRIL.** We have number-
ess testimonials in its favour, which
an be inspected at our office.
NVALUABLE in the KITCHEN
or making **SOUPS** and enriching
SAUCES, GRAVIES, and MADE
DISHES.

NO STOCKPOT REQUIRED.

£100 PRIZE

is offered by the Proprietors of
BOVRIL for the solution of a new
and interesting **PUZZLE,** price 3d.,
or posted to any address in the
United Kingdom, on receipt of 4d. in
Postage Stamps.

SPECIAL NOTICE.

An eminent public analyst is
retained as consulting chemist, and
nothing enters or leaves the factory
without being examined and tested
by him.

EET, E.C.

BOVRIL

Is prepared from PURE BEEF
ONLY, and is admitted by scientific experts everywhere to be the
most perfect form of concentrated
nourishment at present known. It
contains, besides Peptone, a perceptible powder, which is Albumen
and Fibrine, the nutritious constituents of Beef, and by this powder
it may be distinguished from clear
Beef Tea, which is devoid of staminal
properties. ONE OUNCE of these
constituents contains more real and
direct nourishment than FIFTY
OUNCES of ordinary Meat Extract
of Beef Tea. **BOVRIL,** by the
simple addition of a spoonful to a cup
of boiling water, instantly forms a
refreshing, sustaining, and strengthening drink, which has justly been
termed a BOON TO THE AGE. It
is sold everywhere, by the Stores,
Chemists, Grocers, and others, in
Bottle, Tins, and Lozenges; and is
SERVED HOT at the leading
Hotels, Restaurants, Railway Stations, Temperance Bars, Theatres,
and places of Amusement.

SPECIAL NOTICE.

Absolutely purity of everything is
guaranteed.

HEAD OFFICE: 30

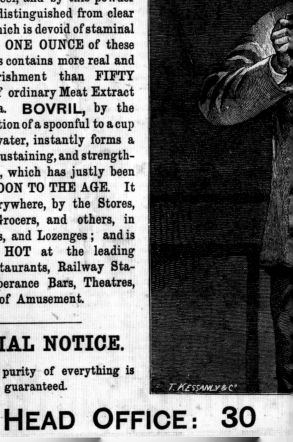

T. KESSANLY & C°

Bovril Prawns

SERVES 2

500g raw tiger prawns
1 teaspoon Worcestershire sauce
1 tablespoon rice flour
2 tablespoons sunflower oil
2 shallots, finely diced
1 clove garlic, finely diced
2 tablespoons Bovril
2 tablespoons runny honey
1 tablespoon muscovado sugar

Put the prawns into a bowl, drizzle with the Worcestershire sauce and then sprinkle over the rice flour. Toss them a few times to coat.

Heat the oil in a large frying pan or wok, add the coated prawns and stir-fry for 3–4 minutes until the prawns have turned pink. Lift them out with a slotted spoon into a warm dish lined with kitchen paper and keep warm.

Into the same pan add the shallots and garlic and sauté until just golden. Then stir in the Bovril, honey and muscovado and add a splash of water. Bring to the boil, stirring so that everything dissolves, until you have a sauce with a consistency to coat the prawns. Remove from the heat, toss in the prawns, turning them a few times, and serve immediately.

MONO MIGHT

Of all the beguiling athleticism and brute strength within the repertoire of film star and martial arts master, Bruce Lee, his one-inch punch and one-handed two-finger push-ups epitomise the extraordinary conditioning of mind and body of which he was capable.

a

b

c

e

h

i

d

f

g

INDEX

j

k

l

G

H

N

THE ADVENTURES OF THE MUSTARD CLUB

Being a selection of the famous advertisements of the MUSTARD CLUB, together with many interesting cartoons and hitherto unpublished documents.

PRICE 6D.

MARMITE
FOR PEOPLE OF GOOD TASTE

"MARMITE" IS GOOD FOR SOUPS SANDWICHES ETC

"BE A SANDWICH-MAN" USE MARMITE

H.P.

N OPEN ECRET—

GOOD GOOD

MARMITE

MARMITE

LYLE'S GOLDEN SYRUP

SAUCE

Good with bacon

LEA & PERRINS' SAUCE

The Original and Genuine Worcestershire

LEA & PERRINS' SAUCE

WAS INTRODUCED
OVER SIXTY YEARS AGO
AND NEVER VARIES
IN EXCELLENCE OF QUALITY.

BOVRIL

puts BEEF into you.

PRESS CAP

TEASPOONFUL TO A T
LING WATER & STIR

LYLE'S GOLDEN SYRUP
in 1lb. 2lb. 4lb. & 14 lb. tins
Abram Lyle & Sons L^{td} SUGAR REFINERS London

BOVRIL

TWO HOUSEHOLD FAVORITES
— ALWAYS IN HOT WATER

HP SAUCE

Lea Perrins Lea Perrins Lea Perrins

By Royal Warrant to   His Majesty the King

THE LABEL.

THE
ONLY
SECURITY
against deception
is to see that

LEA &
PERRINS

is printed in WHITE across the label —
THE ORIGINAL WORCESTERSHIRE.

BY SPECIAL APPOINTMENT
TO THE KING

Colman's

BULL'S HEAD

Mustard

DOUBLE SUPERFINE

ACKNOWLEDGEMENTS

FOR THE MARMITE RECIPE COLLECTION

p24 picture courtesy of Russell Tuck. p38 'Margate Main Sands' picture courtesy of Thanet District Council. p59 screenshot of www.marmiteman.co.uk. All other images courtesy of Unilever Best Foods UK Ltd / Freud Communications. Images of Zippy©, courtesy of FremantleMedia Ltd. Licensed by FremantleMedia Licensing Worldwide. Images on p20, p46, p34, p56 all courtesy of The Robert Opie Collection. All film images courtesy of The Kobal Collection: p12 MGM / The Kobal Collection; p13 Columbia / The Kobal Collection; p25 The Kobal Collection; p27 London Films / The Kobal Collection; p28 Paramount / The Kobal Collection; p32 Paramount / The Kobal Collection; p43 The Kobal Collection; p57 Panda Film / The Kobal Collection; p62 Metro Pictures / The Kobal Collection; p67 RKO / The Kobal Collection

FOR THE COLMAN'S MUSTARD RECIPE COLLECTION

Images on p81, p87, p91, p108, p103, p115, p114, p121, p128, p131, p123 all courtesy of The Ropert Opie Collection. All film images courtesy of The Kobal Collection: p73 MGM / The Kobal Collection; p74 Warner Bros / The Kobal Collection; p79

MGM / The Kobal Collection; p86 Universal / The Kobal Collection; p99 British Lion / The Kobal Collection; p112 MGM / The Kobal Collection; p120 Universal / The Kobal Collection; p126 First National / The Kobal Collection; p125 Paramount / The Kobal Collection. All other images courtesy of © Unilever Archives and Unilever Bestfoods Ltd.

FOR THE LEA & PERRINS RECIPE COLLECTION

All pictures courtesy of Lea & Perrins, except for p140, p149, p158, p193, p166, p170, p186 all © Robert Opie Picture Collection; and p136 © Intergloria / The Kobal Collection; p192 © Svensk FIilmindustri / The Kobal Collection; p154 © ABC/Cinerama / The Kobal Collection; p176 © 20the Century Fox / The Kobal Collection. The publishers would like to thank Lea & Perrins, especially Roma Phulwani and Paul Harvey, and a special thank you to Tony Deakin for all his help and enthusiasm. Thanks also to Robert Opie and to Caroline and Darren at the Kobal Collection.

FOR THE LYLE'S GOLDEN SYRUP RECIPE COLLECTION

The Lyle's trademarks and copyrighted materials used in this book are owned exclusively by Tate and Lyle PLC and are used with permission.

FOR THE HP RECIPE COLLECTION

Images on pages 261, 264, 276, 284, 286, 274, 306, 319 and 322 courtesy of Robert Opie, Museum of Brands, Notting Hill, London. Images on pages 271, 272, 281, 298 and 316 courtesy of The H.J. Heinz Co. Ltd Archive at The History of Advertising Trust (www.hatads.org.uk).

FOR THE BOVRIL RECIPE COLLECTION

All Bovril archive images in this book courtesy of the Unilever Archive, except pages 328, 329, 350 and 355, courtesy of Robert Opie, Museum of Brands, Notting Hill, London.